JEAN GIRAUDOUX

Also published by Hill and Wang

Jean Giraudoux

THREE PLAYS

Translated by

PHYLLIS LA FARGE *with* PETER H. JUDD

❧

VOLUME 2

A MERMAID DRAMABOOK
HILL AND WANG · NEW YORK
A division of Farrar, Straus and Giroux

Manufactured in the United States of America

15   16   17   18   19   20

CONTENTS

SIEGFRIED

A Play in Four Acts

❧

CAST OF CHARACTERS

(IN ORDER OF APPEARANCE)

MUCK
EVA
BARON VON ZELTEN

HERR SCHMIDT ⎫
FRAU HOEPFL ⎪
HERR KELLER ⎪
HERR KRATZ ⎬ *The parents*
HERR *and* FRAU PATCHKOFFER ⎪
HERR MEYER ⎭

GENEVIEVE
ROBINEAU
SIEGFRIED
GENERAL DE FONTGELOY
GENERAL VON WALDORF
GENERAL LEDINGER
PIETRI
SCHUMANN
SERVANT, FOOTMAN, SERGEANT

The action of the play takes place in GOTHA, the capital of post World War I Germany, and on the French-German border. The time is January 1921.

SIEGFRIED

ACT ONE

A luxurious modern anteroom. To the right of a bay window is a white marble staircase covered with a thick red carpet. Through the window Gotha can be seen, blanketed with snow. MUCK, *a steward,* EVA, *and a* SERVANT *are on stage.*

MUCK [*announcing*]. His Excellency General Ludendorff!
 Eva. Not now——ask him to come back at nine.
 Muck. His Excellency, President Rathenau!
 Eva. Tonight at nine. You know perfectly well that this afternoon is sacred for Chancellor Siegfried.
 Muck [*to the* SERVANT]. I'm not having any luck. Try announcing yours!
 Servant [*almost ashamed*]. Herr Meyer!
 Eva. Excellent. Chancellor Siegfried will receive him in a minute.
 Servant. Herr Kratz! Frau Schmidt!
 Eva. Excellent. They're on time, and Chancellor Siegfried will see them all.
 Muck. He's making a mistake.
 Eva. Who asked your advice?
 Muck. Chancellor Siegfried is getting excited for nothing.

EVA *makes no reply but sits down and starts to write.*

 Muck. I've taken a good look at all these would-be parents who've come from every corner of Germany thinking he might be the son they lost in the war. None of them looks the least bit like him.
 Servant. No?
 Muck. I suppose you're going to tell me that family traits are like certain illnesses—they skip a generation?
 Servant [*rearranging chairs and portières*]. Yes, that's what I'd say.
 Muck. They all bring photographs, as if they were en-

trance tickets—photographs of their sons. They show them
to me at the door. One wears glasses; one has a suspicion
of a harelip. Not one looks like the chancellor!

Servant. Perhaps you're not very good at spotting a like-
ness.

Muck. Just the opposite. Take one of those elaborately
costumed or stark naked statues of Lohengrin or Alexander
that you see in museums or theatres, put it in a business
suit, and it would look more like Chancellor Siegfried than
any of them—— You know Lohengrin?

Servant [*vaguely*]. Not well. I've just had a glimpse of
him.

Eva [*interrupting their conversation*]. Is everything ready
for the reception?

Muck. The candelabra is repaired. I replaced the bulbs.

Eva. Is the Chancellor dressed?

Muck. He's dressing. [*To the* SERVANT.] He can't make
up his mind. He doesn't know whether to cut off his mus-
tache, as he did last time. I left him standing in front of
the mirror. I know he's wondering which way he'd look
more like himself. It takes more than the right suit to make
a man look as he did in childhood.

Eva. Bring in Baron von Zelten.

Muck [*surprised*]. But I haven't announced Baron von
Zelten!

Eva. That's precisely what irritates me. Why did you
let him in when I told you not to? Why do you let him
mingle with our visitors and question them?

Muck. I thought I was doing the right thing. He's your
cousin.

Eva. People are saying terrible things about Zelten. His
word is law in every café, in the corridors of every government building, even in the public baths. They say that he
has bought the police and that yesterday evening all the
special agents met at his house.

Muck. You are mistaken. He gave them theatre tickets.
They all went to *Salomé* to study the uniforms of Herod's
guard.

Eva. You may go. I'll wait for him.

MUCK *exits.* EVA *dismisses the other servant. Enter* BARON
VON ZELTEN.

Eva. What do you want here, Zelten?

Zelten. I see you're still taking good care of your nursling. Has he returned from parliament yet?

Eva. Are you for or against us, Zelten?

Zelten. He is back and he has told you of his success, I can see by your face! You're radiant, cousin. If that feeble constitution just adopted by our deputies puts such a glow in the cheeks of a pretty young German, I won't be too stern with her!

Eva. A German girl can rejoice to see Germany saved, can't she? The only word we could use for Germany these last three years was *lost*. It's wonderful now to be able to say *saved*.

Zelten. It's easy enough to interchange adjectives, cousin, especially when they're applied to Germany. You have something to say to me?

Eva. Why did you vote just now against the Siegfried Proposal?

Zelten. The Siegfried Proposal! You might as well accuse me of voting against the Valkyries and the entire German mythology! Just because of the heroic name you gave him, an entire country believes this man can do no wrong. Seven years ago you took it into your head to use the name Siegfried to christen a wounded soldier in your hospital. He had lost his memory as well as his clothes. Even during his subsequent triumphant political career, he has been unable to recall his real name. Everything he says or does benefits from the prestige attached to his namesake! Who's to say that your Siegfried wasn't called Meyer before he was wounded and that the proposal I voted against wasn't anything more than the Meyer Proposal?

Eva. Please remember that you are in the Chancellor's house.

Zelten. The last time I saw you, Eva, six years ago, you were at the rehabilitation center teaching your grown-up baby simple words like *dog, cat, tea,* and *coffee.* Now he's teaching you seductive words like *Constitution, Liberalism, Proportional Representation* or——love, perhaps?

Eva. He has taught me the word *Germany.*

Zelten. Your Siegfried's Germany! I can picture what that's like. A model of social order, with its thirty little kingdoms, its duchies and free towns eliminated. In the past these provided thirty different variations on the themes of culture and liberty. Now he proposes a country divided into equal departments. Budgets, pensions, and insurance will be the country's only adventure. It will be a country just like its creator—entirely theoretical, without a memory or a past. Your child of the void has the heredity of an accountant, a judge, or a watchmaker. Forcing his constitution on Germany is like feeding Siegfried's—the real Siegfried's—dragon an alarm clock so that he can tell time!

Eva. With Siegfried, Germany will be strong.

Zelten [*impetuously*]. Germany does not have to be strong. She has to be Germany. Or, rather, she must be strong in spirit—a giant, but an invisible giant. Germany isn't a humane and social institution, it is a conspiracy of poetic, demonic souls. Whenever a German has tried to make her into a solid, efficient structure, his handiwork has been smashed to a few glittering bits. Whenever a German has had faith in his country's ability to transform thoughts into symbol and deeds into legend, he has constructed for eternity!

Eva. That eternity is now at an end——

Zelten. At an end, Eva! Instead of parading Siegfried through model cities, why don't you take him up into the Alps. Stand with him on the first peak and watch the sun rise. At dawn the Germany of the Holy Roman Empire still lives in the icy air: there's not even a trickle of water in the center furrow of the frozen streams. The only men and beasts abroad—piebald horses, weasels, and pretty chambermaids riding in yellow mail coaches—have not changed since Gustavus Adolphus. There you'll see the very landscape of our Germany in days gone by—a country of conspiracy and toil, pillage and sainthood—so spiritually and poetically endowed that you would expect at any minute, as in a medieval engraving, to see a plump, naked, heavenly child floating in the sky, or else celestial hands joined in prayer. That's where Germany is, in the mountains——

Eva. I'm in a hurry. What do you want?

Zelten. May I see Siegfried?

Eva. Why?

Zelten. That's my business.

Eva. He can't see you.

Zelten. Is he resting?

Eva. Don't pretend that you don't understand. You know what he's getting ready for.

Zelten. I can guess! He's shaving, changing his shirt, brushing his hair, primping as if it were the last toilet of his life, for a meeting which he hopes will furnish him with a family. His earlier interviews haven't discouraged him? He's still hopeful?

Eva. He's hopeful. You don't mind, do you?

Zelten. What about you, are you hopeful?

Eva. Of course.

Zelten. I don't believe you.

Eva. Zelten!

Zelten. Won't you be lost the day when one of these visitors retrieves your pupil from his ideal kingdom to make of him an ordinary Bavarian, or a simple Prussian? What if this German created out of nothing should suddenly have a father! Every virgin in Germany has already recognized him as her legitimate child. And besides, how am I to know that he's not playing a trick on us?

Eva. Are you mad?

Zelten. Siegfried owes his popularity to the mystery surrounding him! The man whom Germany looks to as her savior, who claims to be her very personification, was born to her six years ago in a dressing station without memory, papers, or kit! Nations are childish enough to believe that their great men are not born but just arrive one day by train. In her heart Germany is flattered that her hero is not the result of the humble embrace of an ordinary couple. A statesman whose birth is like the death of a poet—how marvelous! Amnesia has endowed your Siegfried with everyone's past, made him completely noble and—not to be scorned by a politician—completely plebeian. Should he recover his family or his memory, he will become our equal once again. I'm glad to say that I have reason to believe that moment is not far off.

Eva. What do you mean?

Zelten. It's possible that a most unexpected hand will repair the short circuit which cut Siegfried off from his real life.

Eva. Do you know something about Siegfried? Be careful, Zelten——

Enter MUCK.

Muck. Fräulein, it's time for the reception.

EVA *starts up the stairs without concealing her anxiety.*

Eva. Show Baron von Zelten to the door.   [EVA *exits.*
Muck. Is it still set for tomorrow, Baron?
Zelten. Yes, Muck.
Muck. For what time?
Zelten. Late in the afternoon. The signal will be two cannon shots. Remember, Muck, later today there will be a ring at the door. You'll see two foreigners—French people. Do you know how to recognize French travelers?
Muck. Of course. They are all diplomats; they wear morning coats.
Zelten [*slipping him some money*]. See that you find a way to let them in. Tomorrow depends on them. Does it rub you the wrong way to be hospitable to French people?
Muck. Why should it? In the trenches, between attacks we sometimes chatted with the French. It's hard to go on being silent for months on end. Our officers hardly ever spoke. We were far from our families . . . They were all we had. . . . Certainly, I'll hide them.
Zelten. No, no, don't do that. Make them wait here in this hall. One of them is a woman. Get in touch with me as soon as they're here. Then, after I've seen them, tell Siegfried that a Canadian schoolteacher would like to see him. [*A bell rings.*] What's that?
Muck. I must bring in the parents. The Chancellor is coming down.
Zelten. I'll see you later.

Exit ZELTEN. MUCK *opens the door and ushers in the* PARENTS, *a dreary motley group.*

Muck. City planner Schmidt!
Schmidt. Present.
Muck. You can give me your hat, sir.
Schmidt. I'd rather keep it—— It's a prewar hat—— I dressed a little bit as I used to.

Muck. As you wish. Frau Hoepfl—— profession—— independent means!

Frau Hoepfl. Here I am.

Muck. Have you your invitation?

Frau Hoepfl. I already showed it to you, with the photograph.

Muck. That's right. The one with the harelip—— [*Catching himself.*] The suspicion of a harelip—— Bookbinder Keller!

Keller. Present. My eyesight is weak, sir, so I've taken the liberty of bringing along Herr Kratz, our neighbor and pharmacist. He was very fond of Franz.

Kratz [*coming forward humbly*]. Pharmacist Kratz.

Keller. Herr Kratz spoiled him. He made more candies for Franz than he did prescriptions. One has become a well-known delicacy.

Kratz [*bowing*]. Kratz's apple sugar. I brought a little bag for the Chancellor—— That is to say, in any case—— I'll leave it here . . .

Muck. Herr and Frau Patchkoffer—— [*Two country folk come forward.*] I wrote you, Frau Patchkoffer! It seemed to me that there wasn't much point in your coming. You said in your letter that your son was short and dark. Chancellor Siegfried is tall and fair.

Patchkoffer. We've seen all the dark ones in Berlin, at the rehabilitation center.

Keller. But what about his height, Frau Patchkoffer?

Frau Patchkoffer. We've seen all the short men, too. Haven't we, Patchkoffer?

Muck. All right, then, all right.

Frau Patchkoffer. If he hadn't changed, we would have found him before now——

Muck. Herr Meyer!

Meyer. I'm Meyer—— Tell me, sir, what's it like? What happens?

Muck. What happens? Don't worry. It's all over very quickly. You stand in the bay window. The Chancellor comes down the staircase. A chandelier is lighted above him. Those who are nearsighted can go as near as they like, the incredulous can touch him. And, if you don't mind my saying so, five minutes later you'll all leave, thoroughly de-

jected. At least that's what has happened up till now. I
wish you better luck.

Meyer. Thank you. If I told you that I hoped to rediscover my poor Ernst—such a nice boy, but always at the
foot of his class—in the person of our foremost statesman—my Ernst—so good but always in bad with his
teachers—in the person of the man who within a few
months has become Germany's favorite, I'd really be lying—— Tell me, sir, does he have curly hair?

The bell of the outer door rings.

Muck. This way, ladies and gentlemen.

The parents enter the room on the left. MUCK *goes to open
the outer door, ushers in* GENEVIEVE *and* ROBINEAU, *and
greets them obsequiously. He disappears, smiling know-
ingly.*

Genevieve. Won't you tell me where we are, Robineau?

Robineau. Eleven hundred and fifty kilometers from
Paris, Genevieve. Guess where that is.

Genevieve. It's freezing! It's certainly not Nice, that's
certain! Where are we?

Robineau [*wiping his binoculars as he stands near the
stairs with his back to the bay window*]. You can see the
entire town from this window. See—— I'll explain. Tell me
what you see.

Genevieve. No, it's not Nice—— To my right I see a
medieval town with watchtowers, banners flying, and draw-
bridges.

Robineau [*speaking as if to himself, but aloud*]. That's
the National Museum!

Genevieve. Ahead of me I see a Greek temple set in the
midst of some cedars, covered with snow.

Robineau. That's the National Theatre!

Genevieve. And on my left a ten-story building with
windows in the shape of unicorns.

Robineau [*more and more lyrically*]. That's the National
Art Gallery!

Genevieve. Then down there, there's a Florentine palace
with frescoes and arcades.

Robineau. The National Palace!

Genevieve [*turning from the window*]. What else? . . . Where are we, Robineau?

Robineau. In Gotha, Genevieve, we're in Gotha, of course! The town where I met Zelten fifteen years ago one Mardi Gras. He was disguised as a Zulu; I was dressed as Alcibiades. No national prejudices stood in the way of our friendship.

Genevieve. What were you doing in Gotha?

Robineau. What did the French come to Germany for before the war? Philology. I was one of twelve in a Sorbonne raiding party which France loosed successfully on the Saxon dialects after Agadir. I am one of the twelve Frenchmen mentioned in all the German histories of the Middle Ages. You can search all day in their current histories and you won't find the names of twelve of our generals.

Genevieve [*who has taken a seat*]. What about this place? Whose house is it?

Robineau. I don't know. But look, there's someone coming!

The parents pass sadly on their way out, bidding each other dejected good-bys.

Genevieve. I'm afraid, Robineau.

Robineau. Afraid? Of what?

Genevieve. Of being here—— Of having left the Rue du Bac on such short notice yesterday evening and then all of a sudden being here.

Robineau. There's nothing to be afraid of. Zelten sent us Canadian passports. If you feel people looking at you suspiciously, act as if you came from Quebec. Here, I've made you a list of idioms. Are you cold? You're trembling.

Genevieve. A Canadian doesn't tremble from the cold. I'm trembling from fright, Robineau.

Robineau. That's impossible. You're the soul of courage.

Genevieve. Even so, I'm afraid. All night on the train I kept telling myself I was a fool to have obeyed you.

Robineau. Zelten has sent me twenty telegrams in the last few days urging me to look you up and bring you, willing or unwilling, here to this house, today. At three francs a word he's been assuring me that your most vital

interests are at stake. He even claims that the fate of
Franco-German relations could depend on your trip.
Franco-German relations are not to be sneezed at if you're
a student, as I am, of the aspirated "ch" in the Rhineland!
What interests you most in the world?

Genevieve. In the world? Nothing. Since Jacques died,
since he disappeared from the world? Nothing. In fact,
that's why I was open to what you proposed.

Robineau. Then why are you afraid?

Genevieve. Because, for the first time in my life, a bit of
news has reached me.

Robineau. And yet, you've suffered many misfortunes?

Genevieve. Until now, misfortune overtook me in silence. I have no parents; but during my childhood, silence
rather than any event taught me that I was an orphan.
Then I loved Jacques Forestier—— At the beginning of
the war he disappeared. Never once in seven years have I
received word of him, or even a single indication of his
death. This is the first time the fates have paid the slightest
attention to me, made the slightest sign. I'm afraid——
But you don't look too at ease yourself, Robineau.

Robineau [*who does appear nervous*]. No, I'm not.

Genevieve. Why?

Robineau [*anxiously*]. This is the first time since the
war, Genevieve, that I have met any of my German
friends. For seven years I haven't shaken hands with a
German; friendship and Germany no longer went together.
I wonder what it will be like.

Genevieve. Were you fond of him, this German of
yours?

Robineau. Zelten isn't "my" German, but he's German
all right—the epitome of a German. He has all the blatant
faults we ascribed to Germans before 1870—blond hair,
an intimate acquaintance with the creatures of his own
imagination, ignorance of reality, and a sincere sort of
pomposity. But you've seen Zelten, haven't you, in Montparnasse? As a sculptress you must have found him a fine
model!

Genevieve. A fine model? He was missing a rib, judging
by the way he walked.

Robineau. He broke it diving into the Rhine at the
spot where Schumann committed suicide.

Genevieve. One of his ankles was bigger than the other

Robineau. He sprained it jumping off the cliff from which Louis of Bavaria threw himself. He explained to me that he wanted to experience the final seconds in the lives of all Germany's great men. If you see he has a broken nose or a shoulder out of joint, it's certainly the fault of Wagner or Frederick Barbarossa.

Genevieve. Unless it's the fault of a French bullet.

Robineau. Don't rub it in, Genevieve. Don't weight with lead the ghosts that will haunt our conversation.

Genevieve. Ghosts? What ghosts?

Robineau. There are plenty to choose from—from Vercingetorix to Blucher, to mention only those in uniform——

Genevieve. Robineau, I'm going to let you two have the first part of your reunion alone together. I'm tired, and I saw a couch as we came in. Call me if you need me.

Robineau. Then hurry! Here he is!

Exit GENEVIEVE. *Enter* MUCK, *who introduces* ZELTEN, *then exits. The two men remain apart for a moment, studying each other in silence.*

Zelten. Is it you!

Robineau. Is it you!

Zelten. Is it you, Robineau, Hippolyte-Amable?

Robineau. Otto-Wilhelmus von Zelten-Buchenbach, it is I.

Zelten. Is it you, O dark brachycephalic, overweighted with lorgnettes and knitted vests, terrible in the attack?

Robineau. Yes, O essence of culture, distillation of carnage, son of Arminius, it is I.

Zelten. I feel as if I were talking long distance on the telephone, Robineau, with a very bad connection—— Speak right into the telephone! Still, I see you. You haven't changed.

Robineau. Nor have you—— But what have you been doing these last twelve years, Zelten? You, who loved springtime, music, joy, peace—what have you been doing?

Zelten. I have been fighting. I made war against thirty-five nations, but I was locked in combat with only one. And you—mild, bespectacled, freedom-loving inhabitant of imperial or royal libraries—you, my dearest friend, what have you been doing?

Robineau. Fighting, making war against you——

Zelten. Fortunately we were so unskillful, Robineau, that we missed each other. Were you aiming at me?

Robineau. Several times, during an attack, I raised my gun, thinking of you, and fired at the sky.

Zelten. So you did that too! It's probably still over Germany, your bullet, pursuing its course. But, you know, I had an idea you weren't intent on killing your old friend. Every time a bullet missed me, I said to myself—that's good old Robineau firing! I couldn't help thinking that every bullet which hit an object for which it wasn't intended—such as a bottle or a pear still on the tree—was yours. That's what your words used to do. My adjutant was hit in one cheek of his buttocks; everyone laughed—I thought of you. [*He approaches, and assumes the tone of ordinary conversation.*] Hello, Robineau!

Robineau. Hello, Zelten.

Zelten. How are you?

Robineau. All right. And you?

A *silence.*

Zelten. What are you doing these days?

Robineau. I'm finishing my thesis on the dentals.

Zelten. You're still a philologist? The voice of war didn't divert you from our chatter?

Robineau. But what about you? Why did you get in touch with me? What do you want? What are you doing?

Zelten. What am I doing? I'm going on. In Germany one goes on. I'm waging war——

Robineau. War?

Zelten. Not the same kind. Civil war this time. I'm fighting Germany's true enemies. Countries are like fruit —the worms are always inside.

Robineau [*very much the academic*]. You're writing propaganda, lecturing?

Zelten. No, I'm organizing a revolution. Today is the twelfth of January, 1921. I'm working on the revolution of January 13th or 14th, 1921. This is why I got in touch with you. You're only just in time, but you are indispensable.

Robineau. I wouldn't be so sure of that! My presence has always made historical events misfire. History is suspicious of me, as if I were a historian instead of a philologist.

Zelten. Just stay in Gotha three days. Besides, it's not only you I need, it's Genevieve, especially Genevieve. She's here?

Robineau. Yes. She's resting. I had to wake her in the middle of the night. She's sleeping now.

Zelten. She wasn't annoyed at being waked out of a sound sleep?

Robineau. She's never annoyed. But the Spanish flu is raging in Paris. She had been awakened two nights in a row to make death masks of famous men. She's a sculptress, you know.

Zelten. It's for something similar that I'm bothering her this time.

Robineau. What do you mean? Is someone dead?

Zelten. Both living and dead—— You've heard of our Siegfried?

Robineau. Chancellor Siegfried? Everyone in Europe has heard of him. He's your new leader, the man who wants Germany to accept his model constitution and to see things in the light of reason, as he does.

Zelten. What about Forestier? Do you know Forestier?

Robineau. The French writer? Genevieve's friend who disappeared? She was just talking about him—— I know only his work, and very fine it is. He wanted to restore to our language and tradition the mystery, the depth of feeling they had in the past. He was right, too. Every time I read the *Roman de la Rose* I'm more convinced—— But making a place for poetry in France is about as much of a job as making Germany rational.

Zelten. The same man has done both.

Robineau. What do you mean?

Zelten. Siegfried was found in a heap of wounded soldiers. He was naked; he remembered nothing, not even what language he spoke. I believe that Siegfried and Forestier are the same man.

Robineau. My dear Zelten, when a great man dies he changes planets, not countries.

Zelten. If seeing won't convince you, reading will. If you were in Saint Thomas' place, you would have been convinced not by Christ's hands but by the way he signed his name. You've read Forestier's works; well, then, read Siegfried's! The one is an exact copy of the other—the same point of view, style, even turns of speech.

Robineau. But every work of literature is based on plagiarism, except the first—and that was lost long ago.

Zelten. There's nothing more German than a French philologist! I hoped to win you over more quickly with arguments drawn from your own field. As a matter of fact, I was not led to the truth by following the established methods of scholarship.

Robineau. I can imagine. The method you used was the more popular and no less fruitful one of the anonymous tip.

Zelten. How did you guess? A stranger who would not tell me his name informed me that Siegfried had been in the bed beside him in the hospital. He told me that he wasn't a German. He's seen his real name on a tag which he'd found on the stretcher: Jacques Forestier. Damn it all, I know—my story begins where any respectable melodrama ends—but it's not hard for you to see how pleased I am!

Robineau. Not a bit hard. It's a great stroke of luck to change a politician one hates into a writer one loves.

Zelten. It's an even greater stroke of luck to unload onto another country a great man who's in the way in one's own country. I can't wait any longer. My investigations must come to an end today. But in a few minutes we'll get to the bottom of the matter.

Robineau. But what about Genevieve, Zelten? Haven't you thought about her? Where does she come in?

ZELTEN *has rung for* MUCK, *who enters.*

Zelten. Muck, tell Chancellor Siegfried that the Canadian schoolteacher wants to talk to him.

MUCK *bows and exits up the stairs.*

Zelten. There! All we have to do is wait. Siegfried adores foreign academics, especially those from the other side of the Atlantic. He questions them avidly about the administration of universities and prisons, and about coeducation.

With such irresistible bait he'll be down in a minute to see Genevieve.

Robineau. Down? What do you mean "down"?

Zelten. This is his house. He's upstairs on the second floor. Call Genevieve.

Robineau. Not for anything. We must prepare them first—— You can kill a sleepwalker if you shout his name, even in a foreign language.

Enter GENEVIEVE.

Zelten. No need to call her; here she is. You don't have to ring for the servants of destiny.

Genevieve. Well, now, Baron von Zelten, what is it you wish?

Robineau. Nothing, Genevieve. We'll tell you tomorrow.

Genevieve. What is it you want, Baron?

Zelten. Could we talk about the subject which causes you the most pain, the most grief?

Genevieve [turning to ROBINEAU]. Oh!

Robineau. Yes!

Genevieve. About Jacques?

Zelten. Yes, about Forestier—— Could we talk about him? It won't be too painful for you?

Genevieve [very unaffected and quiet]. Let's talk about Forestier. Has his body been found? Do you want me to identify it? What did I say, Baron? Why are you looking at me that way?

Zelten. I am always entranced whenever I see a human being approach a serious event with the voice and manner required.

Genevieve [sitting down, with a trace of a smile, between ZELTEN *and* ROBINEAU, *who are still standing].* Yes, other people have said that about me. I have precisely the dignified manner suitable for receiving word that my son or my mother has died or that my father is bankrupt and dishonest. But the misfortune, the true misfortune, is that I have had neither parents nor children. Tragedy has never taken me on. I'm Phaedra without a stepson, without a husband, and without scruples—a cheerful Phaedra. That doesn't leave much material for destiny.

Zelten. What about Forestier?

Genevieve. Oh, yes, Forestier—— We knew each other for two years, from 1912 to 1914. It would have been natural if I had to worry while he was at the front, grieve when he died, and fall heir to his glory—— But you can be sure that such a positive destiny was denied me: we quarreled a month before the war. By a slight, slight quarrel, destiny kept me from quarreling with life itself, from mourning—— Beneath every mourner's weeds is an opportunity I never had.

Zelten. Why didn't you make up when the war was declared?

Genevieve. We were both counting on his getting a five-day pass. Now we have to count on religions that offer a life after death. But I've always avoided playing any official role—— I was an illegitimate child; I would have hated being a widow.

Zelten. He isn't dead. Just missing!

Genevieve. Missing and found. The earth swallows up the bones of great men and then redistributes them, transformed into marble, to every corner of their homeland. Every bone of his body has already reappeared: his head, in granite, stands in a square in Limoges; and his right hand, in alabaster, holds a laurel sprig in Orléans.

Zelten. If he disappeared, he can just as well reappear.

Genevieve. You can imagine that that's what I tell myself now and again.

Zelten. Have you ever had a presentiment that he might return?

Genevieve. Not one. Quite the opposite. I never see him in my dreams. Nor does he obsess me when I can't sleep. I haven't received from him a single one of the messages the dead send to the living——

MUCK *returns, crosses the room bowing to* ZELTEN, *and exits.* ROBINEAU *becomes increasingly agitated. An anguished silence is broken by the sound of a door being opened on the landing upstairs.*

Zelten. What if he returned? What if all of a sudden he came down these stairs?

Genevieve [*smiling*]. I've quarreled with him.

SIEGFRIED'S *voice is heard.*

Zelten. Listen!

Genevieve. What is it? What do you mean? That's Jacques' voice! [*The voice is no longer heard from upstairs.*] Whose voice was that?

Zelten. That was the master of the house, Chancellor Siegfried.

Genevieve [*going to stairs and calling*]. Jacques!

Silence.

Genevieve [*returning*]. Explain——

Robineau. Zelten believes that he has discovered that Siegfried, who was found in a state of amnesia in a mass of wounded men, is none other than Forestier.

SIEGFRIED *opens the door at the top of the stairs.*

Genevieve. Who's that coming down?

Zelten. Siegfried.

Genevieve [*not daring to look at him, talking to herself*]. That's not his step!—— Or else he's carrying something very heavy! Yes, it is his step. The way he walked when he carried me—— What could he be carrying that's even heavier than I am? That's his voice! And that's his shadow! [SIEGFRIED *reaches the foot of the stairs, accompanied by* EVA.] Ah! It's he!

Exit ZELTEN, overjoyed.

Robineau. Quiet! You could kill him.

GENEVIEVE *withdraws to the back of the room.* SIEGFRIED *bids* EVA *good-by with a friendly gesture.*

Genevieve. Look at the way you're dressed, Jacques!

SIEGFRIED *moves toward* GENEVIEVE, *who has withdrawn to the back of the stage near the bay window. He greets her in the German style, lightly clicking his heels.*

Siegfried [*presenting himself*]. Siegfried. [GENEVIEVE *nods in acknowledgment.*] I thought you would be old. A very old woman. No, I don't dare tell you my plan. [GENEVIEVE *keeps looking at him.*] I hope I'm not mistaken? You're the French-Canadian lady I was told wanted to see me? [GENEVIEVE *nods affirmatively.*] Can you understand what I'm saying? I know my French isn't fluent; in fact, that's the only reason I dare speak to you. I would like to take lessons. Every evening around six I take an hour to myself. Would you care to do me the service of coming at that time? Starting tomorrow?

Robineau. Say you will.

GENEVIEVE *nods.*

Siegfried. I hope I won't be taking lessons from a lady who is mute?

Robineau. Don't worry, sir. But the lady is hesitant——

Siegfried. The lady is your wife? I'm sorry, I didn't know——

Robineau. Oh, no! The lady and I are only friends, but I know she's never given lessons before. She's wondering whether she's qualified. [*Becoming confused.*] French as it's spoken in Canada presents certain significant differences from French as it's spoken in France. In Quebec we call a *tram* a "car," and an *overcoat* a "topcoat."

Siegfried [*who has approached him*]. *Snow*—how do you say *snow?*

Robineau. Snow? We say snow . . . Why do you mention snow?

Siegfried. And *winter?*

Robineau. Winter—— Just like summer—— I mean that there are the same words for the seasons that there are in France.

Siegfried. Then there's no need to worry. I don't need an idiomatic vocabulary—and it's just too bad if I develop a Quebec accent. [*With a gesture he invites* GENEVIEVE *to sit down. As she seems not to understand, he turns back to* ROBINEAU.] Life is becoming so ridiculously specialized that I need to relax with broad conversations on broad themes. Canadian French, coming from a country of wide rivers and extremes of weather and seasons, is just what I need—— What about *silence,* mademoiselle? How do you say *silence* in Canada?

Genevieve [*slowly, as if in a dream*]. How do you say it in German?

SIEGFRIED *goes toward* GENEVIEVE, *who moves away from him.*

Siegfried. Stille! Silentum!

Genevieve. We say "silence."

Siegfried. Even the words of the new world are open and pure!

Robineau. Excuse me, but these words are French, after all.

Siegfried. Yes, I know they're French, but in your mouth they take on something of the unknown. In France the word *snow* has never touched as much snow as it has in Canada. You took from France a word which she used for only a few days out of the year and with it lined your entire language.

Genevieve. Until tomorrow, then. [*Very rapidly, as* SIEGFRIED *is already near the door.*] Look how you're dressed, Jacques!

Siegfried. Did you speak to me? I see I don't understand you at all well when you talk fast.

Genevieve. How fast should I speak tomorrow?

Siegfried. Let's experiment. Recite a speech from some well-known play. I'll tell you when I can't understand. Then we'll know how fast you should talk.

Genevieve [*after starting toward him and then stopping herself, recites, slowly at first, then very quickly, but at the end almost falters*]. When spring came, when the lindens along the Boulevard Saint-Germain first unfurled their leaves, we used to go to the Café de Cluny—just the two of us—every day at five o'clock. You used to order a Chambéry-Fraisette. At six you went back to the *Action Française* where you wrote up the events of the day in the Chamber of Deputies from the royalist point of view. Then you went to the offices of the *Lanterne* where I picked you up at eight o'clock after you had finished writing a piece on proceedings in the Senate from the socialist point of view. So passed two years of our life, Jacques.

Siegfried. That's a little fast. I can catch the words, but not the sense—especially of such a long speech. Is it from a tragedy or a comedy?

Robineau. All the genres are combined in the modern theatre.

Siegfried. Until tomorrow, then, mademoiselle. I'm sure we'll find our proper tongue somewhere between your amazing silence and your rapid speech. Our meeting has given me great pleasure. [*He bids her good-by, clicking his heels.*]

Genevieve [*holding herself in check*]. Jacques!

Eva [*appearing on the landing*]. Siegfried!

Siegfried [*gesturing vaguely in the direction of* Eva *and excusing himself with a smile*]. I must go!

Curtain.

ACT TWO

A study in SIEGFRIED's *house. It is furnished in late nine-teenth-century style, which has since been supplanted in Germany by American chrome modern. Frost can be seen on the wide bay window. Snow falls outside. Throughout the act the music of a nearby piano is heard on which a pianist is practicing German romantic music. As the curtain goes up General de* FONTGELOY, *in a black and white uniform, is standing, apparently waiting. A bell rings.* EVA *enters, shows the general into a hall, then goes to open the door. Enter* ROBINEAU.

ROBINEAU. We've come for the lesson, mademoiselle.

Eva. I'll tell the Chancellor.

Exit EVA. *Silence. With a gesture* GENEVIEVE *calls* ROBI-NEAU's *attention to the room.*

Genevieve. This is scarcely the way I pictured the temple of forgetfulness.

Robineau. Did Forestier have better taste?

Genevieve. Exactly opposite to this.

Robineau [*a little crossly because, unlike her, he is enchanted by the heavily Germanic atmosphere*]. What do you mean, opposite? Forestier had an armchair and a desk, didn't he?

Genevieve. Of course he did, but the armchairs were just the opposite of these armchairs, the table of this table—the lamp was the opposite of this lamp——

Robineau. This furniture, my dear, is the work of Kohlenschwanzbader.

Genevieve. I could have guessed——

Robineau. These busts are by Weselgrosschmiedvater.

Genevieve. I'm not a bit surprised. And who made the electric light?

Robineau. Then what is it that surprises you?

Genevieve. Until we came here, a minute ago, I couldn't really imagine that Forestier was alive. I came here feeling that I would have to make my way down into some dark, shadowy retreat—a study halfway between the one Fores-

23

tier had in Paris and the one he'll have in Hades. I came to dislodge a mummy, to descend into a royal tomb. And this is what I find.

Robineau. Comfort is what you find.

Genevieve. Comfort never occurred to me when I thought of Forestier's ghost. I see I've been wrong to go on thinking ever since yesterday that he lived without chairs, without a clock, without an inkwell. My God, they give him red ink to write with: he hates that! And look at this cigar; he smokes a cigar now! He detests cigars. I'm sure they've made him do the two things he most abhors: go without a hat and wear suspenders. Steel yourself, Robineau! This tomb is pretty set in its ways; we're going to have to turn things upside down. Take away these smoker's knickknacks first of all!

Robineau. You're out of your mind—these little accessories are delightful!

Genevieve. And so practical!

Robineau. Yes, practical. Look, you take a match from this squirrel, strike it on Wotan's back, and then you light a cigarette which you've taken from the belly of this swan. You tap the ashes into this Walkyrie and you throw the butt in this bear—— You've got to admit that this string of legendary animals and heroes which the Germans include in even the most humble aspects of their lives are lively and amusing. And look at that copper frieze—female centaurs pursued by gnomes! They're full of life, aren't they?

Genevieve. So full that they need killing.

Robineau. Well, in any case, sit down.

Genevieve. No, thank you. Nothing will reconcile me with this furniture. And anyway this chair is reserved. There's an inscription on the cushion.

Robineau. It's the fashion in Germany to embroider proverbs. [*He approaches in order to read the proverb.*] Why it's the cushion itself talking!

A dream in the night,
A cushion in the day.

Genevieve. Who asked its opinion? And what's that embroidered on the table cover? Another proverb?

Robineau [*reads*]. "Falsehood is the jockey of misfortune."

Genevieve. You really believe a self-respecting new sideboard or a self-respecting new tablecloth would utter such clichés of their own accord? It's pure hypocrisy, this babbling of stools, this prattling of whatnots! If this furniture must speak, why doesn't it have a real conversation, the way they do in the *Tales of Hoffmann*. The sideboard could sing a Tyrolean air and the cushion could tell us what it thought about the backside of the people who have sat on it!

Robineau. First sit down, Genevieve.

Genevieve. It's when she's silent that I seem to understand your Germany. Last night when you took me around the town and pointed out to me its gabled houses and belfries, the only inscriptions I saw were patches of moonlight. The town was mute and so was the river we saw—frozen to the bottom, forced into silence. Yet I understood them both, town and river—their age, their strength, what they were saying. What have you got there, Robineau?

Robineau [*puts something on the shelf of a bookcase*]. Time bombs. Two books in French which I found in a bookstore. There weren't many to choose from. This is a manual for breeding and stocking trout. This is a comedy by Legouvé. I don't claim they will have an immediate effect on Siegfried, but he'll see them—he'll read them. How do you intend to approach him?

Genevieve. I don't know. I was intending to ask your advice. It's a problem.

Robineau. A serious problem. What about beginning with the imperfect subjunctive?

Genevieve. I didn't mean the French lesson. I'm thinking of what I must reveal to him.

Robineau. But that's what I am too—— Believe me, Genevieve, I've been teaching foreigners of all sorts for ten years, and, whatever they were—Scandanavians, Brazilians —or however formal our relationship had been until then, all I had to do was to explain the imperfect subjunctive and we felt relaxed, congenial, almost tender—— In fact, Genevieve, the imperfect subjunctive has given birth to one or two exceptionally tender relationships.

Genevieve. Don't joke, Robineau. Help me decide what to do. Keep in mind the role I'm playing. I'm carrying a dagger hidden in my dress; what have I come here to do

but to kill Siegfried? Isn't that so? But if I've come to kill
the enemy king in his tent, don't I deserve the confidante
that playwrights always give Judith and Charlotte Corday?
I need a friend to tell me what they're always being told:
that there's no evading one's duty, that life is short—all
those truths which would in this country have been embroidered on Socrates' or Danton's cushions. Come on!
Reel them off to me!

Robineau. But this will be a murder without a wound
and without a corpse.

Genevieve. That's just it! I'm going to inflict an invisible wound, and spill colorless blood. I'm afraid.

Robineau. There's no need to rush things. It takes
twenty lessons to learn French.

Genevieve. That's even worse. Instead of murdering
Siegfried, you're advising me to subject him to a slow
death. What are you doing now?

Robineau. I'm substituting tobacco for his cigarettes.

Genevieve. Yes, Robineau, I know you think that if you
exchange Siegfried's comb for a Parisian comb, each
piece of furniture in this room for one from Forestier's
apartment in Paris, every dish he eats for a French dish,
a landscape of hop fields for a landscape of vineyards,
every German for a Frenchman, that if you do all this,
you'll succeed in replacing Siegfried with Forestier.

Robineau. Yes, I believe that's the way to do it!

Genevieve. I know it's not a method I can even attempt
to follow. I didn't have the heart to put on any of the
jewels he used to know or one of the ones he gave me. I
didn't choose the perfume he used to love. Fortunately the
fashions this season do not have any specific character.
Never before have the couturiers dressed us as they have
this winter, for eternity. I've had my hair cut short since
he saw me. This is the first time I've been reduced to
looking so little like myself. These styles diffuse my per-
sonality, disperse it. I can get at Forestier only by way of
abstractions and eternal truths. I'm mobilizing everything
that is most rarefied and impersonal in myself. I fear, my
dear Robineau, that we'll be talking a lot less about the
imperfect subjunctive than we will about life and death.

Robineau. But you'll tell him who he is, won't you?

Genevieve. Who he is now? But I'm not sure. Oh! Look at this, Robineau! [*She indicates a framed painting.*]

Robineau. The portrait?

Genevieve. The portrait of the woman!

Robineau. It's only a painting——

Genevieve. Dear painting! It's one of Vermeer's women. Oh, Robineau, look at her and be grateful. Just seeing her restores my confidence.

Robineau. She looks like you!

Genevieve. He had a similar reproduction in his study in Paris. No doubt it's the only object his former and present lives have in common, but at least it exists! All is not lost, Robineau, if this little Dutch girl found a way of rejoining him across such a dark void!

Robineau. I can leave you now; you've found your confidante.

Genevieve [*who has unhooked the painting and is examining it*]. Of course the frame is different. Forestier's was a plain wooden one. Siegfried's seems to be of bone, ivory, and aluminum, with the corners made of pinchbeck. What sort of frame must I wear in order to register on his retina?—— You're going? Just a minute. Take these cushions with you—I don't want any inanimate object talking during my lesson! And take these flowers, too. To-day let him reap only artificial flowers. Let the dwarfs capture these female centaurs here in this drawer. Frolicking between gnomes and gods is forbidden in the presence of Frenchmen. [*She turns out a light.*]

Robineau. Why so dark? You can't recognize anyone in the dark.

Genevieve. Oh! How quickly we'd recognize each other if we were blind! [*She pushes* ROBINEAU *out of the room. Once alone, she replaces the Vermeer portrait and places the roses from the bodice of her dress before it.*] Now, O ghost of Forestier, return!

SIEGFRIED *enters abruptly.*

Siegfried. Good afternoon, madame.

Genevieve [*surprised, drawing back*]. Please—— mademoiselle.

Siegfried. May I ask your name?

Genevieve. Prat—— My family name is Prat——

Siegfried. And your given name?

Genevieve. Genevieve.

Siegfried. Genevieve—— Am I pronouncing it correctly?

Genevieve. A little slowly, but it's all right for a start.

Siegfried. Let me repeat what we've said so far. You want me to go back over our conversations from time to time, don't you? It's easy this time. Our conversation was a model dialogue. Let me sum it up in as few words as possible: I have before me Mademoiselle Genevieve Prat?

Genevieve. None other. [*She sits down.*]

Siegfried. What did you do in Canada?

Genevieve. In Canada? We had—what everyone has there—a farm——

Siegfried. Where was it?

Genevieve. In the country—— [*He laughs.*] Near a town——

Siegfried. What town?

Genevieve. What town? You know people don't pay much attention to names in Canada. It's a large country, but everybody feels near to everyone else. We used to call our lake "The Lake," and our town "The Town." No one remembers the name of the river—I'm sure you're going to ask me about the immense river which crosses Canada—it's just "The River"!

Siegfried. The postmen must have a hard time——

Genevieve. People don't write much. When they do, they deliver their own letters by sleigh.

Siegfried. What did you do on the farm?

Genevieve. What everyone does in Canada: look after the snow.

Siegfried. I understand. It was a snow farm. Those are your farming clothes?

Genevieve. We're rich. We had a few profitable years when it was very cold.

Siegfried [*suddenly very serious*]. Why are you fooling this way?

Genevieve [*laughing*]. Why are you forcing me to pretend to be something I am not? Can't you see I'm not Canadian? But my nationality won't have the slightest effect on our lesson! We shall simply make every sentence negative instead of positive. I am not Canadian. I have never shot a grizzly bear, etc. You will learn just as much.

Siegfried. Who are you?

Genevieve. A riddle will give you good practice. I do not kill grizzly bears, but I design my own dresses. I do not ski, but my cooking has made me famous. Who am I?

Siegfried. You are French? Why didn't you tell me?

Genevieve. I thought the teacher was supposed to ask the questions!

Siegfried. You are right. The trouble is that there is nothing to me except questions. My questions grasp at every bit of flotsam within reach and hold on for dear life. You've heard my story?

Genevieve. What story?

Siegfried. There are few subjects on which I can speak without having to ask questions: taxation in Germany since 1848 and the legal status of the individual in the German Empire since the year 1000 are the only two areas on which I have anything to say. I hardly think you are eager to know more about either.

Genevieve. You'll see one day! But now, ask all the questions you want.

Siegfried. I should not have asked you who you are! Now there's nothing left to ask. A first name followed by a last name answers every question. If I ever rediscover my name, it will be my reply to every question. Yes, I am so-and-so. Yes, winter has come but my name is so-and-so. How good it must be to be able to say: "It is snowing, but I am Genevieve Prat."

Genevieve. It's cruel of me to contradict you, but unfortunately I don't agree. To me every human being is condemned to a terrible anonymity. A man's name, title, and rank are artificial and impermanent; they do nothing to reveal what he really is, even to himself. You may not believe me, but I find it more upsetting to be in the presence of an ordinary man than in the presence of a victim of amnesia.

Siegfried. Then I seem to you to be the only man in this world who is not anonymous?

Genevieve. That's going a little far . . .

Siegfried. I am being difficult; forgive me. At any other time I would have wanted to conceal from you for a few days longer the shadowy world in which I live. No one can

do me a greater kindness than to remain ignorant of what
has happened to me. At another time I would have told
you that I was descended from the true Siegfried, that my
godmother had just twisted her ankle, and that my aunt's
aunt was in town for a few days. You would have believed
me, and the peace and quiet so necessary for the study of
irregular verbs would have ensued.

Genevieve. That's right; we are forgetting the lesson.
Question me, sir, since you like to ask questions. Ask me
the sort of question one discusses with one's teachers as
well as with people one doesn't know very well—a question
like, "What is art?" or "What is death?" It's a good way
to learn useful vocabulary.

Siegfried. All right. What is life?

Genevieve. You sound like a character in a Russian
novel. But I can give you an answer: life is a dubious adventure for the living, but it is a completely agreeable experience for the dead.

Siegfried. What is it for those who are dead and living
at the same time?

Genevieve. Must you make our lesson so gloomy? Let's
open our text to another chapter. Let's learn the words
you'll need at the barber. Or, here are the names of some
animals and the cries they make. Don't you want to know
what sort of a noise the screech owl makes in French?

Siegfried. If you wish. I want to make you happy—not
that you seem unhappy. You are gentle and gay and full
of smiles, yet I can't help sensing in you something akin to
my own melancholy. What I have been saying seems to
echo within you.

Genevieve [*looking him directly in the eyes very seriously*]. My fiancé was killed in the war. My life ended
where yours began.

Siegfried. I'm sorry. Even so I would change places with
you.

Genevieve. Let's change, then.

Siegfried. Don't say that. If only you could understand
what it means to me, how it delights me to receive a little
of that past which you carry around so lightly. It is always
with you, layer upon layer: your childhood, your adolescence, your youth. Just by coming into this house, you have
shown me something of all this. You are still garlanded

with the songs your mother sang to you, with the first sonata you ever heard, with the first opera you attended. You are crowned with your first memories of the moon, the sea, forests, and flowers. You would be terribly mistaken to give up these riches; if you take my place you will have to tell the night and the stars, "Night and stars, I never saw you for the first time." [*He smiles.*] I suppose you know them well after all these years?

Genevieve. You carry nothing of your life with you? You are not aware of love or ambitions in your past?

Siegfried. No. And yet I cannot help feeling that there are parts of my heart which are hidden from me. I value myself enough to believe that I could not have reached my present age without my fair share of love and longing. I have not yet dared to unlock these hidden places. I am waiting to do so.

Genevieve [*in a voice full of feeling*]. For not much longer, perhaps.

Siegfried. Sometimes I think you are right. Sometimes destiny solves mysteries of human life which men don't solve for themselves. A famous diamond is lost and destiny makes it turn up in an apple; a ship is lost and a hundred years later destiny finds its wreck. Only inadvertently does God allow a blot on his account book. He is most meticulous. He will be furious when he notices that there are two dossiers for the same Siegfried. I'm counting on the elements to point out my plight to him. They are incorrigible gossips—— [*He looks at her tenderly from a distance.*] But you are not one of the elements, you're human; don't you have anything to tell me?

Genevieve [*very seriously*]. I am thinking up a sentence for you.

Siegfried. Yes, you are right; we should return to the lesson—return to ourselves. [*He goes to her and bends over her.*]

Genevieve. You are returning from a great distance, and at the same time from nearby.

Siegfried. I am studying you, a stranger, as closely as I do my own image each day in the mirror—— Forgive me—— You are a mystery to me, but a so much more captivating and tender mystery, a so much more delightful one than my own. What a pleasant, restful task to wonder who

this young woman is, whom she has loved, what she is
like!

Genevieve. What she is like——

Siegfried. How quickly one develops second sight for
other people's lives! I can see you as a child, skipping rope.
I see you as a young girl reading at your desk. Then I see
you beside a still pond, perfectly reflected in it, and beside
a flowing stream, with your reflection broken into a
hundred bits—— Dear Genevieve, your life has not been
completely happy. I see you as a young woman kneeling by
your fiancé's grave——

Genevieve. No—— He disappeared——

Siegfried. Oh! I'm sorry—— Was he an officer?

Genevieve. He became an officer during the war. It was
in his bright, light blue officer's uniform that he disappeared—that uniform which our countrymen were foolish
enough to believe would be invisible to the enemy. Not that
it helped him to be found—— He was a writer—— He was
one of those who foresaw the war; he wanted France to
prepare herself. [*She rises.*]

Siegfried. He hated Germany?

Genevieve. He would have liked a peaceful Germany.
He was sure she would be defeated. He looked forward to
being able to respect her once again.

Siegfried. What did he say about her? Don't be afraid:
I never knew the Germany you are talking about. I am a
German, but one only six years old.

Genevieve. I don't know anything about politics.

Siegfried. Are you being modest?

Genevieve. He used to say, if I remember correctly, that
the Germans were a great people—hard-working, passionate, with an immense capacity for poetry. But he said
that they often sang a false note with more feeling than a
true, that they were brutal, bloodthirsty, without compas-
sion——

Siegfried. Did he tell you how young their two-thousand-
year-old empire is, how vigorous their art is, despite its
preciousness? Did he tell you how conscientious and upright the Germans are despite their reputation for hypocrisy?
Did he describe the spiritual and artistic discoveries they
have made despite their lack of taste?

Genevieve. Of course now and then he did speak favorably of Germany—he adored the song of the Rhine maidens and he liked the German ideal of love. But he used to say that, during the past century when everything German was the fashion, the Germans had failed to preserve a sense of simplicity. He said that Germany should have been true to her instincts, her soil, and her heritage. Instead, he said, pedantic scholars and megalomaniac rulers had convinced Germany that she was superhuman, gigantic. Often in the past Germany had created a new image of human dignity; this time she has created a new image of pride and suffering. There! Now I've told you what Jacques used to say—— Oh, yes, one more thing: he blamed Germany for accusing the whole world of her own mistakes.

Siegfried. Did he tell you that we Germans are critical of ourselves? Did he say that Germany has almost always been the first to see the truth about herself? Did he explain to you the real causes of the war? Did he explain that the heart of Germany was exploding and that it was a passionate heart despite the horror and destruction it caused? Did he explain Germany's mad passion for the world, the way in which she wants to wed the entire earth, the way she lusts for the universe? No other people have loved the world with all its flora and fauna as the Germans have. The world's best zoos and biggest telescopes have been made by Germans. The world's greatest explorers and geologists are Germans. They are scattered on every continent, and wherever they go, they bring the sound of the music they love—as well as the aroma of the roast goose they insist on eating for Sunday dinner. But their exodus resembles the nuptial flight of bees. Did your friend Jacques explain this to you? Did Jacques tell you that it is love which drives them over the face of the earth?

Genevieve. Jacques! How do you know his name?

Siegfried. You told me a minute ago—— Tell me about Jacques—— Tell me his last name. I still have so few acquaintances from other countries! Let me find one in the past, where I used to live. What was he called?

Genevieve [*facing him*]. Forestier.

*Siegfried. F*o or *F*a?

*Genevieve. F*o. Like *forest.*

Siegfried. What did he look like?

Genevieve. Tall. Auburn hair. A wonderful smile. My

description sounds vague but, in fact, it's so precise that you could pick him out of a crowd.

Siegfried. Do you have a picture of him?

Genevieve [*hesitating at first*]. Yes, I have one.

Siegfried. At your hotel?

Genevieve. No, here——

A bell rings. EVA opens the door abruptly.

Eva. The commander in chief wants you, Siegfried. It is urgent.

SIEGFRIED *excuses himself with a smile, bows, and goes out with* EVA. GENEVIEVE *remains alone for a minute, facing the audience. She is distraught. General de* FONT-GELOY *enters, trying to be quiet, but* GENEVIEVE *hears the sound of his spurs.*

Fontgeloy. What about me, Genevieve Prat, do you recognize me? [GENEVIEVE *studies him in silence.*] Don't you and I share a certain family resemblance? [GENEVIEVE *continues to study him.*] I am tall and dark; I speak French without an accent. [*He grasps her hands somewhat roughly.*] Who am I?

Genevieve. A Prussian officer.

Fontgeloy. Wrong! A French gentleman. [GENEVIEVE *still looks at him.*] I am another Forestier, or another Siegfried, as you wish. But a Siegfried who was able to retain his name and his memory. A perfect memory. For two and a half centuries it has been perfect. [*He clicks his heels.*] Jacques de Fontgeloy, descendant of the first Protestant to be driven out of France by Louis XIV and commander of the Death's Head Brigade of the hussars.

Genevieve. The Death's Head Brigade? I thought that was a thing of the past.

Fontgeloy. I am their general, and their patroness is not far off.

Genevieve. Patroness and general—what do they want of me?

Fontgeloy. You can be sure, mademoiselle, that you have nothing to fear from either one of us. I have come to beg you to depart before Siegfried returns. This is all I ask of you; please do not object. You have come too late to detach him from Germany. It is as if you were to try to uproot the Fontgeloys.

Genevieve. It is flattering to France to have another country fight so obstinately for people who slipped out of her ranks.

Fontgeloy. Slipped out! The Fontgeloys did not slip away. They were chased out, given notice that their service as Frenchmen was ended. One fine day my ancestor was ordered to leave the country within a week, to give up his family, his estates, his place in society. But no gentleman would wait a week after such an insult. He departed at once; but once he had crossed the frontier, he killed the two royal guards who had followed him as if they had been riffraff. They were no longer his countrymen.

Genevieve. I can see that it is not amnesia which is keeping his descendants in Germany.

Fontgeloy. No, they are kept here by what they remember. They are kept here by memories of despotism and persecution, and by a distaste for a bureaucracy which is the slave of petty tyrants whose names you recite with reverence.

Genevieve. Yes, men like Loubet and Fallières.

Fontgeloy. Let me finish my story. My ancestor settled near the frontier and took in all the exiles from France. According to their abilities, he helped them settle in Prussian towns which needed notaries or burgomasters or surveyors. The exiles strengthened Prussia at her weak points, but there was one place they did not fill. Now the man for this place has been found at last. We will not let him go. I have been charged to tell you this. He will remain or he will die——

Genevieve. Once again?

Fontgeloy. It is unfortunate, isn't it, that a man's life has not mattered very much in France for the last ten years? But he will be killed by what you want to reveal to him. Remember, he is still ailing. If he does not kill himself in a frenzy, someone else will kill him. If he discovers who he is, his strength will fail and his new life will dissolve. He will die and his death will be unforgivable. And now, mademoiselle, follow me, if you wish to save Siegfried from misfortune. I am under orders to have you de-

ported. My men have your friend the philologist in their
custody already. He is trying to win them over by talking
to them in thirteenth-century dialects.

Genevieve [*sitting down*]. Are there many men like you
in Germany?

Fontgeloy. Do you like statistics? You are not like a
German. On the first of August, 1914, there were fourteen
generals, thirty-two colonels, and three hundred officers in
the Prussian army alone who were descended from French
émigrés and exiles, all aristocrats who emigrated or were
exiled. In the commissary corps there were a fair number
of untitled Frenchmen as well.

Genevieve. I had no idea that the wars between France
and Germany were civil wars.

Fontgeloy. Civil wars! Since the reign of Louis XIV we
have never crossed the French frontier except under orders.
I haven't given up hope of setting up headquarters one day
at the Fontgeloy manor near Tours, which still stands, I
have heard.

Genevieve. Yes, it is still there—on the road from Tours
to Chenonceaux——

Fontgeloy. Don't bother to describe it to me.

Genevieve. You would love it. There are roses and aristolochia and jasmine everywhere.

Fontgeloy. Aristolochia? What is aristolochia?

Genevieve. It is a low, creeping plant, a suitable emblem
for certain twentieth-century Frenchmen.

Fontgeloy. Why are you looking at me that way?

Genevieve. I am sure you will think I'm peculiar, but
I'm trying to imagine what you look like naked.

Fontgeloy. Completely naked?

Genevieve. Yes. Let's forget for a minute your stories of
exiles and émigrés. You must be the only one who is interested in them these days. I am a sculptor, Monsieur de
Fontgeloy. The human form is my model and my Bible.
Under your uniform I recognize the body which we sculptors give to Racine and Marivaux—— My countrymen are
known for the refinement and sophistication of their
manners, but they are modeled after men like you—men
of energy, daring, and, if I may speak sternly for the first
time in my life, sternness. Your forehead and the sharp look
of your mouth are very French. Even your sternness is very

French—— After all, one must remember that France wasn't always a soft-living country with every Frenchman dressed in silks and satins—— Still, the sight of you gives me all the more respect for the two centuries since you left France. At least they've worn off her rough edges.

The telephone rings. The sound of cannon fire follows.

Fontgeloy [*thinking aloud*]. The telephone can wait. [*He goes to the window. The artillery fire ceases. He returns and answers the telephone.*] A vote of censure? What vote of censure? They are calling for a vote? Calling for what vote? War? What war?

The sound of artillery fire once again. Enter General von WALDORF *and General* LEDINGER, *wearing heavy military overcoats, as* FONTGELOY *puts down the receiver.*

Waldorf. Not war, Fontgeloy, revolution!
Fontgeloy. Who? The Communists?
Waldorf. No, Zelten.
Fontgeloy. Don't joke!
Waldorf. Zelten has occupied the Residency and seized power.
Ledinger. Power? There's no power to be seized these days in our country.
Waldorf. Be serious, Ledinger! He has at least the power to put us in prison. We're marked men. I have a car waiting for us outside. Siegfried is calling Berlin, and as soon as he has finished we shall leave for Cobourg, where my brigade is stationed. We shall attack this very night.
Fontgeloy. But what troops does Zelten have?
Ledinger. The kind of troops that always support a so-called liberal revolution—all those who keep order, the police and the fire brigade. But this time they are heavily reinforced with drug addicts and cubists.
Waldorf. I beseech you, Ledinger. You artillery staff officers have an unbearable way of making light of serious events.
Ledinger. Forgive me, Waldorf, but at a moment like this it's not a question of artillery versus infantry!
Waldorf. It is always a question of artillery versus infantry.
Ledinger. I don't follow you.

Waldorf. It isn't the first time an artillery man can't
follow what is being said, even when it's only a foot soldier
talking to him. What I mean, Ledinger, is that we
wouldn't be in our present difficulties if, at a decisive moment in the past, the army hadn't had an infantry chief-of-
staff who began this tradition of treating everything serious as if it were a joke.

Ledinger. Perhaps he was incompetent?

Waldorf. No. On the battlefield he won what others
counted on losing when they looked at the map. And, as
a matter of fact, he lost where others would have won.

Ledinger. Was he a coward?

Waldorf. The soul of bravery. I saw him refuse to be
defeated by Schlieffen himself on manoeuvers in Silesia.

Ledinger. What was wrong with him then?

Waldorf. What was wrong with him? His definition of
war was incorrect! War does not depend on strategy, muni-
tions, and audacity alone. Its success or failure depends
on the way it is defined from the outset. An exact chemical
formula must be made for it.

Ledinger. I am precisely of your opinion, Waldorf, and
I assure you that my definition of war has been proved.
It saved Prussia twice, once from the Russians and once
from Napoleon. I stand at attention to enunciate it: War
is the Nation!

Waldorf. That is the formula which lost us the last war!
What exactly do you mean by nation? Do you lump together the Potsdam grenadiers with the cartoonists for the
socialist newspapers, the Death's Head Brigade of the hussars with cinema magnates, the aristocracy with the Jews?

Ledinger. Every thinking, feeling, working man is part
of the nation.

Waldorf. Why not push your formula to its furthest
extreme and say, "War and the Brotherhood of Nations
are one!" It would be scarcely more ridiculous. Your definition of war compromises the rights of the general staff.
We alone have the right to make war. You are trying to
make war democratic, so that an ordinary German can declare war whenever he wants to. In the last war the nation
was so flattered with this military version of universal
suffrage that it was completely united in an enterprise
which should have remained in our hands. Sixty million

people participated in the war effort, but as a result you lost control of the war itself. Parliamentary government runs the same risks. If only you had subscribed to the definition of war which my master taught me! Then you would have been victorious! You know the formula I mean; it is used as an epigraph in all our secret manuals; whenever it is spoken every one of us, soldier or civilian, becomes more sharply conscious of his honor and his usefulness to society: "War is Peace!"

Fontgeloy. You are wrong, Waldorf. I appreciate your master's achievements, of course, even though he was so meticulous that he assigned his hussars' trouser straps to a different supply train than their trousers. And I recognize that your definition has the right point of view: believe me, it has not often occurred to a general staff to differentiate between peace and a state of war. But there is only one word which has the same weight as the word war, which will equal it in a formula. Only one which is worthy, only one which can present the monster of war in all his glory! That word is part of our definition—a formula which deceived neither the Grand Electors nor Bismarck. Our definition is a moral precept! A piece of practical advice useful to the soldier in all circumstances! This is our formula: "War is war!"

All three draw their swords.

Waldorf. You are wrong! You are wrong! Your definition is redundant. It is as if you said General de Fontgeloy is General de Fontgeloy.

Fontgeloy. Exactly! Even this definition of me which springs so easily to your lips is not redundant. I am sure that even you realize that coming from you it means: This intelligent man—he must be intelligent since he's a general—is a stupid man since he's not on the right staff level.

Enter a SERVANT.

Servant. The Chancellor is waiting for your excellencies downstairs at the door.

Fontgeloy [*severely, to* GENEVIEVE]. Silence is one with silence, mademoiselle.

Genevieve. And death is one with death, no doubt?

Fontgeloy. Exactly.

Exit Fontgeloy, Ledinger, Waldorf. *Enter* Siegfried, *quietly, dressed for departure. Throughout the following conversation,* Genevieve *keeps looking anxiously at the door, where* Fontgeloy *appears from time to time.*

Genevieve. Did you forget something?

Siegfried. Don't I look like someone who forgot something on purpose? Don't I look as if I had left behind my umbrella just so that I could come back for it?

Genevieve. It is snowing. I don't know of anything which will protect you against snow.

Siegfried. Your prediction came true. Revolution has broken out. My work of the last seven years is threatened; everything that I have tried to accomplish may be destroyed. My future seems as blank as my past. Don't be angry at me for having left my courage, my self-confidence, my will here with you so that I would have an excuse to come back for them.

Genevieve. That makes three umbrellas you've forgotten! I'm afraid you are not very well organized!

Siegfried [*studying her*]. Let me look at you!

Genevieve. Have I changed so much in a quarter of an hour?

Siegfried. Seeing you again I notice everything I didn't see at first, things I have never seen in you or anyone else —those sad lips which are even sadder when they smile, that somewhat heavy brow which looks as if it might combat everything that was light and gay in the world. Yes, now I see you—— Speak to me——

The sound of artillery fire is heard.

Genevieve. More important voices are calling to you.

Siegfried. They are not calling to me; they are nothing more than echoes of what I feel. [*He tries to take her hands.*] What have such soft hands touched to become so tender?

Genevieve [*drawing away*]. Earth. Mud. I am a sculptress.

Siegfried. It is snowing. For some time now destiny has been hoping that it will be forgiven if it cloaks revolutions in snow. Think of Moscow, Budapest, and Munich. These days Pilate washes his hands in snow. Today snow makes every German walk as quietly as death itself. And I can tell you it takes a good thick snowfall to silence the spurs of my three generals.

Genevieve. They are waiting for you—— Farewell.

Siegfried [*approaching*]. Why is it that I can't answer you?

Genevieve. Have I asked a question?

Siegfried. Everything about you asks questions except your mouth and your words. Human beings are like timid punctuation marks sprinkled among the incomprehensible sentences of life. Eva is an exclamation point, and for this reason I once liked her. She lent emphasis and an atmosphere of enthusiasm to her surroundings, to a piece of furniture or a landscape. You are a question mark. Your calm and your simplicity are questions. Your dress is a question. I would like to see you when you are asleep—— What an urgent question your sleep must be! Only the confession of a secret would be a worthy answer for the insistent questions I sense in you, and I have no secrets to confess.

Genevieve. Farewell.

Siegfried. Or, if I have one after all, it is so insubstantial that I am scarcely aware of it.

Genevieve. Don't tell it to me.

Siegfried. Even those words ask a question. Here then is my secret since you demand it of me. It's nothing—— But it is the only bit of me which my friends and Eva and the president of the Reich and sixty million Germans don't yet know—— It's nothing—— It's a word——

Genevieve. Farewell.

Siegfried. Yes, I won't go yet. It is the only word out of my entire vocabulary which seems to come not from my present life but from my past. You will see that it is insignificant, even ridiculous. But whereas every other word, however beautiful and subtle, finds a response only in my brand new self, this word strikes a chord in a heart and senses which are hidden in my past. A blind man feeling sunlight on his face must experience the same anguish and the same comfort.

Genevieve. Is it a name?

Siegfried. It is not even a noun. It is a simple adjective. The spirit of my former life was unable to will anything more than an adjective to my new life. It is the most banal, ordinary, almost vulgar epithet, but it is my entire family, my past. It sums up the mystery of my life. It will go with me when I die. It is my only baggage.

Genevieve. I must go——

Siegfried [*turns away, his eyes half-closed*]. Now and then I hear people in the street say it without knowing that they are doing so. To me they are playing with fire. Most writers avoid it, but fortunately Goethe uses it frequently —you can see why I think he is a master. The critics reproach him for using this word, saying that it is a cliché. When I read this word I can see Mignon's flesh beneath her gown, Helen's flesh beneath her robes. It's the word— God, how banal it is, how superficial, it doesn't sound right at all, you'll laugh—it's the word *ravishing*. [*Repeats, his eyes closed.*] *Ravishing*.

Genevieve. I'm laughing.

Siegfried [*turning to her*]. It was this which I wanted to say to you, Genevieve. Perhaps it is equal to a whole secret to have had the courage to tell you this minute fraction of a secret. Farewell. [*He kisses her.*] But now that I have spoken it, I am discovering new uses for it: a ravishing hand, a ravishing girl——

Genevieve. You must go——

Siegfried. Thank you. Farewell.

Curtain.

ACT THREE

The same setting as in the first act. MUCK, *a* FOOTMAN, ZELTEN.

MUCK [*reading self-importantly into the telephone from notes that he is holding in his hand*]. The truth is that during the last century Germany has often failed to give a proper value to her own deepest virtues and has placed too high a value on the daily routine of her life.

Footman. They are coming in crowds.

Muck. As a result she has made a bad name for herself in history while making an immense contribution to civilization——

Footman. The house will be full before the Chancellor has returned from parliament.

Muck. As a result she mistakes the respect and deference which are accorded her instinctive and spiritual life as a nation for homage to the transitory achievements of her daily life—— [*Changing his tone.*] Is that sufficient? Is that the only passage of the Chancellor's speech which you were missing? Excellent—— I am always at the disposition of any representative of the Wolf Agency—— [*To the* FOOTMAN.] What do you want? The Chancellor will be back in five minutes. Whom have you still to find place for?

Footman. The conductors of the choral groups which are going to sing as they parade by.

Muck. Are there many of them?

Footman. Forty.

Muck. Put them in the large reception room. Who else?

Footman. The defenders of the Weimar Constitution.

Muck. How many of them are there?

Footman. Seven—only one delegation.

Muck. Put them in the small study.

Enter ZELTEN.

Zelten. What about me, Muck? Where will you put me?

Muck. Here in this house? You, Baron?

Zelten. Where else can you suggest I go? This is virtually the only place where no one would think to look for me. Did you attend the session?

Muck. I was there.

Zelten. Parliament has asked me to leave the country for a while, I understand?

Muck. That is right.

Zelten. Was it Siegfried who introduced the bill?

Muck. No, but he supported it.

Zelten. And no one protested?

Muck. Your absence turned everyone against you. Your own party thought that you had abandoned them.

Zelten. I was a prisoner in my room, Muck. I was watched by two soldiers. I was not able to escape until a few minutes ago, and then it was too late to attend the session. But it will go on here, I assure you.

Muck. Here? You're not planning to stay here, are you? The Chancellor is going to pass through here. Hear that shouting! He's coming now.

Zelten. What was Siegfried like in his moment of triumph? Was he modest and calm in a manner befitting a noble soul?

Muck. He was tired and happy. For the first time I felt that he was happy. For the first time he seemed to forget himself, to lose himself in events, to believe in the future.

Zelten. There's seldom anything to be gained by losing oneself in events. But you say he was happy? Excellent. I shall stay here, Muck. I want to examine what brought happiness into his face.

Muck. You are frightening me. I hope you aren't armed. What do you want to do to him?

Zelten. What was done in the old days to every imposter. Flay him alive as they did in the Middle Ages. Is there a telephone downstairs in your office?

Muck. Yes.

Zelten. Go down and call Mademoiselle Genevieve Prat. Say that you are calling for the Chancellor. Tell her to come at once for his lesson.

Muck. His lesson! The Chancellor would never have a lesson at such a moment!

Zelten. On the contrary, it will be good for him to have

to translate his overheated ideas into a new language. It will cool him down a bit. Go down and call her. Hurry.

Muck. I hear the Chancellor, Baron. His Excellency is coming up the stairs. [*Exit* MUCK.

Zelten. Excellent! The Chancellor deigns to come upstairs!

Enter SIEGFRIED, *accompanied by* EVA, FONTGELOY, *and* WALDORF.

Siegfried. You are late, Zelten.

Zelten. That is a matter of opinion. I am sure that just at this moment your companions think that I am early.

Siegfried. What do you want here? Don't you know that you must leave Gotha before tomorrow?

Zelten. I shall have left it, and not alone. But so far no one has done me the honor of giving me any official notice that I must leave.

Siegfried. I am giving it to you now.

Zelten. You are giving it to me? May I ask who has authorized you to do so? In whose name are you acting?

Siegfried. Who has authorized me? It's simple. I am acting in the name of Germany.

Zelten. You are acting in the name of Germany? There is nothing simple about that. Not every man who wishes to act in her name succeeds in doing so. Isn't that true, Eva?

Siegfried. Leave Fräulein Eva out of this. She has nothing to do with our problem.

Zelten. That is where you are wrong. She has a great deal to do with it.

Siegfried. I forbid you to speak a single word against her.

Zelten. Against her? I have nothing to say against her. Quite the opposite. I admire the way she has sacrificed her youth, her conscience, to her idea of Germany.

Siegfried. That's enough. You may go.

Zelten. Go? I wouldn't dream of it! I intend to leave in style. I am abdicating today. I have always thought that the abdications in history were far more moving than the coronations. I am looking forward to experiencing the full humiliation and grandeur of my abdication.

Siegfried. Save your histrionics for the cafés of Paris.

That's where you picked up your lamentable comic opera notion of our country in the first place.

Zelten. It will not be long before you will agree with me that I deserve a more solemn farewell—— I shall have left Gotha an hour from now, Siegfried, as you wish; but you will be wrong if you think that I have been driven out by you, or by Germany. I shall continue to believe that all true Germans love small principalities and great passions. I had prepared two fine manifestoes on this subject. I was planning to plaster them over your posters on supplementary taxation and the administration of prefectures, but even my last weapon failed me: I ran out of paste. It is neither your decisive spirit, nor your orders, clever as they are, which are driving me out of my country, and marshaling the people behind you against me. It is two telegrams addressed to Berlin which my agent intercepted. Here they are. Be kind enough, Waldorf, to read the first aloud.

Waldorf [after glancing at SIEGFRIED *to see if he concurs].* "Morgan Rockfeller to President Reich. If Zelten controls in Gotha, we cancel phosphates contract."

Zelten. Here is the second. It's from London.

Waldorf. It's addressed to Herr Stinnes. "If Zelten remains in power, we will start a run on the mark."

Zelten. That's all, but these two threats which the Center and Catholic parties have organized against me correspond to excommunication in the old days. These days phosphates bring us to Canossa—— I intercepted no other messages; no one wired, "If Zelten is president, German musicians refuse to play Beethoven's symphonies——" "If Zelten is regent, German philosophers no longer capable of defining the categorical imperative——" "If Zelten is king, German schoolgirls refuse to pick bilberries to the tune of blackbirds——" But I won't insist any further. I made one last effort to keep Germany from becoming a modern corporation and I failed. For all I care the Rhine can flow on quietly under a coating of crude oil. And that leaves you and me, Siegfried. Will you ask these generals to leave the room?

Siegfried. No, they are my witnesses.

Zelten. With all their decorations they look as if they were holding an inquest. They have caught me *flagrante delicto* with Germany. Yes, I have committed adultery with her, Siegfried. Her perfume still clings to me—that odor of dust and roses and blood with which she fills the air the moment one tries to rule even the least of her principalities. I have enjoyed everything that she offers her lovers—melodrama and a power over the souls of men. She will never give you anything more than the delights of a farmer's cooperative; you will be nothing more than her servant. Dismiss your generals. I have something to say to you alone.

Siegfried. I am not in the mood nor do I have the right to have a private conversation with you.

Zelten. Let them stay, then. You are the only one who will suffer. In any case it is quite right that they should be here. Every time destiny prepares to strike she has a rush of blood to the head and crowds her target with men in uniforms. When Oedipus learned that he was married to his own mother and that he had killed his father, he tried to rally around him all the senior officers of his city.

Waldorf. We are general officers, Zelten!

Ledinger. May I put an end to this farce, your Excellency?

Zelten. Look at Eva's face, Ledinger, and you will see that this is no farce. The lips of the heroine are pale, a minute wrinkle runs across her brow, her hands are joined but they do not seem to know each other—these are the marks of tragedy, not comedy. Why, this is the moment when the stagehands fall silent, and the prompter lowers his voice, and the spectators, who naturally have guessed everything before Oedipus and before Othello, shiver at the prospect of learning what has been known from the beginning of time. I mean the civilian not military spectators, for you haven't guessed a thing, have you, Waldorf!

Waldorf. Muck! Muck!

Siegfried [*stepping between them*]. No, let him speak!

Zelten [*turning to* SIEGFRIED]. He has guessed!

Eva. Don't listen to him, Siegfried. He is lying!

Zelten. He has guessed! He knows that it has something to do with himself. The two ravens which hovered above the head of the true Siegfried have appeared at this moment above the head of his stand-in.

Siegfried [*close to* ZELTEN, *speaking in a controlled, rapid tone*]. That's enough of your flowery language. Say what you have to say.

Zelten. Forgive me. Germans love metaphor. However, I shall avoid it henceforth with you.

Siegfried. What you have to say is something to do with me—Siegfried?

Zelten. Not with Siegfried, with you.

Siegfried. With my past?

Zelten. With your past.

Siegfried. Has enmity brought you to this point?

Zelten. I am not your enemy. Unlike you, the rest of us politicians spend our hatred only on our compatriots.

Siegfried. Have you discovered my true name?

Zelten. I have discovered neither your name nor your family, but the witty insinuations I have been lavishing on you for the last minute or so should have given you a clue to what I mean. I have discovered what I had suspected for a long time. I have discovered that he whose judgment is entirely intellectual, who speaks from his mind rather than from his heart, whose calculations are always rational is not a German!

Siegfried. I don't believe a word you are saying, Zelten.

Zelten. That doesn't astonish me. This is not one of my good days. Even the Germans themselves are overwhelmingly critical of me today.

Siegfried. Must I use force to make you come to the point?

Zelten. The point? But I've said all I am going to say. I want to get across the frontier alive. In any case my role is at an end. It is up to Eva to continue this scene.

Eva. I despise you, Zelten.

Zelten. You will be a sturdier soul than I if you do not find yourself despised too in a few minutes.

Eva. I don't know what he is talking about, Siegfried.

Zelten. Eva knows everything, Siegfried. She can give you the details concerning your arrival at her hospital. She can describe to you the accent of your wordless moaning. She will tell you that you were wearing the identification tag of a foreign army on your arm. It is not my job to supply the truth in such small quantities.

Ledinger. That's enough! Get out!

Zelten [*going in the direction of the door, then turning back*]. Ah, Siegfried, it is too bad that you don't like metaphor or fables. I would like to tell you the one about the fox who slipped into a flock of birds. When they flew up he found himself all alone out in the open. They're already raising their wings, Siegfried; their feathers are stirring. The bird Goethe, the bird Wagner, the bird Bismarck have already extended their necks for flight. Eva has only to make a move and they will be gone!

Ledinger. Get out!

Zelten. And so, too, the bird Zelten departs!

[*Exit* ZELTEN.

Siegfried [*impassive*]. Gentlemen, the farce is done. Return to your posts. I shall remain here. Keep me informed and consult me if necessary.

Ledinger. Certainly, your Excellency. What will the regimental band play as it comes into the city?

Siegfried. What a strange question. Our anthem, the German anthem!

Exit LEDINGER *and* WALDORF. SIEGFRIED *goes to* EVA *and, taking her hands, looks at her intently.*

Siegfried. Am I German, Eva?

Eva. What do you mean, German?

Siegfried. Am I German, Eva?

Eva. From the bottom of my heart I can say to you, yes, Siegfried, you are a great German.

Siegfried. There are certain words which cannot be qualified with an adjective. Try telling a dead man that he died a great death. Am I German, Eva?

Outside the sound of a crowd acclaiming SIEGFRIED. *Fanfares.*

Eva. Let them answer you.

Siegfried. No, I want you to answer this time. Was I German when you leaned over me in the hospital, when you saved me?

Eva. You asked me for water in German.

Siegfried. Every soldier who goes into battle knows the word for water in the language of the enemy. But did I have a foreign accent when I asked you for water? You told me once that you were able to tell by his moaning what country and even what province a wounded man came from. Remember that I, too, moaned.

Eva. You were courage itself. [SIEGFRIED *starts for the door.*] What are you doing, Siegfried?

Siegfried. I am going to speak to the crowd and denounce myself to them.

Eva. Siegfried!

Siegfried [*returning to her*]. I am answering to that name for the last time.

Eva. Yes, you are right; I may as well tell you now that your identity was determined forever by the course of the war. While you lay there without knowing or remembering anything, without any past, without any language, with nothing but the helpless thrashing of a poor wounded beast, perhaps then you were not German.

Siegfried. Who was I?

Eva. Neither the head doctor nor I knew.

Siegfried. You swear?

Eva. I swear.

Enter the SERGEANT.

Sergeant. Mademoiselle Genevieve Prat.

Siegfried. You had better go.

EVA *goes slowly up the stairs. Enter* GENEVIEVE, *exit* SERGEANT.

Genevieve. Did I just pass Zelten with a soldier on either side of him?

Siegfried. Yes, that was Zelten.

Genevieve. Is he going to be shot?

Siegfried. Don't worry. He is being escorted to the train which will take him to the country where he belongs.

Genevieve. Where is that?

Siegfried. At the crossroads of the Boulevard Montmartre and the Boulevard Montparnasse.

Genevieve. But that's impossible——

Siegfried. Not at all!

Genevieve. I meant the two boulevards. They run parallel, Chancellor—one at the north of the city and the other at the south, so it is hardly likely that they would ever intersect. [*She approaches him.*] One day you must come to Paris and see how the boulevards are laid out. Why did you ask me to come? Are you ready for a lesson?

Siegfried. A lesson?

Genevieve. You seem tired. Why don't you sit down? Let us sit down on this couch. It looks out over Gotha as if it were made for tourists. Isn't the town hall ravishing! It was built in 1574, wasn't it? It looks so much older than the bell tower, and that was built in 1575, I believe.

Siegfried. How learned you are.

Genevieve. My learning dates from yesterday. After I saw you I longed to learn about this country and its history; I wanted to learn about this city and its life. I have been thinking that perhaps in exchange for my French lessons you could give me German lessons and teach me something about Germany. I want to stay here and study with one of your sculptors. I would like to have a little German girl as a model. I would like to see you often if you enjoy seeing me. I hope to be able to speak to you in your own language a few months from now. Is German hard for a foreigner to learn?

Siegfried. It took me six months——

GENEVIEVE *looks at him with astonishment. The German anthem is heard outside.*

Genevieve. What are they playing?

Siegfried. That's the German anthem.

Genevieve. Is it the custom to get up when it is played?

Siegfried. Yes, unless one is out of breath, defeated by life, or a foreigner. [GENEVIEVE *stands up.*] You're getting up? Life hasn't defeated you, even a bit?

Genevieve. I am standing to honor the anthem of the country of great music. I am confident that I, too, shall become a musician like every one of you. It's not hard to become a musician, is it?

Siegfried. I owe my career to the crime of war. It took me six months——

There is a silence.

Genevieve. What a mysterious language French is when spoken by a German. What's wrong with you? I saw you

a little while ago with the crowd all around you. Everyone praised your youth and strength.

Siegfried. The name of Siegfried is decidedly unlucky
in this country, Genevieve. This body full of youth and
strength is that of a German who is dying.

Genevieve [afraid]. Dying!

Siegfried. Eva has just admitted that she deceived me.
I'm not a German. [GENEVIEVE *gets up.*] Why are you getting up? No anthem is playing now. Yes, that's as it should
be. Silence is my national anthem. [A *long silence.*] What
an interminable anthem!

Genevieve. How you are suffering!

Siegfried. A death of this kind is never painless. Perhaps
those who have a family, a home, a memory can lose their
country without suffering too greatly, but my family, my
home, my memory is Germany. To protect me from the
nothingness of my past, those who cared for me in the
hospital had nothing to give me but Germany, but they
gave me all of her. Her history was my only youth, her
glories and defeats my only memories. She gave me a
glittering past with which to light my dark, formless childhood. Now that light has gone out.

Genevieve. My dear friend!

Siegfried. Every light has gone out. I'm not afraid of the
night. I'm afraid of that obscure being which is taking
shape within me, taking my shape, obscuring the last
vestiges of myself. I dare not think any more.

Genevieve. Don't do that! Lift your head and look at me.

Siegfried. I don't dare move. If I move the very structure
of my life will crumble. Lift my head? Only to see all these
heroes on these walls all of a sudden become strangers and
enemies and the landscapes foreign. Think, Genevieve, what
a seven-year-old child would feel if the great men, the cities,
and the rivers of his history book were suddenly to become
indifferent to him. Look at them, they are rejecting me.

Genevieve. That's not true.

Siegfried. I am no longer German. But it's simple
enough to change everything. My famous victories are no
longer Sedan and Sadowa. The stripes on my flag are no
longer horizontal. The Orient and the Occident can continue in their courses without me. Events in history which

I believed to be examples of loyalty and honor may seem treasonous and brutal.

Genevieve. Half the human race can change its name and sometimes its nation without suffering—at least half! All women!

Siegfried. That rustling and fluttering I hear, it's nothing, nothing but the wings of sixty million creatures and their millions of ancestors and their millions of descendants flying off and leaving me, as Zelten said they would just now. I have only to think of one of the great men I loved so much for him to fly off. Ah, Genevieve, I shall not tell you the names of the two who are abandoning me at this instant.

Genevieve. If they are truly great men, they will be visible from your new country.

Siegfried. My new country! Ah, when I lay there, why didn't Eva force me to ask again and again for water! Why didn't she force me to repeat it, even if my thirst became unbearable, until she could tell what accent colored my words, until she could tell if I pictured a blue sea when I called for water or a mountain torrent or a lake and thus revealed my native country. She condemned me to an eternal thirst by hurrying to give me a drink in that way. Now I hate her.

Genevieve. She thought she was doing right. You meant a great deal to her. She gave you what she thought was the finest country. She had no choice.

Siegfried. I can choose now. Don't leave me, Genevieve. It consoles me not to be with any of the friends I made in my second existence whom I shall have to give up. It consoles me to be with you.

Genevieve. To be with a stranger?

Siegfried. If you want to put it that way. I must put all the associations which the words *friend* and *relation* have for others into the word *stranger*. Everything in my life is collapsing, but there is something in your face and in your presence which is permanent and stable.

Genevieve. Is there nothing that you notice in this stranger's face?

Siegfried. I see that she is pale and flushed at the same time, a sign of great emotion.

Genevieve. There are many reasons why I am flushed. But what would I look like if I were not flushed. Would I still be a stranger to you?

Siegfried. What do you mean, Genevieve?

Genevieve. Can't you guess why Zelten summoned me here, why, since yesterday, when I saw you again, my heart has leaped within me?

Siegfried. When you saw me again?

Genevieve. Destiny errs in confiding her mistakes to a woman. I can no longer keep silent, whatever may come. I don't mind that I have so little sense of the dramatic that I am simply going to speak, one after another, the three sentences which I have been burning to tell you ever since I saw you. I was silent only because I thought what I was going to say would kill you. It is possible that, if I said them in a certain order, these sentences would seem natural to you, even acceptable, but I can't think what order that would be. I shall just say them all at once: you are French; you are my fiancé; you are Jacques.

Eva *has entered during the last few words of* Genevieve's *speech. She approaches the two.*

Eva. Siegfried! [Siegfried *turns toward her.*] It is I, Siegfried. [Siegfried *gestures wearily.*] If it was a crime to have shared my country with you, forgive me, Siegfried. [Siegfried *makes a vague gesture.*] If it was a crime to have taken in a waif abandoned on Germany's doorstep, to have clothed him with the nation's sweetness and nourished him with her strength, then forgive me.

Siegfried. All right. Let me alone.

Eva. You are ours, Siegfried, by right of adoption, by right of friendship, by right of the care we gave you. For two weeks I watched over you day and night, before you regained consciousness. You did not come from another country, you came out of nothingness.

Siegfried. That country has charms of its own.

Eva. If I had known that destiny was going to restore your country to you, I would not have given you mine. But I learned the truth only yesterday. I lied to you for the first time today. I was wrong to do so. I should have revealed everything to you myself, but in any case what you have learned cannot change anything.

Siegfried. That's enough, Eva. Farewell.

Eva. Why farewell? You're remaining with us, aren't you?

Siegfried. With you?

Eva. You are not leaving us? You are not abandoning us?

Siegfried. Us? Whom do you mean by us?

Eva. I'm speaking for all of us—for Waldorf, Ledinger, for the thousands of young people who lined the route when you returned from parliament a little while ago. I'm speaking for all those who believe in you. I am speaking for Germany.

Siegfried. Leave me, Eva.

Eva. It is not like me to leave you when you are stricken.

Siegfried. What are you referring to?

Eva. Your true heart, your conscience. I have had a day's head start to find my way in the mist you are now entering. By tomorrow you will see clearly once again. Your duty lies here. During the last seven years not a single memory from your past has come to the surface. Never once has anything from your past signaled to you. There's not a cell of your body which is not new, not a single taste or habit has led you back to what you left. Nothing from your past has a right to any hold over you. What have you to say, mademoiselle?

Genevieve. Nothing. I shall remain silent.

Eva. Your silence seems to speak. It seems louder than our voices.

Genevieve. Everyone has a right to his own language.

Eva. I implore you. Please look at me. We are engaged in a battle, you and I. Don't look straight ahead of you like that.

Genevieve. Each of us has his own manner.

Eva. Why do you despise a woman who is fighting for her country when you are fighting only for yourself? Why are you silent?

Genevieve. I am silent because, in the past, only silence prevailed over my enemies.

Eva. You are silent because every one of your words, if you were to speak, would be petty and egotistical.

Genevieve. I was silent, too, because I thought that anything you and I might say, Siegfried might have heard from louder voices. But you may be right after all. Perhaps the only comfort that we can give him is that we two strangers, one French, one German, act out the inward duel which is destroying him. Here, I shall even offer you my hand so that he will understand that the forces tearing him apart are not irreconcilable.

Eva. I would not dream of taking your hand. By what right are you here? Who asked you to come here; this country does not need you.

Genevieve. A German asked me.

Eva. Zelten?

Genevieve. Zelten.

Eva. Zelten is a traitor to Germany. You see now what he is, Siegfried. His plot did not aim to correct the errors of the past, but to rob the country of you, its greatest hope —you to whom it has given what it did not always give to its kings, power and respect.

Siegfried. That is just what I now deny myself. Please, I beg you both, leave me alone.

Eva. No, Siegfried.

Genevieve. Why, Jacques?

Siegfried. Have neither of you a name for me halfway between Siegfried and Jacques?

Eva. There is no halfway point between duty and the demands this woman symbolizes.

Genevieve. Symbolizes? A Frenchwoman is too much a creature of fashion ever to be a symbol, ever to be anything but vibrant and suffering although dressed in the latest style. But in any case you are wrong. If Jacques had to choose between duty and love, he would have chosen long since. If you are willing to forget that there is an element of duty in love and of love in duty, then it's easy to choose between the two. Characters in tragedies make the choice all the time. But Jacques must choose between a magnificent life which does not belong to him and the nothingness which does. Any man would hesitate.

Eva. His choice is between a country which depends entirely upon him and a country where his name is written only on marble, between a country where the flags bear his crest and a country where no one, peasant or politician, awaits him. Here he can help save us from chaos; there his return will mean nothing beyond a few headlines in the morning papers. Is that not true?

Genevieve. It is true.

Eva. His family is dead, aren't they?

Genevieve. Yes.

Eva. He has no sons, no nephews?

Genevieve. No.

Eva. He was poor? He had no house in the country? He didn't own a handful of French soil?

Genevieve. No.

Eva. Where does your duty lie, Siegfried? Sixty million people depend on you here. In France, there is no one?

Genevieve. No one.

Eva. Come, Siegfried——

Genevieve. But no, there is someone—— Perhaps *someone* is putting it too strongly, but in any case a living creature.

Eva. Who is it?

Genevieve. A dog.

Eva. A dog?

Genevieve. His dog. How unfeeling of me not to have thought of him! Your dog is waiting for you, Jacques. Everyone else—your friends, your professors, your pupils—have given you up. Even I felt justified in giving you up. After all, in giving you up, I was giving up my own life. The disappearance of a man in wartime is an apotheosis, an immediate ascension to paradise. There is no body in a death of this sort and so there is no need for a burial, keening or wailing—or even grief—for the missing person seems to have returned to dust faster than the bones of those who die an ordinary death. He seems to have been mingled with his native earth and air, to have become part of them—— But your dog did not give you up. He is still waiting for you.

Eva. That's ridiculous.

Genevieve. It's even more ridiculous than you can imagine: the dog is a poodle. He is white and, like all white dogs in France, he is called Black. But, Jacques, Black is waiting for you. He sits at the door of the closet where your clothes hang; he sniffs an old bottle of your shaving lotion. I take him for a walk every day. He's always looking for you. I admit that sometimes he tries to dig you out of the ground. But most of the time he looks up in the air for you just at the level where people's faces are. He does not believe that your substance is scattered atom by atom through the earth and air of the nation. He is waiting for you to return whole, in one piece, as you were.

Eva. This joke has gone far enough.

Genevieve. Yes, I know. You want me to talk about France. You think it is infamous of me to use a poodle to tempt Siegfried.

Eva. Why must you make light of such an important moment?

Genevieve. I ask you to forgive me if I find no other personification for France than a poor little poodle without even a pedigree. But I am not accustomed to battles such as this, and I can think of nothing else to say to Jacques. The grandeur of Germany and the grandeur of France are an obvious subject for a gifted orator. I don't deny that it's dramatic that one man should epitomize the conflict between the only two nations which stand not only for two different ideals of beauty and two different ways of doing business but for two different concepts of good and evil. But dramatic as your situation is, Jacques, it does not matter for the moment.

Eva. May I ask what does?

Genevieve. What matters now, Jacques, is the conflict between the crowd outside which is calling for you, and— if you let me put it this way—your poodle and that muffled dumb life which still hopes for your return. You see I was not quite truthful when I said that only your dog awaits you—— your lamp waits for you, the monogram on your stationery waits for you, the trees outside your apartment on the boulevard, the cognac in your decanter, and your suits—they are out of fashion now, but I mothproofed them every year. You would be comfortable in those suits, Jacques. There is an invisible garment woven around us from our earliest years; it is made of the way we eat, the way we walk, the way we greet people, woven of tastes and colors and perfumes which our senses spin in childhood. This garment is our true homeland; since coming here I have seen that it is this which you long for. I know why you are perpetually ill at ease. The difference between the wasps, the sparrows, the flowers in this country and those in your own is minute, but no matter how minute it is unacceptable to you. Even the fragrances of flowers vary a little from country to country, and you will not be happy once again until you rediscover your own animals, your own insects, your own plants. Even if your memory never returns, you will be happy, for these things are the warp on which your life is woven. In France it is only the human beings who do not await you. Here men alone know you; nothing else is aware of you, nothing else has guessed at your nature.

Eva. Even if you begin to wear those old suits of yours once again, you will not be able to break out of the circles which seven years in Germany have ringed round you, any more than a tree can break out of the rings of its growth. Anyone who has frozen under the hoary touch of a German winter and has been warmed back to life by the youthful caress of a German spring—in all Europe there's no spring as dazzling—is henceforth insensitive to moderate climates and to moderate emotions. The world of cafés and boulevards is no longer your world; you have become accustomed to our giant beech trees, our gabled and timbered cities; you have learned that the soul can never be satisfied unless it is seized by a paroxysm of emotion, a fit of love for the beauty of the world. Germany has given you a heart which has no limit to what it can feel; I beg you not to exchange it for that precision instrument, that alarm clock, the heart of a Frenchman!

Sounds of music and shouting for SIEGFRIED *from the crowd outside.*

Eva. Choose, Siegfried. Do not be blackmailed by a past which you no longer have any knowledge of, a past which can supply a whole arsenal of weapons to be used against you. Do not allow yourself to be weakened by flattery or accusations drawn from this past. It is you, yourself, and no dog, which this woman is using as bait to tempt you back to France, but it is a version of yourself which is lost forever; you will never know it again, never recover it. Do not sacrifice yourself to a ghost.

Genevieve. Choose, Jacques. You saw that I wanted to hide everything from you for months, if necessary, until a less brutal opportunity presented itself. Fate did not want it to be so. I am waiting for your verdict.

The crowd shouts for SIEGFRIED *outside. Searchlights beam on the outside of the house.*

Eva. Beware, Siegfried! Our friends are waiting for me to return. They will be coming to you, trying to persuade you by force. Now, while there is still time, let friendship persuade you. Look. Listen. Those lights are all in your honor. The crowd is calling for you. Listen to them. The choice is between light and darkness. Which will you choose?

Siegfried. How can a blind man choose?

Curtain.

ACT FOUR

A station at the frontier, divided into two parts by a gate and a table on which baggage can be examined. The German station is as luxurious and clean as a bank. The French station, like all French stations, has a stove and a ticket booth barred so that it resembles a prison cell. It is just before dawn. The French customs inspector is reading a newspaper.

French customs inspector PIETRI, GENEVIEVE

GENEVIEVE. Has anything of any interest happened lately in France, Inspector?

Pietri. Well, yes. Today the station master at Bastia was promoted. He's gone as far as a man of his rank can go.

Genevieve. I meant in Paris.

Pietri. No. There were no promotions in Paris. He is only fifty-five years old. If he were retired now with a merit promotion, it would be unprecedented.

Genevieve. Perhaps you could tell me the name of your hero?

Pietri. His name is Pietri, like mine, but he is more fortunate than I am. When he was sixteen, he helped an old lady cross the tracks. She turned out to be Gambetta's mother. Since then he has been able to take his pick whereas I have had the ill luck to find two lengths of lace in a suitcase belonging to the wife of the president of the senate. [*He continues to read his newspaper.*]

Genevieve. Could you tell me, Inspector, why are all the customs inspectors in France Corsicans?

Pietri. Only the Corsicans have yet understood that France is an island.

Genevieve. What's more, they perfume the entire frontier of France with garlic—— Is that herring and garlic you are cooking there?

Pietri. No, it's my *café au lait*—— You're pretty talkative, aren't you, mademoiselle!

Genevieve. I have had to be so silent for the last few days! It never occurred to me that I had a particular gift

for talking to Corsicans or customs inspectors, but as a
matter of fact I do feel like chatting this morning.

Pietri. Do me a favor and don't keep hovering on the
imaginary line.

Genevieve. On the imaginary line?

Pietri. That's a technical expression used by customs
inspectors. It means the frontier. It's that yellow line
which cuts the waiting room and disappears over there between the restaurant and the men's room.

Genevieve [*moving*]. Is it dangerous to stand on it?

Pietri. Don't get me wrong. I didn't mean to imply that
you were doing it on purpose. But all day long a band of
maniacs keep sliding a foot under that gate or straddling
the line. Sometimes a doctor from Berlin comes to observe
them. Sadists he calls them. Don't ask me what they get
out of this sadism of theirs. I was customs inspector for the
port of Nice and I assure you it was not my idea of fun
to go wading across the frontier all the time.

Genevieve. Perhaps you don't care for ocean voyages.

Pietri. And I don't like traveling on land any better——
I'm right here on the border but I've never set foot in
Germany—— Well, come on over, since your papers are
all in order, and warm up.

Genevieve [*sits down near the stove*]. Your stove doesn't
go out during the night!

Pietri. Go out! We don't burn the stuff they dig out of
the ground around here. You have to be a customs man to
know where good things come from! The coal we burn is
real Carmaux coal; it comes all the way from the south of
France.

Genevieve. Wouldn't you prefer central heating, such as
they have next door?

Pietri. Would you prefer it? Would you like to be warm-
ing your hands at their radiator? And I can tell you, not
an hour goes when the station-master's dog from the other
side doesn't try to come across and warm himself at the
stove; I kick him back, of course. That swan that's supposed to be out swimming in front of the restaurant is even
worse; he's always waddling across the line.

Genevieve. What will travelers think to see two heating
systems in the same waiting room?

Pietri. They will know that Germany has a central heating system and France has an individual heating system. I'm astonished that no one has thought to install a separate smoking system for smokers. I know that our railroad authorities are intriguing with the Franco-German Customs Union and the German railroad administration to have radiators installed in my part of the station. When that day comes, I'm quitting.

Genevieve. It would be a shame if you had to quit. It must be interesting to be a customs inspector.

Pietri. As of now, it's the only way to become a sergeant inspector—— Are you taking the eight o'clock train, mademoiselle?

Genevieve. I hope to. If the person I am waiting for arrives on the train from Gotha.

Pietri. So you wasted your time talking to me just to make the minutes go faster.

Genevieve. I haven't wasted my time. You can't imagine what a world of good it has done me to hear about merit promotions, liver complaints, and food with garlic. It's like taking a deep breath of pure oxygen for a French person to hear of such things.

Pietri. But we didn't talk about liver complaints.

Genevieve. Yes, yes. It was included in what we talked about even though we didn't mention it. In any case, I'm hungry and thirsty. It was talking about apéritifs that did it.

Pietri. But we didn't talk about apéritifs.

Genevieve. That's strange. I thought we talked of nothing else—— Yes, for the first time in three days, I'm hungry. I would like a bacon omelet and a roast chicken.

Pietri [*grumbling*]. The German restaurant is open. They make a specialty of meatballs flavored with cumin, but they mix a lot of bread with the meat.

The German customs inspector, Schumann, *enters and hastily dusts off a leather-covered banquette.*

Pietri. Guten Tag, Schumann.

Schumann [*speaking with a heavy German accent*]. Bonchour, Pietri.

Pietri. I thought we had agreed to start dusting at the line and drive the dust away from the line toward the doors. You keep your dust for your country, I'll keep mine.

Schumann. Pardon me.

Pietri. Who are those two men in overcoats pacing back and forth on your platform? I warn you I'm going to search them. In January people always try to smuggle in toys. Just yesterday I caught two mecano sets in your sister's luggage. I'm sure those two outside have their pockets full of tops.

Schumann. Not a chance of that—— They are both generals. They came by private train in order to get here ahead of the train from Gotha. They are waiting for someone——

GENEVIEVE, *seeing the two generals go by, leaves and disappears quickly into the restaurant on the German side.*

Pietri. You could have closed the door, mademoiselle. [*Sneezes.*] People don't realize that they leave the customs inspector sitting in a draft if they leave the gate to the frontier open!

Enter LEDINGER *and* WALDORF, *escorted by* SCHUMANN.

Waldorf. Will he come through here?

Schumann. All travelers bound for France come through here, your Excellency. His train is pulling into the station right now. Have your excellencies any orders for me?

Waldorf. We shall return to Gotha by the first express. Reserve our seats.

Schumann. Right, your Excellency. Two seats?

Waldorf. No. Three.

Exit SCHUMANN.

Ledinger. Was he disguised when he left, Waldorf?

Waldorf. No, but he was dressed in black—in mourning for himself. He'll make a sad figure against the snow.

Ledinger. Is the woman with him?

Waldorf. They didn't see each other again. She disappeared a few hours before he did. He left alone, without any baggage.

Ledinger. I heard that he destroyed all his papers. Is that true?

Waldorf. Those he destroyed were not important—his

free pass for German museums, his permits for cut-rate seats at the opera or hiring boats on the Bavarian lakes. There are a fair number of the fine things in life for which he will now be paying the full tariff.

Ledinger. He left no letter?

Waldorf. He left two. One for the tax collector, paying what he owed up until yesterday. The other was to the mayor, leaving everything he possessed to the various charities of the city. You can't say he didn't act as if he were dying, Ledinger!

Ledinger [*looking out the window*]. Here's the dead man coming now!

They both rise and face the door. SIEGFRIED *enters and stops when he sees the generals.*

Waldorf. Good morning, your Excellency.

Siegfried. Good morning, Waldorf—— Did you come here to bid me farewell?

Waldorf. No, your Excellency.

Siegfried. Did you want to see me once again where Germany first found me, in the cradle of my German life, in a station?

Waldorf. No, your Excellency.

Siegfried. Then you came to keep me from leaving, to take me back with you?

Waldorf. Yes.

Ledinger [*advancing a few steps*]. We have come to beg you, my dear Siegfried, to change your decision.

Siegfried. Decision? What have I decided?

Waldorf. Have you decided on what country to take as your own?

Siegfried. That decision was made the day I was born.

Ledinger. You were born twice, Siegfried——

Siegfried. You only die once and you're only born once.

Ledinger. The time is growing short, Siegfried. In a few minutes it will be time to catch the train.

Siegfried. I, too, have a train to catch. [LEDINGER *rushes abruptly toward* SIEGFRIED.] What's wrong, my dear Ledinger?

Ledinger. Come back with us, my friend. You are suffering. You have lost weight. Come back with us.

Siegfried. Yes, I am thinner, Ledinger. It is the gift of

France as much as the loss of Germany which has made me thin. A convalescent like me should be given a miniscule country, not a large one. I have been amputated from Germany and grafted on to France; I would have to have an extraordinary sense of balance not to have somewhat lost my equilibrium. I confess that the day before yesterday I dreamed of disappearing, of seeking asylum in some third country that was neither France nor Germany, a country that I would have selected because it had no neighbors, no enemies, no ceremonies inaugurating memorials to the dead, no dead. A country with no war in its past and no war in its future. But the more I looked for such a country on the map, the more attached I felt to the countries which are full of suffering and tribulation, the more clearly I understood my mission.

Waldorf. What is this mission?

Siegfried. To be a functionary—that and nothing more. It's not for nothing that I come from the country of functionaries. My mission is to serve.

Waldorf. That is the motto of all those who love to command. Germany alone responds to commands.

Siegfried. I want to serve my country.

Ledinger. If you want to serve, my friend, then come back with us. Germany is the only country to which one can devote oneself completely. It's the only country in the world where people are still obedient, respectful, disciplined, in a youthful, vigorous fashion. At the slightest sign from you our country would discover new strength: a resurgence of that cruel virginity of spirit which justifies outbursts of violence and makes sacrifice possible. Everything that Germany experiences is like a dose of tonic for an already healthy child. At a single word from the leader who serves our state, our rivers, instead of coursing toward the north, become obedient canals crossing Germany from east to west. At a single word sixty million faces turn to the Orient or to the Occident, where new nations will rise up. If you, a leader, abandon Germany for another country, you will resemble a gardener who leaves land where his plants flower in a day for one where they flower only once in a century. If you wish your work to bear fruit, do not abandon Germany, above all to serve France.

Siegfried. Is it so difficult to serve France?

Ledinger. It's impossible for a man who wants to mold the soul of a country—and shape its future.

Siegfried. Why, Ledinger?

Ledinger. France is unique in that its destiny is so precise, so well defined, that only dreamers can believe that they lead her, and only hypocrites can persuade the people that they control her destiny. It's the only country in the world where the future always seems to conform to the past. The course that her institutions, her rivers, and her people take has been established for so long that the French no longer respond to the voices of their leaders but to their own interior voices. What would you find to do in a country where all that is left to the government is to make small improvements in central heating and public health? It is her artisans who serve France, her writers, her engineers, her engravers. She is served by her miniaturists, for decoration and more decoration, even if it only covers a square centimeter, is the only way she can be served today. The annual or even monthly succession of governments which has become a ritual should prove to you that her best leaders are content to alternate as the substitutes for an invisible and silent destiny.

Siegfried. I intend to serve her. I am a good gardener. I can make things grow on unpromising land.

Waldorf. Are those your last words on the subject, Excellency?

Siegfried. Those are my last words, and that is the last time you will call me "Excellency."

A silence.

Waldorf. So be it, Siegfried. We have no other course but to accept your decision. But in retaliation I believe we must ask a sacrifice of you. May I go on? [SIEGFRIED *gestures his assent.*] Here you are within a step of the frontier, but every German believes that you are still in the heart of Germany. The mails are clogged with letters addressed to you. Your name lies at the center of every German heart. We think it would be criminal to destroy what you have achieved by telling the people who have put their faith in you that you are no longer theirs, that you are abandoning them.

Siegfried. I understand. You prefer to tell the German people that I no longer exist.

Waldorf. Wouldn't it be more useful and more noble for the German people to believe that you left them in the same mysterious fashion as you came? It is quite possible that the love the German people bear you might be changed first into bewilderment and then into an ugly scandal between France and Germany. This can be avoided if Ledinger and I testify that during the uprising we saw you fall into the flames of a burning house.

Siegfried. Is that your view as well, Ledinger?

Ledinger. Yes, Excellency.

Siegfried. No one would be surprised? You don't think that it would make matters far worse?

Ledinger. Certainly not! There is no event for which a nation is better prepared than the death of one of its leaders. They cannot imagine that a friend with whom they have shared their daily sausage and sauerkraut can ever die, but the death of a great scholar, or a great general, is, for those who love him, proof of a divine, enduring element in his character. Those who envy him are flattered to have outlasted him.

Siegfried. I detest flattery. Siegfried will live.

Ledinger. Please believe Waldorf, your Excellency. He is right. I agree with him, except that I would favor a death that would have no political overtones. Siegfried's glory should be above party politics. I would favor an accidental death, perhaps a fall into a river, or, better yet, a fall into one of those completely clear, though bottomless lakes.

Siegfried. You are generous, my friends, to offer me a glorious death. I am aware I have a choice of deaths. I can go up in flames, like a phoenix, in a splendid, exotic conflagration. I can die in the manner of our romantic heroes by plunging into one of those lakes, into which Ledinger is thoughtful enough to push me. By the way, those lakes are frozen over at this time of year. My death comes with a bonus, a bonus rarely accorded the dead—life. I do not accept. A statue in Munich for Siegfried, a broken column in Paris for Forestier—I would be worse than useless being twice dead.

Ledinger. You prefer instead to live in the shadow of two ghosts?

Siegfried. I am not planning to live in the shadow of anything. Siegfried and Forestier will live side by side. I shall try to be worthy of the two names and the two destinies which chance has given me. You can't cut a man's life in half to make two perfect lives as you can the body of a worm. No two lives are so contrary, so inimical in what they have contained of suffering and experience that they cannot be fused one day into a single life; there are no elements so diverse that they cannot be joined in the heart of a man. Perhaps before long my lost memory and my two countries will become part of a single existence. Perhaps everything I have known and everything I have not known which has caused me suffering and at the same time such joy will be forged into a single meaningful whole. I cannot believe that in the human heart, where the most contrary vices and virtues exist, only the word *German* and the word *French* cannot compose their differences. I refuse to dig trenches in my heart. I am not returning to France as if I were a last prisoner—the last prisoner of war to be released—but as if I were the first beneficiary of a new human insight, of a new development in the history of man. Farewell. I hear the whistle of your train. Siegfried and Forestier bid you farewell.

Waldorf. Farewell, Siegfried. Good luck. But remember how hard it is to see Zelten, who wanted to ruin Germany, and the man who wanted to save her take the same train a day apart, bound for the same refuge.

Siegfried. I am not at all to be pitied, Waldorf, for my place of exile is my homeland.

Ledinger. Farewell, Siegfried. Good luck. Remember the mask which the French wore during the war—remember that, even though it protected them from poisonous gas, it often prevented them from seeing and breathing.

Siegfried. I shall wear no mask as a Frenchman, just as I was a German unencumbered by a memory.

The generals bow ceremoniously and exit. Once alone SIEGFRIED *walks toward the French side of the station and, without noticing that he is doing so, goes through the gate. The customs inspector,* PIETRI, *accosts him.*

Pietri. What are you doing there!
Siegfried. Are you speaking to me?

Pietri. What do you think you're doing there?

Siegfried. What do you mean "there."

Pietri. Well, you're in France now, you know.

Siegfried. Ah, I am in France——

Pietri. Can't you see the yellow line that runs under the gate? That's the frontier.

Siegfried. I crossed it?

Pietri. Yes. Get back on the other side.

Siegfried. But it's France that I'm entering! Here are my papers.

Pietri. You can't enter France until 7:34. It is now 7:16. [*Before going back through the gate,* SIEGFRIED *warms his hands at the stove.* PIETRI *speaks more kindly.*] Did you come into my waiting room to warm yourself or to enter France?

Siegfried. Why do you ask?

Pietri. If you want to warm yourself, you can reach over the baggage rack. I don't care if your hands are in France——

Siegfried. Thank you. [*He warms his hands, leaning on the baggage rack and looking out over the landscape on the French side where the sun is dawning.*] Is that the first town in France over there?

Pietri. Yes, that's the village.

Siegfried. Is it big?

Pietri. It's the size of all villages, eight hundred and thirty-one inhabitants.

Siegfried. What's it called?

Pietri. It has the same name as all villages—Blancmesil-sur-Audinet.

Siegfried. What a beautiful church! How pretty that white house is!

GENEVIEVE *comes out of the German restaurant. She speaks with her back turned to* SIEGFRIED *and the village.*

Genevieve. That's the town hall.

SIEGFRIED *turns and studies her, astonished.*

Pietri. You are familiar with the village, mademoiselle!

Genevieve. And that overgrown brick chalet between the yew trees halfway up the hillside, with the porte-cochère and the veranda, is the chateau.

Pietri. You're from these parts?

Genevieve. And at the end of the avenue lined with lindens there is a statue. It's a statue of either Louis XV or Louis XIV.

Pietri. Wrong, it's of Louis Blanc, a great man of the Left.

Genevieve. And on the first Sunday of the month, the firemen test their equipment on that scaffolding at the corner of the fair grounds. Their claxon is off key.

Pietri. You know Blancmesil better than I do, mademoiselle.

Genevieve. No, I don't know Blancmesil. I have never seen it. But I am French and I know my own people. [*Sound of a bell.*] Is that the train?

Pietri. No, that's the call for heavy baggage. Follow me.

Genevieve. We have no heavy baggage.

Pietri. Did you send it ahead?

Genevieve. Yes, seven years ahead.

Pietri. Seven years? Then that's not a matter for the customs. You'll have to see the checkroom.   [Pietri *exits.*

Siegfried. What are you doing in this station, Genevieve?

Genevieve. I am looking for someone, Jacques.

Siegfried. The man you are looking for is not here.

Genevieve. Don't believe that. Wherever I am, he is. You seem surprised that today I am almost gay, scarcely gloomy at all. I am gay because I see and hear the man you call invisible and mute.

Siegfried. Why have you followed me here?

Genevieve. I have been following you since the day before yesterday, Jacques. I took a room across the street from your room. From my window I watched you all night. You hardly slept.

Siegfried. Jacques slept. Siegfried was wakeful.

Genevieve. You stayed on the balcony until dawn. That was a silly thing to do in such cold weather. I didn't dare call out and tell you to go back inside. I thought that perhaps you were talking with some mute, invisible being, with the German night, perhaps?

Siegfried. I thought I was alone.

Genevieve. No, I was there. I saw everything. Even when the snow fell, you stayed on the balcony. You were entirely white with snow. When you put out your hand to the night, your hand was covered with snow. That's a strange way to bid Germany farewell.

Siegfried. However, no other farewell cost me as much. Snow is the same on every continent and the stars are the same all over Europe, but last night they spoke to me of Germany. The voice of the river that ran through Gotha would have sounded the same anywhere, but it spoke to me of Germany. The living, like the dead, lay shrouded in snow; only the statues in the public squares pierced the winding sheet which bound the whole world in whiteness. The wind held sway and I could not leave it any more than I could stop looking at the gleam of the moon on the snow. The great men, the history, and the customs of a country speak to all people but last night I learned that the way the rays of the moon fall on the land is unique to each people; no one can take it from them. I learned so much in the course of the night that, when the sky began to grow pale yesterday morning, the last seven years of my life began to grow pale too, and I felt that I was ready to say good-by.

Genevieve. You have comforted me, Jacques. I feared a far more terrible struggle in your heart. I imagined that you would contrast every glorious incident of your temporary country's history with the glories of your redis-covered homeland. I had sworn to myself that I would keep silent. It would have been repugnant to me to slip a weapon to one of the combatants, be he Bayard or Napoleon. But since it was a combat between dawn and dusk, a competition between a river and the light of the moon, I have no further scruples.

Siegfried. Why did you follow me?

Genevieve. Why did you flee from me, Jacques? You didn't think that I could let you return to France without giving back to you everything I have of yours, every memory and habit which had been left in my care for seven years, which I cared for faithfully? You didn't think I would let you embark on your new life totally blind? Siegfried is safe and sound now. Let's think of Forestier. It is he who must be refashioned. Trust yourself to me. I know everything about you. Jacques used to be very talkative.

Siegfried. You have a long task ahead of you.

Genevieve. Long? We have only ten minutes. That's

more than enough time for me to return to you your
original virtues here on the threshold of your new life.

Siegfried. And my faults?

Genevieve. They will return of themselves; you have only
to live with someone you love. I want you to be able to
answer, should you be questioned by a customs inspector,
a curious customs inspector who asks you if you are courageous, if you are a spendthrift; I want you to be able to
tell him what dishes you prefer to eat. At the moment you
seem uneasy. You resemble a horseman who does not know
the idiosyncracies of his mount. This uneasy look must
disappear today. Come here, Jacques. I'm going to release
you from all the secrets that you do not understand. [*She
sits down on a bench and draws him to her.*] Come here.
Nothing in Jacques has changed. Every one of your eyelashes is miraculously still in place on the edge of your
lid. Even when I first knew you, before you experienced
such suffering, there was this same little crease half bitter
and half smiling at the corners of your mouth. It was the
pleasures of life that put the crease there. Everything in
your face which you think is the trace of suffering is just
as likely to be the result of joy. That scar on your forehead
is not a remnant of the war, but of a fall from a bicycle
one day when you were picnicking in the country. Even
your gestures have a longer lineage than you would think.
If your hand goes up now and then to your neck, it's because you used to adjust your necktie continually. And
don't think that the tick in your eyelid comes from what
you've been through; the tick started when you started
against my advice to wear a monocle. I bought the kind of
tie that you used to wear yesterday, before leaving Gotha.
Here, put it on.

Siegfried. The customs inspector is watching us.

Genevieve. You used to be bold and courageous, but you
were always afraid of customs inspectors who looked at you
and neighbors who listened to you. It wasn't Germany that
made you so careful and suspicious. When we spent hours
boating on the Marne, just the sight of a fisherman's hat
would make you fall silent as you rowed.

Siegfried. Row? I know how to row?

Genevieve. You know how to row, you know how to

swim, you know how to dive. Once I saw you dive and
stay under for an entire minute. I thought you'd never
come up! It seemed a century! You see, I have already
given you back one of the four elements. When we see a
stream from the train, you will be able to look at it with
your former assurance. It was with you that I saw the sea
for the first time. Have you seen it again?

Siegfried. No.

Genevieve. And mountains! You can't imagine what a
good mountain climber you were. At every crag I used to
unload onto you a piece of clothing or a bit of equipment.
You would arrive at the summit draped with knapsacks
and parasols and I would be almost naked.

There is a pause.

Siegfried. Where did I meet you?

Genevieve. On a street corner, near a river.

Siegfried. I suppose it was raining? Was I a bit bold, like
all Parisians, and did I offer you my umbrella?

Genevieve. It was a beautiful day. I have never seen such
sunshine. Perhaps you thought that the light of the sun
and the sky would be too much for me; you wanted to
protect me. I agreed to let you accompany me. We walked
along the Seine. Throughout the rest of that day I discovered you just as you are discovering yourself today. By
evening I knew your favorite composers, and wines, and
the writers you most admired. I can tell you which they
are, if you wish. Next day you took me for a drive in your
automobile along nearly the same route. I imagine myself
taking the same promenade for the rest of my life.

Siegfried. My automobile? I know how to drive?

Genevieve. You know how to drive. You know how to
dance. There is nothing you don't know. You know how
to be happy.

There is a pause.

Siegfried. Did I love you?

Genevieve. You alone knew. I was hoping to know myself when you returned.

Another pause.

Siegfried. Were we engaged, Genevieve?

Genevieve. You were my lover. [*Another pause.*] You know how to be cruel. You know how to deceive. You know how to lie. With one word you know how to fill a heart to overflowing. With one word you can extinguish the hopes of a whole day. Don't worry——you're hardly unique in being gifted with these qualities. Despite your excellent memory, you know how to forget. You know how to betray.

He goes to her.

Siegfried. I know how to take you in my arms?

Genevieve. The customs inspector is listening to us. That's right, adjust your necktie——

Siegfried. I know how to hold you closely?

Genevieve. Jacques, where love and friendship are concerned it is your hope for the future which is the real past. If there is love in your heart, don't hold yourself back from loving.

Siegfried. Did I know how to make you happy? What did we talk about?

Genevieve. You used to ask me about my own past. You were jealous. You didn't believe that my childhood could have been so empty. In those days our roles were reversed —your life had been far fuller than mine.

A pause.

Siegfried [*still holding* GENEVIEVE]. Who are you, Genevieve?

Genevieve. What did you say, Jacques?

Siegfried. Who are you? Why are you smiling?

Genevieve. I am smiling?

Siegfried. Why are you weeping?

Genevieve. Because now I know that Jacques will return. Who am I? At last you are no longer searching for yourself, but for another—— You are saved. Ah, Jacques, you need look no further for our past, for the last three days have given us a new one, and happy are those whose past is completely fresh. These three days have made ten years of my life disappear. They have become the source of all my feelings, of both sadness and joy. Do you remember how you clicked your heels when we first met? Tell me, do you put little bits of metal on them so that they will click, or are the Germans themselves made of steel? Our meeting seems so long ago, but how clear it is in my mind. You had placed a beautiful salmon and green handkerchief in your breast pocket to please your Canadian visitor. Don't tell me you've forgotten?

Siegfried. No, I remember.

Genevieve. And do you remember our lesson? Do you remember how hard on me you were about the snow, and how ironical you were about my farm clothes?

Siegfried. I remember. You were wearing a pearl-gray hat with a mouse-gray ribbon to please your German student.

Genevieve. Did I please him?

Siegfried. Do you remember my sudden return, just before the uprising, and our farewells and that umbrella which I had forgotten on purpose, the one which was to protect me against anxiety and despair? How I needed that umbrella, Genevieve!

Genevieve. The storm is over now, Jacques.

The station bell rings.

Siegfried. Here is the train. Let us go. You go first, Genevieve.

Genevieve. Not yet.

Siegfried. But that's the German signal to close the barriers.

Genevieve. That's the French signal for the engine to be moved onto the turntable. I have one more word to say to you.

Siegfried. Say it when we're across the line.

Genevieve. No, I must say it on this side of the line. Do you remember, you who remembers everything, that I have never called you by your German name?

Siegfried. My German name?

Genevieve. Yes. I swore to myself that I would never speak it, that even torture would not wrench it from my mouth.

Siegfried. You were wrong; it's a beautiful name. What do you want?

Genevieve. Want? Come here. Leave that gate——

Siegfried. All right.

Genevieve. Are you listening to me, Jacques?

Siegfried. Jacques is listening to you.
Genevieve. Siegfried!
Siegfried. Why Siegfried?
Genevieve. Siegfried, I love you.

Curtain.

AMPHITRYON 38

A Play in Three Acts

CAST OF CHARACTERS

(IN ORDER OF APPEARANCE)

JUPITER
MERCURY
SOSIE
TRUMPETER
WARRIOR
ALKMENA
AMPHITRYON
ECCLISSE
LEDA
ECHO
CELESTIAL VOICE
DANCERS
CROWD

AMPHITRYON 38

ACT ONE

Thebes. A terrace near the palace. JUPITER *and* MERCURY *are on stage when the curtain rises.*

JUPITER. There she is, my dear Mercury.

Mercury. Where, Jupiter?

Jupiter. See that lighted window where the breeze is stirring the curtain? That's where Alkmena is! Don't move. Any minute you may see her silhouette.

Mercury. That's enough for me. I admire you, Jupiter. When you love a mortal like Alkmena, you forsake your divine talents. You're willing to trample around in the dark through all these brambles just to see Alkmena's silhouette, when with your ordinary vision you could so easily pierce the walls of her room, not to mention her nightgown.

Jupiter. And I could then touch her body with invisible hands, enfold her in an embrace she could not feel. No, Mercury!

Mercury. That's the way the wind makes love, and of course the wind encourages fecundity just as you do.

Jupiter. You know nothing about earthly love, Mercury.

Mercury. How could I fail to when you always force me to appear as a human. Remember, I'm the one that always ends up with the lady in waiting. To win a woman in the first place one must please her, then undress her, and then somehow get her clothes back on her. Finally, so that she will allow you to leave her, you've got to annoy her—— It's a whole trade in itself.

Jupiter. But it is the rituals of earthly love which provide the pleasure. I fear that you know nothing of them.

Mercury. No, I'm aware of them.

Jupiter. First you follow her, matching your steps with hers at an easy pace so that your two bodies fall into the same rhythm.

Mercury. Obviously; that's rule number one.

Jupiter. Then with a leap press your left hand to her breast, the seat of both virtue and weakness. With your right hand cover her eyes so that the lids, the most sensitive part of a woman's body, know that you long for her by the heat of your hand. She will open her eyes and take pity on you for the sad destiny portrayed on your palm—for you would agree, wouldn't you, that you must make a woman pity you in order to win her?

Mercury. Rule number two. I know that one by heart.

Jupiter. And now loosen her belt, carry her to the divan, and place a pillow under her head.

Mercury. That's the third and last rule.

Jupiter. And then—what's it like? What's it like?

Mercury. Nothing special, to tell you the truth. Just the way it is with Venus.

Jupiter. Then why do you bother to come down to earth?

Mercury. Why not? It's a green and pleasant planet, although I admit it has a stench all its own, something like the stench of a wild beast.

Jupiter. Look! The curtain! Quick!

Mercury. Yes, there she is!

Jupiter. But that silhouette seems larger than Alkmena!

Mercury. Look, it is breaking in two. It was two people embracing. I hope, for your sake, that it is only her husband. Watch, he's kissing her again. He's a giant, isn't he?

Jupiter. Yes. That's Amphitryon, her one and only love.

Mercury. Now I see why you give up your divine vision, Jupiter. It's better to see shadows than to be face to face with a man and wife.

Jupiter. Look how loving she is, my dear Mercury.

Mercury. And docile, too, it would seem.

Jupiter. Ardent.

Mercury. And satisfied, I'll bet.

Jupiter. Faithful.

Mercury. Faithful to her husband or faithful to herself, that's the question.

Jupiter. The shadow has disappeared. Alkmena is probably lying there languorously, listening to the nightingales.

Mercury. Don't be jealous of the birds, Jupiter. You know perfectly well that they are disinterested spectators of a woman's love. You have disguised yourself as a bull upon occasion, but never as a nightingale. Make no mistake, it's the husband of that fair lady who is a threat to you.

Mercury. She has blonde hair and pink cheeks which are always a little flushed by the sun.

Jupiter. You're making it up, or did you spy on her?

Mercury. A little while ago, while she was taking her bath, I simply resumed my god's vision——— Don't be angry —I'm myopic once again.

Jupiter. You're lying! I can tell by your expression. You can see her! The phosphorescence of a woman is reflected even on a god's face. Please tell me, what is she doing?

Mercury. I do see her, that's true.

Jupiter. Is she alone?

Mercury. Amphitryon is lying down. She's bending over him. She's holding his head in her hands and laughing. She kisses him, and then she lets his head fall, her kiss made it so much heavier.

Jupiter. And her husband?

Mercury. He's swarthy. His chest is tanned.

Jupiter. I was asking you what he was doing.

Mercury. Stroking her as one strokes a young horse. After all, he's a celebrated horseman.

Jupiter. And Alkmena?

Mercury. Now she's run away. Here she comes back again, carrying a golden jug. She's going to pour cold water on her husband's head. You could make it ice cold if you wanted.

Jupiter. That might stimulate him—I don't want that!

Mercury. Well, boiling water, then.

Jupiter. But that would set Alkmena on fire, so much does a wife make a husband part of herself.

Mercury. Well, then, just tell me what you're intending to do with that part of Alkmena in which Amphitryon does not participate.

Jupiter. Embrace her, make her fruitful.

Mercury. But how? The hard thing when you set out to seduce a virtuous woman is getting her behind closed doors. Her best protection is a half-opened door.

Jupiter. Then what's your plan?

Mercury. My human or my divine plan?

Jupiter. What's the difference?

Mercury. The divine approach would be to take her up to our level, let her repose on a cloud, and then, a few minutes later, pregnant with a hero, she could return to earth.

Jupiter. That way I would miss the most precious moment of a woman's love.

Mercury. Is there more than one? What do you mean?

Jupiter. Her consent.

Mercury. Then do it the human way: in the door, into the bed, and out the window.

Jupiter. But she loves only her husband.

Mercury. Then take his form.

Jupiter. But he's always around. He never stirs from the palace. When there is no war to be fought, no one is more of a homebody than a soldier like Amphitryon.

Mercury. Get rid of him then. There is only one way to make a warrior leave home.

Jupiter. War?

Mercury. Have someone declare war on Thebes.

Jupiter. But Thebes is at peace with all her enemies.

Mercury. Then have a neighboring friend declare war on her. It would scarcely be an unusual way for neighbors to act. You must not forget that we are gods. When we are on earth, fate forces us to extremes humans never know. The very least we are forced to do is to pile up a few thousand miracles—and all to win from Alkmena that one moment which the most awkward of mortal lovers could obtain with a calf-eyed smile. Get a courier to bring news of war. Then send off Amphitryon with his army. Assume his form and give me the form of Sosie, who will have departed with him. I can tell Alkmena, discreetly of course, that Amphitryon is only pretending to leave and that he will return to the palace during the night. But look out! Someone's coming! [*Enter* TRUMPETER *and* SOSIE.] Let's hide. No, no, Jupiter, you don't need a special cloud! To make ourselves invisible to creditors or to the envious, and even to our own worries, we can take advantage here on earth of a great democratic institution—in fact, democracy's only success—the night.

[*Exit* JUPITER *and* MERCURY.

Sosie. Are you the trumpeter of the day?

Trumpeter. You can call me that, yes. And who are you? It seems to me I know you from somewhere.

Sosie. Do you really? I am Sosie. What are you waiting for? Blow!

Trumpeter. What's it say, your proclamation?

Sosie. You'll soon hear.

Trumpeter. Someone lost something?

Sosie. Someone has found something! Blow, I tell you!

Trumpeter. You don't think that I am going to blow without knowing what for, do you?

Sosie. What does it matter to you? You can play only one note on your trumpet.

Trumpeter. I may play only one note on my trumpet, but I compose hymns.

Sosie. One-note hymns! Hurry up. Look, there's Orion!

Trumpeter. Orion or no Orion, I want you to know that I am famous among one-note trumpeters. I imagine a whole musical development in silence and make my one note the conclusion. Can you think of a greater enhancement for a single note?

Sosie. Hurry up, the town's falling asleep.

Trumpeter. The town's falling asleep, but my colleagues, I want to emphasize to you once again, are wildly jealous of me. I have heard that at the trumpet academies they are now training students exclusively in the technique of silent music such as mine. You must tell me the nature of the lost object so that I can compose an appropriate silent air.

Sosie. Peace is the topic.

Trumpeter. What peace?

Sosie. That interval between two wars which is called peace. Every evening Amphitryon has me read a proclamation to the Thebans. It's a carry-over from his campaigning days. He's replaced the order of the day with the order of the night. There are proclamations on the various ways of protecting oneself against insects, thunderstorms, and hiccups. There is one on urban problems and one on the gods. This evening he wants to speak to the people.

Trumpeter. I see. Pathos? The sublime? Listen.

Sosie. No, something discreet. [*The* TRUMPETER *raises the trumpet to his mouth, marks a few measures with his hand, and, finally, blows.*] It's my turn now.

Trumpeter. One turns toward the audience when one reads a speech, not toward the author.

Sosie. Not if the author is a ruler. Besides, they're all asleep over there. I don't see a single light. Your trumpet didn't carry.

Trumpeter. They heard my silent hymn, that's all I care about.

Sosie [*declaiming*]. O Thebans! This is the only proclamation that you can hear while you are asleep. My master, General Amphitryon, wants to speak to you of peace. What is more beautiful than peace? What is more beautiful than a general who speaks to you of peace? What is more beautiful than a general who speaks to you of freedom from war during the peace of the night?

Trumpeter. Than a general——?

Sosie. Quiet.

Trumpeter. Two generals.

Just behind Sosie, *slowly climbing the stairs which lead to the terrace, rises a gigantic* Warrior, *fully armed.*

Sosie. Sleep on, Thebans! How good it is to sleep in a country trenches do not gut, where the laws are not in jeopardy, among birds, dogs, cats, and rats that do not know the taste of human flesh. It is good to wear the face of the nation, not as if it were a mask to frighten those of a different race, but as if it were perfectly suited to smiles and laughter. It is good to forsake your assault ladder and scale one's days on the rungs of breakfast, lunch, and dinner, with nothing more than the cares of private life to worry you. Sleep on! The panoply of your bodies, asleep, outstretched, naked, encumbered only by a navel, is more beautiful than the finest suit of armor. Never was a night as clear, as fragrant, as sure—— Sleep on——

Trumpeter. We are asleep.

The Warrior *reaches the top step and approaches.*

Sosie [*taking out a parchment and reading*]. No war threatens! The only prisoner is a roebuck captured on the Thracian border. Near Mount Olympus we grew green wheat in arid meadows and enveloped syringa bushes in clouds of bees. A golden age is at hand! The Aegean has become familiar to us; it no longer oppresses us with its vastness nor do the heavens weigh down our hearts. Our wise men can now begin to interpret the signs exchanged between temples and the stars, trees and houses, animals and men—— We are threatened by centuries of peace. Cursed be war!

The WARRIOR *is now behind* SOSIE.

Warrior. What's that you're saying?

Sosie. I said what I had to say. Cursed be war!

Warrior. Do you know to whom you're talking?

Sosie. No.

Warrior. To a warrior!

Sosie. For what kind of war? There are wars and wars——

Warrior. But only one kind of warrior. Where is your master?

Sosie. In that room over there, the one where there's a light.

Warrior. Such a brave general. Is he studying the battle plans?

Sosie. Of course! He is stroking them, caressing them——

Warrior. Such a great strategist——

Sosie. They lie beside him, ready for his embrace.

Warrior. That's the new approach. Bring him this message immediately! Tell him to arm himself at once. Are his weapons in order?

Sosie. They're a little rusty, but the nails they hang on are new.

Warrior. Why do you hesitate?

Sosie. Can't you wait until tomorrow? His horses are already asleep for the night. The night is so peaceful that they are lying down like humans. The watchdogs are snoring in the doorway, and above them an owl perches.

Warrior. Animals are wrong to trust man-made peace.

Sosie. Listen! You can hear the land and the sea resound with the echo of peace.

Warrior. That's just when war breaks out.

Sosie. War!

Warrior. The Athenian army has crossed the frontier.

Sosie. That's a lie! They're our allies!

Warrior. Put it any way you like. Then it's "our allies"

who are invading. They are taking hostages and torturing them. Wake up Amphitryon!

Sosie. If it were only sleep from which I must awaken him and not happiness as well! What bad luck, on the very day of the peace proclamation!

Warrior. No one heard you read it. Go wake him; and you, there, stay here. Sound your trumpet!

Exit SOSIE.

Trumpeter. What theme?

Warrior. War!

Trumpeter. I understand. Something pathetic, sublime?

Warrior. No, youthful! [*The* TRUMPETER *sounds his one note. The* WARRIOR *leans on the balustrade and shouts.*]

Warrior. Thebans, awake! Hear the one proclamation which you cannot hear asleep! Answer my cry, all those who are strong and sound in body! Leave the sweating, panting mass of sleepers! Take up your arms! Put on your armor! Human flesh must have iron added to it to make the true alloy of courage. What's it all about? It's war!

Trumpeter. Listen to them shout.

Warrior. Freedom, brotherhood, opportunity: that's war! You, the poor, mistreated by fortune, take vengeance. You, the rich, learn the great joy of casting in your fate—your riches, your pleasures, your women—with the destiny of your country. Gamblers, come gamble your life! Blasphemers, war gives you a free hand to attack the statues of the gods, and you, the perverted, to take your pick among the laws of the land. You, lazy ones, to the trenches! In war there's plenty of time to sit around. You hard-working ones, war is yours to manage. If you love handsome children, remember that after a war more boys are born than girls, except, of course, to the Amazons. Ah, I see over there in that cottage the first lamp war has lighted. There's a second, and a third; there are lights everywhere! The first fire of the war, setting household after household ablaze! On your feet! Who would prefer peace to the glory of hunger and thirst, of wading through mud, and dying in the service of one's country?

Trumpeter. Me.

Warrior. You have nothing to fear. Civilians exaggerate the dangers of war. I've heard that what every soldier believes as he goes off to war will be true. This time there will not be a single death, and whatever wounds there are will be in the left hand, except for the left-handed. Fall in! You are no longer scattered individuals; you belong to a modern nation, and duels have been replaced by war. Ah, the stink of peace! Peace accepts the death of the old, the sick, the weak, whereas war takes only the vigorous, men in their prime—— That's right. Eat and drink before you go. Ah, how good that bit of rabbit pâté washed down with white wine tastes. There you sit, between your tearful wife and the children who, one by one, crawl out of bed as once they came from the womb. War! We salute you!

Enter SOSIE.

Trumpeter. Here is Sosie.

Warrior. Is your master ready?

Sosie. He is. It's my mistress who is not quite ready. It is easier for a man to clothe himself for war than a woman for parting.

Warrior. Is she the kind of woman that weeps?

Sosie. No, smiles. Those who weep recover more quickly than those who smile. Here they come.

Warrior. On our way!

Exit SOSIE, WARRIOR, TRUMPETER. ALKMENA *and* AMPHITRYON *enter*.

Alkmena. I love you, Amphitryon.

Amphitryon. I love you, Alkmena.

Alkmena. That's just the trouble! If only we hated each other ever so little, we would not feel so sad right now.

Amphitryon. We can't deceive ourselves, dearest wife. There's not the least bit of hate between us.

Alkmena. You are so sure that you have a perfect wife that you're always a little absent-minded with me. Will you think of me when you're far away? Promise?

Amphitryon. I'm thinking of you already, my dear one.

Alkmena. Don't look at the moon that way. I'm jealous of it. What can you possibly find to think about that vacant face?

Amphitryon. What does this blonde head want me to think?

Alkmena. Twin thoughts: perfume and memory——

Goodness, you shaved? Men shave these days to go to war?
You imagine you'll look more fearsome with a pumiced
cheek?

Amphitryon. I'll lower my helmet. There's a Medusa
carved on it.

Alkmena. That's the only portrait of a woman I'll allow
you. Oh! You cut yourself, you're bleeding! Let me drink
the first blood of this war—— Tell me, do you still drink
your adversaries' blood?

Amphitryon. To our mutual health, yes.

Alkmena. Don't tease. Lower your helmet so I can look
at you with an enemy's eye.

Amphitryon. Prepare to tremble!

Alkmena. How mild Medusa is when she has your eyes.
Do you like the way her hair is braided?

Amphitryon. Those are serpents, carved of pure gold.

Alkmena. Real gold?

Amphitryon. The purest gold, and the cabochons are two
emeralds.

Alkmena. Wicked husband, how you flirt with war! You
wear jewels and shave for her, and for me you let your
beard sprout. You never wear pure gold at home. And your
greaves, what are they made of?

Amphitryon. Silver; and the chasing is platinum.

Alkmena. Aren't they a little tight? Steel greaves are
more flexible when you run.

Amphitryon. Have you ever seen a general run?

Alkmena. The fact is that there's not a sign of your
wife about you. You would dress just this way for an as-
signation. Admit it, you're going to fight the Amazons. If
you died in battle, dear husband, no sign of me would
be found on you. How vexing! I'll bite you on the arm before you leave—— Which tunic are you wearing under
your armor?

Amphitryon. The rose-colored one, with the black braid.

Alkmena. So that's what I see through the joints whenever you breathe—it makes your skin the color of the
dawn. Take a deep breath and let me have another glimpse
of this bright flesh peeking through the armor, black as
night. You're not going yet, are you? You love me?

Amphitryon. Yes—— I'm waiting for my horses.

Alkmena. Raise Medusa a little. Look at the stars, they've never been brighter. How lucky they are to be able to guide you.

Amphitryon. Generals are not guided by the stars.

Alkmena. I know. It's admirals that use the stars. Which one will you choose so that we both can look at it every night at this hour? We shall be looking at each other even though the intermediary is so distant and impersonal.

Amphitryon. Let's choose. There's Venus, our friend.

Alkmena. I don't trust Venus. I shall look after our love on my own.

Amphitryon. There's Jupiter, a fine name!

Alkmena. Isn't there a nameless star?

Amphitryon. That little one down there. All the astronomers call it the anonymous star.

Alkmena. Still, that is a name. Which one shone on your victories? Tell me about your victories, my dear one. How do you win them? Tell your wife the secret! Do you win by charging, shouting my name, breaking through the enemy ranks? For it is only beyond them, isn't it, that you can recover everything you've left behind—house, children, and wife?

Amphitryon. No, my dear.

Alkmena. Well, tell me, then!

Amphitryon. I win by enveloping their left wing with my right wing; then I isolate their right wing with three quarters of my left wing. With the remainder of my troops, I am free to maneuver, and victory's mine.

Alkmena. How beautiful! It sounds like birds fighting. How many battles have you won, dear eagle?

Amphitryon. Only one.

Alkmena. One victory has made you more celebrated than a lifetime of victories for other warriors. Tomorrow will be your second victory, won't it? You are going to return, aren't you? You won't be killed?

Amphitryon. You must ask the fates.

Alkmena. You won't be killed. That would be too unjust. Generals should not be killed!

Amphitryon. Why?

Alkmena. What do you mean, why? They have the most beautiful women for wives, the finest palaces, and, after all, they are famous! The weight of the greatest treasure in all Greece holds you, my dear husband. You can't die. You have Alkmena.

Amphitryon. For that reason I shall think of Alkmena, the better to kill my enemies.

Alkmena. How do you kill them?

Amphitryon. I strike with my javelin, I fell them with my spear, I plunge my sword into their bodies and leave it in their flesh.

Alkmena. Then you're left unarmed after killing a man just like a bee after he bites? I won't be able to sleep—your method of fighting is too perilous. Have you killed many men?

Amphitryon. Only one.

Alkmena. How good you are. Was he a king or general?

Amphitryon. No, a simple soldier.

Alkmena. How modest. You are not one of those people who are snobbish even about the people they kill. Did you hesitate for a minute before striking him with your sword so that he could recognize you and understand the honor being done him?

Amphitryon. Yes, he looked at Medusa and his bloody lips smiled a sad, respectful smile.

Alkmena. Did he tell you his name before dying?

Amphitryon. He was nameless. Unlike the stars there are quite a few anonymous soldiers.

Alkmena. Why didn't he tell you his name? I would have raised a monument to him, here in the palace. I would have seen that its altar was always covered with flowers and offerings. No shade in the underworld would have been more spoiled than the shade of the man my husband killed. Dearest, I'm glad that you're a man of one victory and one victim. Perhaps that makes you a man of only one woman. [*Horses' hooves are heard.*] There are your horses. Embrace me.

Amphitryon. No, my horses canter; that's a gallop. But I can kiss you anyway. Careful, dearest, don't press yourself against me so hard! You'll hurt yourself. I'm an ironclad husband.

Alkmena. Can you feel me, through your armor?

Amphitryon. I can feel your warmth through the joints. Where an arrow might strike, you reach me. And you?

Alkmena. A body can be a suit of armor as well. Often, when I lie in your arms, you seem colder and more distant than today.

Amphitryon. Yes, I have felt you sadder and more desolate in my embrace than now, even though I was leaving for a hunt and not a war. Look, you're even smiling! I almost think that this sudden declaration of war has relieved you of some anxiety.

Alkmena. Didn't you hear that child crying a few mornings ago under our window? Didn't you think that was a bad omen?

Amphitryon. A thunderclap in a clear sky or a three-pronged fork of lightning, they're bad omens!

Alkmena. The sky was clear and the child was crying. I can't think of a worse omen.

Amphitryon. Don't be superstitious, Alkmena. Stick to omens approved by the augurers. Did your serving maid give birth to a web-footed daughter?

Alkmena. No, but recently my heart has been fluttering, and once I found myself weeping, just as I was about to laugh. I have been worrying that our happiness was threatened in some terrible way. Thank God it was only war that was coming. I am almost relieved; at least the perils of war are straightforward. I prefer enemies who carry swords and spears.

Amphitryon. What do you fear other than war? We're lucky enough to be young on a young planet where the wicked have not developed beyond elementary wickedness: rape, parricide, incest. We are loved here in Thebes. We two will be united against death when it comes to find us. What could threaten us?

Alkmena. Our love! I was afraid that you were deceiving me. I imagined you in the arms of other women.

Amphitryon. Many other women?

Alkmena. One or a thousand, what does it matter—the deceit was the same. You were lost to Alkmena.

Amphitryon. You are the most beautiful woman in Greece.

Alkmena. That's just it. I wasn't afraid of Greek women. I feared goddesses and foreigners.

Amphitryon. What?

Alkmena. I feared goddesses the most. When they appear suddenly from the sea or the heavens, all pink without any rouge, pearly without powder, with their youthful breasts and their glowing eyes, it is hard to resist them, is it not? You are lifted all of a sudden by their embrace as they enfold you with arms and ankles whiter than snow and stronger than crowbars.

Amphitryon. Hard to resist for anyone except me, I'll admit.

Alkmena. But like all gods they become irritated over nothing and they are very possessive. I don't think you could ever have loved one.

Amphitryon. Nor have I ever loved foreign women.

Alkmena. But they love you! They love every married man, every man who belongs to another, even to science or to fame. They arrive in our towns with their elegant baggage; the beauties are almost naked beneath their silks and furs, the ugly ones wear their ugliness arrogantly as if where they came from it was beauty. The minute they turn up that's the end of household peace, particularly if you've got an artist or a soldier as a husband. The exotic can win any man from his hearth. Like magnets these strangers attract precious stones, rare manuscripts, beautiful flowers, and the caresses of husbands. They are in love with themselves because they remain strangers to themselves. This is what I feared for you, dear husband, when I was tormented by those omens. I feared that you might hear the names of seasons, fruits, and pleasures spoken in a new accent. I feared a new boldness in the gestures of love and I feared a stranger's perfume. It was a stranger I feared! But now it is war that's come, almost a friend. I owe her the courtesy of not weeping in her presence.

Amphitryon. O Alkmena, dearest wife, never fear! When I am beside you, you are my stranger, but in battle I will think of you as a wife. Wait for me without fear. I will soon return, and that will be forever. Every war is always the last of wars. This one is between neighbors; it will be brief. We shall live happily in our palace, and when we are very old, I shall ask a god to change us into trees like Philemon and Baucis.

Alkmena. Would you enjoy growing new leaves each year?

Amphitryon. We would be evergreens. Laurel would suit me.

Alkmena. And we will grow old and be cut down and burned?

Amphitryon. And the ashes of our branches and our bark will mingle!

Alkmena. In that case why bother to be trees? We can mingle the ashes of our flesh and bones at the end of our human lives.

Horses' hooves are heard.

Amphitryon. That's the sound of my horses this time. I must go.

Alkmena. Are you sure it's not the clatter of your ambition, your leader's pride, your taste for bloodshed and adventure?

Amphitryon. No, only Elaphocephale and Hypsipilia, my horses.

Alkmena. Then go! I want to see you drawn by these handsome steeds.

Amphitryon. Aren't you going to say anything else?

Alkmena. Haven't I said everything? What do other wives do?

Amphitryon. They pretend to joke. They hold out your shield and say: "Come back on your feet or on this!" They shout after you, "Fear nothing! Do or Die!" Has my wife no talent for such sublime phrases?

Alkmena. I fear them. They're made to be remembered only by future generations. Everything I say perishes softly when it reaches its mark in you. Amphitryon, I love you; Amphitryon, come back soon! Anyway, there's not much room left in a sentence once one has pronounced your name, it's so long.

Amphitryon. Then put the name at the end. Farewell, Alkmena.   [*Exits.*

Alkmena. Amphitryon!

She leans for a moment on the balustrade while the sound of the horses' hooves grows more distant. Then she turns and starts toward the palace. MERCURY, *disguised as* SOSIE, *accosts her.*

Mercury. Alkmena, my lady——

Alkmena. What do you want, Sosie?

Mercury. I have a message for you from my master.

Alkmena. What do you mean? He's still within calling distance.

Mercury. But he doesn't want anyone to hear what I have to say. My master has ordered me to tell you, first of all, that he's pretending to leave with the army, and second, that he will return this very night as soon as he's given his orders. The staff will have its headquarters only a few leagues away. The war doesn't promise to be of much consequence, and every evening Amphitryon will return, but secretly.

Alkmena. I don't understand you, Sosie.

Mercury. My master has ordered me to tell you, my lady, that he's only pretending to leave with the army.

Alkmena. How stupid you are, Sosie. You don't understand secrets. The minute you hear a secret, you must pretend that you didn't.

Mercury. Very good, my lady.

Alkmena. In any case I didn't understand a word of what you said.

Mercury. You must wait up at night, Princess, until my master comes, for he has ordered me to tell you——

Alkmena. Shhh, please Sosie, I'm going to sleep now.

Exit ALKMENA. MERCURY *signals to* JUPITER *who enters dressed as* AMPHITRYON.

Mercury. Did you hear them, Jupiter?

Jupiter. What do you mean, "Jupiter"? I'm Amphitryon!

Mercury. Don't think you can fool me. One can see you're a god at twenty paces.

Jupiter. It's an exact copy of his clothes.

Mercury. As if it were a question of clothes. And, in any case, you haven't even got the clothes right. Look at them. You've just come out of the brambles and there's not a single tear on you. I can't see any sign of that baggy, worn look which even the best earthly materials begin to develop the very first day one puts them on. You're wearing immortal clothes. I'm sure that they are waterproof, dye-fast, and that if a drop of oil fell on them from a lamp it wouldn't leave a spot. These are real miracles to a good housewife like Alkmena, and she would be sure to notice. Turn around.

Jupiter. You want me to turn around?

Mercury. Men, like gods, imagine that women only look at them from the front. They adorn themselves with mustaches and swell their chests. They don't realize that women pretend to be dazzled by this splendid front while sneaking a look at the back. When their lovers get out of bed or leave the room, they can see whether they are weak or tired by looking at their backs: stooped or hunched, the back cannot lie. But your back is more seductive than your front. We must make a few changes.

Jupiter. The gods never turn their backs. Besides, it will be night, Mercury.

Mercury. That remains to be seen. It won't be night if you continue to glow like a god. Alkmena would never recognize her husband in this glowworm.

Jupiter. All my other mistresses were deceived.

Mercury. No, not a one, take my word for it. Admit to me that you have never been loath to reveal yourself by some miraculous exploit or by a sudden blaze of light which makes your body translucent and does away with all the bother of oil lamps.

Jupiter. Even a god can enjoy being loved for himself.

Mercury. I fear that Alkmena will refuse you this pleasure. In any case you must keep the shape and appearance of her husband.

Jupiter. I will, to start with, then I'll see. You would never believe, dear Mercury, the ways in which a faithful wife can surprise one; and, as you know, it is always faithful women whom I love. As god of justice I deem that they deserve this reward, and, let me tell you frankly, they count on it. A faithful woman looks to the spring, a good book, perfume, earthquakes, and divine revelation for the experience others find in a lover. They deceive their husbands, so to speak, with the entire world, men excepted. Alkmena will be no exception to this rule. At first I will do my best to appear to be Amphitryon, but before long I shall begin to question her as skillfully as I can about flowers, animals, the winds, and the rain. In that way I shall learn what preoccupies her imagination and I shall take its shape—and thus be loved for myself. Are my clothes all right now?

Mercury. It's your body itself which should be faultless. Come over here in the light so that I can see if you're sufficiently human. A little nearer, I can't see.

Jupiter. How are my eyes?

Mercury. Your eyes, let's see. They're too bright. They're all iris with no cornea, not a trace of a tear duct. Remember, you may have to weep. You're not using your optic nerve, you're looking at the world directly through your skull. And a human glance is not as bright as the sun; it corresponds exactly to complete darkness in our heaven. And didn't you have pupils in your eyes in your previous adventures on earth?

Jupiter. No, I forgot. Are pupils like this?

Mercury. No, no, not phosphorescence. Not like a cat! I can see your pupils through your eyelids when you wink. No one can be reflected in eyes like that. Make them so they mirror the world.

Jupiter. I'll use quartz, flecked with gold.

Mercury. And now for your skin!

Jupiter. My skin?

Mercury. It's too smooth, too soft. It's like a baby's. You must have skin on which the wind has blown for thirty years, which has plunged through sea and air—in short, a skin which has some flavor to it, for it will be tasted. Haven't other women remarked that Jupiter's skin had the taste of a baby's?

Jupiter. If so, their caresses were no more maternal.

Mercury. You'd never be asked back with skin like that. And, tighten it up—you're floating in it!

Jupiter. But it hurts so. If I tighten it, I feel my heart beat and my arteries pound and my veins swell. I feel as if I were turning into a sieve, an hourglass of blood. The rhythm of human life is enough to kill me. I hope that mortals do not suffer so.

Mercury. On the day they're born and on the day they die.

Jupiter. How disagreeable to feel yourself being born and dying all at once.

Mercury. No less so when the two processes are separate.

Jupiter. Now have you the impression of being in the presence of a mortal?

Mercury. Not yet. Above all what I notice in men is the way in which their bodies change from second to second. They grow old incessantly. I can even see the light in their eyes aging.

Jupiter. I'll try. And to get used to the idea, I'll repeat, I'm going to die, I'm going to die——

Mercury. No, no, that's too quick. I can see your hair growing, and your nails growing longer, your wrinkles deepening. There, there—slower, slow down your heart. At that rate you're living the life of a dog or a cat.

Jupiter. How about this?

Mercury. Your heartbeats are too far apart now. That's the rhythm of a fish. There—there—that's the medium gallop, the canter that Amphitryon knows his horses by, and Alkmena her husband's heart.

Jupiter. And your last counsel?

Mercury. What about your brain?

Jupiter. My brain?

Mercury. Yes, your brain. You must replace divine ideas with human conceptions. What are your thoughts? What are your beliefs? What do you make of the universe now that you are a man?

Jupiter. What do I make of the universe? I believe this flat earth is entirely flat, that water is water and nothing more, that air is air, nature nature, and mind mind—— Is that all?

Mercury. Do you long to part your hair and keep it in place with oil?

Jupiter. As a matter of fact, I do.

Mercury. Have you the notion that you alone exist and that you can be sure only of your own existence?

Jupiter. Yes, and it's very strange to be thus imprisoned in oneself.

Mercury. Do you believe that you could die one day?

Jupiter. No. My friends will die, poor souls, but not me.

Mercury. Have you forgotten all the women you loved in the past?

Jupiter. Me? Love? I never loved anyone!—— Except Alkmena.

Mercury. Very good. And what do you think of the heavens?

Jupiter. The heavens? I think that they are mine, and I'm much more sure of it now that I'm a mortal than when I was Jupiter. And I think the solar system very small and the earth immense. Suddenly I feel more handsome than Apollo, braver and more amorous than Mars. For the first time, I believe myself, I see myself, I feel myself to be the real master of the gods.

Mercury. Then you're a true man. Go to it!

MERCURY *disappears.* ALKMENA *appears on her balcony.*

Alkmena [*wide awake*]. Who's that knocking? Who's that disturbing my sleep?

Jupiter. A stranger whom you'll be glad to see.

Alkmena. I know no strangers.

Jupiter. A general.

Alkmena. Why is a general abroad at this hour? Is he a deserter? Has he been defeated?

Jupiter. Defeated by love.

Alkmena. If he chooses not to attack another general, that's the risk he runs. Who are you?

Jupiter. Your lover.

Alkmena. You're speaking to Alkmena, not her chambermaid. I have no lover. Why are you laughing?

Jupiter. Didn't you look out the window anxiously a little while ago into the night?

Alkmena. Yes, and I can tell you exactly what the night is like—mild and fine.

Jupiter. A little while ago, didn't you pour some icy water from a gold jug onto a warrior stretched out on his bed?

Alkmena. Ah, so it *was* icy! So much the better. Maybe I did.

Jupiter. And didn't you murmur while looking at a man's portrait, "If only I could forget him while he is away"?

Alkmena. I don't remember. Perhaps——

Jupiter. Standing here under the stars, don't you feel your body unfold and your heart contract as you think of a certain man who, I admit, may be very stupid and ugly?

Alkmena. He is very handsome, and far too witty. In

fact, I have only good things to say of him. And I do remember the gold jug and I did see him in the shadows. But what does all this prove?

Jupiter. That you have a lover and he is here.

Alkmena. I have a husband, and he is away. And no one will enter my room except my husband, and even he, if he refuses to tell me his name, will not enter.

Jupiter. But even the heavens disguise themselves at this hour.

Alkmena. How dense you are if you believe that night is day masked and the moon a counterfeit sun, if you believe that wifely love can masquerade as an illicit passion.

Jupiter. A wife loves out of duty, and duty leads to constraint, and constraint kills desire.

Alkmena. What was that?

Jupiter. The name of a demigod, desire.

Alkmena. We love no half gods here. We leave demigods to those who are betwixt and between: young girls in their teens, and wives whose eyes wander from their husbands.

Jupiter. You're being impious now.

Alkmena. Sometimes I'm even more so, for I rejoice there is no god of conjugal love on Olympus. I rejoice in being a creature whom the gods did not foresee. No god hovers over my joy, the heavens are clear above me, so, if you're a lover, I'm sorry but you'll have to go. You seem handsome and strong, however, and your voice is pleasant. How I would love that voice if it spoke of fidelity and not of desire! How I would love to lie in those arms, were they not a trap which would snap shut brutally on its prey! Your lips are bright and ardent, but they won't convince me. I shall not open my door to a lover. Who are you?

Jupiter. Why do you not want a lover?

Alkmena. Because a lover is always nearer to love than to his beloved. Because I prefer my joy to be without limits, my pleasure to be without reticence, my abandon unconfined. Because I want neither slave nor master. Because one would be badly brought up to deceive a husband even with himself. Because I like to keep my windows opened and my bed nicely aired.

Jupiter. For a woman you're awfully sure of your reasons. I congratulate you. Open the door!

Alkmena. I will not open it unless you are the one beside whom I awaken every morning, whom I allow to sleep ten minutes after my day has begun, he whom my glance cleanses before sun or water touch his face. Are you the one whose footsteps are so familiar to me that I can tell whether he is shaving or dressing, thinking or daydreaming? He with whom I breakfast, dine, and sup, he who always takes a breath a millionth of a second ahead of me? He whom I see fall asleep ten minutes before I do every evening with a sleep snatched from the very quick of my own life? Unless you are this man, I shall not open the door. Who are you?

Jupiter. I must resign myself to telling you. I am your husband.

Alkmena. What? It's you, Amphitryon? Don't you realize how imprudent you are coming back here?

Jupiter. No one at the camp suspects a thing.

Alkmena. It's not the camp I meant! Don't you know the risk a husband runs when he appears without warning after going away on a trip?

Jupiter. Don't try to joke with me.

Alkmena. Haven't you heard that this is the moment when faithful wives welcome their lovers, gasping with pride and fear, into their clammy arms.

Jupiter. Your arms are empty, and cooler than the moon.

Alkmena. I gave him time to flee while we were bantering. Right now he's on the way into Thebes, fuming and cursing, with his tunic slapping his bare legs.

Jupiter. Open the door to your husband.

Alkmena. You think you can come in, just because you are my husband? Have you presents for me? Have you jewels?

Jupiter. Would you sell yourself for jewels?

Alkmena. To my husband? With delight. But you have none.

Jupiter. I see there is no use my staying.

Alkmena. Stay, Stay!—— On one condition, however, Amphitryon, one specific condition.

Jupiter. What do you wish?

Alkmena. Let us now at night take the marriage vows

which we took in daytime. For a long time I've been waiting for this opportunity. I don't want the stars, the gentle winds, and the night's company of moths and shadows to imagine that I am receiving a lover this evening. Let us celebrate a nocturnal marriage, at the hour when so many illicit unions are consummated. Begin!

Jupiter. Take vows without priest or altar, in the emptiness of the night? What good is that? If only you knew how feeble humans appear to the gods, Alkmena! They swear their oaths and brandish their fire to no avail; they don't call forth a single thunderclap.

Alkmena. A little shimmering heat lightning is all they ask for. Raise your hand, with your index finger bent.

Jupiter. With the index finger bent! But that's the most terrible of oaths! The one which Jupiter uses to scourge the earth with plagues.

Alkmena. Bend your index finger, or be gone.

Jupiter. Then I must obey you. [*He raises his arm.*] Molten pitch, swarms of grasshoppers, and plagues of boils, restrain yourselves! This wild little Alkmena is forcing me to use this gesture.

Alkmena. I'm waiting.

Jupiter. I, Amphitryon, son and grandson of deceased generals, father and grandfather of future generals, indispensable buckle on the belt of war and glory!

Alkmena. I, Alkmena, whose parents disappeared, whose children are not yet born, poor isolated link of the human chain!

Jupiter. I swear to act in such a way that the sweetness of the name Alkmena will survive as long as the clamor of my name!

Alkmena. I swear that I will be faithful to Amphitryon, my husband, or else that I shall die!

Jupiter. What?

Alkmena. Die!

Jupiter. Why mention death when it has nothing to do with the matter? I beg you, don't say that word. Don't say die!

Alkmena. I've said it. And now, dear husband, we've said enough. Our ceremony is over and I permit you to come upstairs. How complicated you've made things this evening! I was waiting for you, the door was open. You had only to push it. What's wrong? Are you hesitating? I suppose you want me to call you "lover"? Never!

Jupiter. May I really enter, Alkmena? Truly, do you want me to?

Alkmena. I order you to, dear love!

Curtain.

ACT TWO

Darkness. MERCURY *alone is illuminated, reclining at the front of the stage.*

MERCURY. At my post here by Alkmena's bedroom, I observed a sweet silence, a tender resistance, and a gentle struggle. Now Alkmena carries within her the young demigod. But Jupiter has never lingered so long with any other mistress. I don't know whether this darkness is beginning to weigh on you, but I'm tired of prolonging the night around here, especially when I think that the rest of the world is already bathed in sunlight. It's midsummer and seven in the morning. Everywhere the world is inundated with the day. A flood of light a thousand leagues deep covers everything, even the sea. Every house is tinted rose by the sun except the dark mass of this palace. I can't put off waking my master any longer; he hates to be hurried when he leaves, and I know that he will want to reveal to Alkmena that he is Jupiter as he gets out of bed in order to enjoy her astonishment and pride. With that in mind I've already suggested to Amphitryon that he come surprise his wife at dawn, so that he will be the first to know what has happened. He deserves this small courtesy, and in this way there will be no ambiguity. At this moment the excellent general is stealing out of his camp; he's off at a gallop and he'll be here at the palace within an hour. Give me a choice of your rays, sun, so that I can set this darkness on fire. [*The sun shows him a sample.*] Not that one! Not a sinister green light on lovers who are just awakening. You don't want each to think that the other is a corpse! And not that one either—violet and purple arouse the senses. Keep them for this evening. There we are—saffron! There's nothing like saffron to counteract the insipid quality of human skin. Go to it, sun.

Exit MERCURY. ALKMENA's *room is revealed, flooded with sunlight.* ALKMENA *is already up.* JUPITER *is lying on the couch asleep.*

Alkmena. Wake up. dearest. The sun is high in the sky.

Jupiter. Where am I?

Alkmena. Where no husband believes he can be when he wakes up—in your own house, in your own bed, near your wife—nothing more than that.

Jupiter. And what do I call my wife?

Alkmena. Her name is the same by day as it is by night —Alkmena.

Jupiter. Alkmena, the tall, fair, dimpled woman, who never says a word while making love?

Alkmena. That's the one. And she never stops talking once dawn comes, and now she's going to throw you out, husband that you are.

Jupiter. Tell her to be quiet. And come here.

Alkmena. Easy, there! A dimpled woman is like a dream: one can only embrace her at night.

Jupiter. Close your eyes and it will be night.

Alkmena. No, no, that's not a real night. Get up, or I'll call my maid!

JUPITER *gets up and looks out at the landscape through the windows.*

Jupiter. What a divine night!

Alkmena. Your adjectives are weak this morning, my dear.

Jupiter. I said "divine."

Alkmena. You can say a divine meal, or a divine roast of beef; I can't expect you to be imaginative all the time. But for a night like that you could do better.

Jupiter. What could be better?

Alkmena. Almost any other adjective except *divine*— that really is trite. *Perfect,* for example, or *charming,* or, best of all, the word *agreeable*—it suggests so many pleasant sensations: what an agreeable night!

Jupiter. The most agreeable night we have spent, wouldn't you say?

Alkmena. I'm not sure.

Jupiter. What do you mean, you're not sure?

Alkmena. Have you forgotten our wedding night, dearest? Have you forgotten how light I was in your arms, how we found that we loved each other alone together in the dark for the first time? That was our most beautiful night.

Jupiter. It may have been our most beautiful night, but certainly this one was the pleasantest.

Alkmena. Do you think so? And what about the night when that big fire broke out in Thebes, when you came back gilded by the dawn and warm as bread fresh from the oven. That was our most pleasant night, without a doubt.

Jupiter. Then this was the most astonishing.

Alkmena. Why astonishing? What about night before last after you saved that child from the sea? You returned glistening with seaweed, your skin tasting of salt, and all night long in your dreams you grappled with me, trying to save me from drowning. Now, that was astonishing. No, I think if I were to choose an adjective for this night, my darling, I would call it "conjugal." There was something comfortable about it, secure. Never did I feel so sure I would find you once more in the morning, refreshed, and hungry for your breakfast. For once I didn't have that divine apprehension that you might die any minute in my arms.

Jupiter. And now who's using the word *divine.*

Alkmena. Well, with apprehension I always do.

A silence.

Jupiter. What a pretty room!

Alkmena. You appreciate it most in the morning when you have no right to be here.

Jupiter. How clever men are to have invented windows to bring daylight into their homes! No other creature can do that!

Alkmena. That's not very modest of you. You're the one who invented them.

Jupiter. And what a fine landscape!

Alkmena. That you can praise—you didn't invent it.

Jupiter. Who did, then?

Alkmena. The master of the gods.

Jupiter. And may one know his name?

Alkmena. Jupiter.

Jupiter. How well you pronounce the names of the gods! Who taught you to chew on them as if they were heavenly food? You're like a lamb who has plucked a branch of yellow broom and chews it, head in the air. But it is your mouth that perfumes the flower. Say it once again. They say that the gods often appear if called in this way.

Alkmena. Neptune! Apollo!

Jupiter. No. What you said first—say it again.

Alkmena. Let me graze over the whole of Olympus. I like to name the gods in couples. Mars and Venus, Jupiter and Juno—— Then I can picture them passing along the crest of the clouds, hand in hand for eternity. That must be beautiful!

Jupiter [*ironically*]. How jolly! So, you approve of Jupiter's handiwork—these cliffs and rocks, you find them beautiful?

Alkmena. Very beautiful. But I wonder, did he make them on purpose?

Jupiter. What?

Alkmena. You do everything on purpose, darling, whether you graft a cherry branch onto a plum tree or invent a double-bladed saber. But do you think that Jupiter really knew on the day of creation what he was going to make?

Jupiter. Of course he did!

Alkmena. He created the earth. But the beauty of the earth recreates itself every minute. It's ephemeral, that's what is extraordinary about it. Jupiter is too substantial, too grave to have made anything ephemeral.

Jupiter. Perhaps you have the wrong idea of creation.

Alkmena. No more inaccurate an idea than I have of the end of the world! I'm equally distant from both, and I have no better memory of the past than I have foreknowledge of the future. Can you picture it, darling?

Jupiter. Yes, I see it! In the beginning Chaos reigned. Jupiter's real touch of genius was to have thought of dividing Chaos into the four elements.

Alkmena. We have only four elements?

Jupiter. Four, and the first is water—but it was not the easiest to create, let me tell you. It seems simple enough when you first look at it, but to think of creating water, to conceive of water, that's something else again.

Alkmena. What were the goddesses' tears made of at that time, bronze?

Jupiter. Don't interrupt. I want you to have a clear picture of Jupiter. He might appear to you all of a sudden.

Wouldn't you like him to tell you all this himself, in all his grandeur?

Alkmena. He must have explained it all so often. You make it more amusing.

Jupiter. Where was I?

Alkmena. We were almost finished. Original Chaos, that's where we were.

Jupiter. Ah, yes! Suddenly Jupiter conceived of a force that would be at once elastic and incompressible, which would fill every empty space and deaden all the shocks in the still unsettled atmosphere.

Alkmena. That's foam, isn't it?

Jupiter. No. But once he had created water, it came to him that he should edge it with shores, irregular in shape, so that the force of storms would be broken. He planted the seas with the rocky continents so that the eyes of the gods would not be continually irritated by the dazzling waters. So earth was created with all her wonders——

Alkmena. Pine trees?

Jupiter. Pine trees?

Alkmena. Parasol pines, cedars, cypress, all those blue and green clumps without which a landscape doesn't exist. And Echo?

Jupiter. Echo?

Alkmena. You sound just like her. And color, did he create all the colors?

Jupiter. The seven-hued rainbow, that's him!

Alkmena. I was thinking of russet, purple, and green, the color of a lizard—those are my favorites.

Jupiter. He left those to the dyer's art. But, using the various vibrations of the others, the shock and countershock of the atoms, the refraction and counterrefraction of light, he webbed the world with a thousand different nets of sound and color which can be perceived or not (for after all, what does he care?) by human eyes and ears.

Alkmena. That's exactly what I was saying.

Jupiter. What you were saying?

Alkmena. Yes, he never did a thing except to plunge us dumfounded into a world of illusions in which we must make out as best we can on our own, my dear husband and I.

Jupiter. That's blasphemy, Alkmena. The gods can hear you!

Alkmena. They don't hear in the same way that we do. I'm sure that these supreme beings don't hear my chatter above the beating of my heart—it's such a simple, direct heart. And anyway, what would they have against me? I have no reason to be particularly grateful to Jupiter because he created four elements instead of the twenty we require. After all, creation is his profession; in contrast, my heart overflows with gratitude for my dear husband, Amphitryon, who found a way, between battles, to create a system of pulleys for windows and invented a new method of grafting fruit trees. You changed the taste of cherries for me, and you've had your workmen build me a new pantry. You are my creator! Why are you looking at me that way? Can't you take a compliment? Don't you have any pride? Or am I too down to earth?

Jupiter [*rising, very solemn*]. Wouldn't you like to be less so?

Alkmena. Then I couldn't be close to you.

Jupiter. Didn't you ever wish to be a goddess, or nearly a goddess?

Alkmena. Certainly not. Why would I?

Jupiter. So that you would be honored and revered by all.

Alkmena. Isn't it better to be admired as a simple woman?

Jupiter. Your body would be lighter, you could walk on the wind and on the water.

Alkmena. That's what every wife does, weighted down by a good husband.

Jupiter. You would understand the reasons for things, see other worlds.

Alkmena. I've never been interested in my neighbors.

Jupiter. You could be immortal, then!

Alkmena. Immortal? What good would that do?

Jupiter. What good? Why, you wouldn't die!

Alkmena. And what would I do if I didn't die?

Jupiter. Live forever, dear Alkmena, as a star; you will shine in the night until the end of the world.

Alkmena. And when's that?

Jupiter. Never.

Alkmena. And a delightful evening that would be! And you, what would you do?

Jupiter. A voiceless shade, melting into the mists of the underworld, I would rejoice to think of my wife glowing up there in the dry air.

Alkmena. You usually prefer the treasures that can be shared. No, my dear, I hope the gods don't ask me to be a star. The night air is not good for a fair complexion. How wrinkled I would become if I were immortal!

Jupiter. But how cold you would be if you were dead!

Alkmena. I'm not afraid of death. It's the stake one puts up in order to play the game of life. Since that Jupiter of yours, rightly or wrongly, created death on earth, I shall be faithful to this planet of mine. In every fiber I am one with other men, animals, and plants, so much so that I must share their destiny. Don't speak to me of immortality until there is an immortal vegetable. It's treason for a human to become immortal. Besides, when I think of the rest death will afford from all our petty fatigues, our cheap annoyances, I'm grateful for its abundance, its plenitude. Think of being kept waiting for sixty years for badly dyed clothes and badly cooked meals! To come at last to the still pond of death is recompense out of all proportion. Why are you looking at me all of a sudden so respectfully?

Jupiter. You are the first true human I've ever met.

Alkmena. That's my particular specialty. You don't know how right you are. Of every one I know I am the only one to accept and love my fate. There is not a twist or a turn of human life which I don't accept from birth to death. I even accept family dinners. My appetites are moderate and controlled. I'm sure that I'm the only human being who sees fruits or spiders as they really are and finds in every joy its true taste without exaggeration. It's the same way with my sensibility. I lack that gaming, erring spirit which, when affected by wine, love, or a beautiful landscape, longs for eternity.

Jupiter. But wouldn't you like to have a son somewhat less human than yourself, an immortal son?

Alkmena. But it's human to desire an immortal son.

Jupiter. A son who would become a great hero, who even as a child would grapple with lions and monsters.

Alkmena. As a child? He should have a turtle or a water spaniel as a companion.

Jupiter. Who would kill enormous serpents who came to strangle him in his cradle.

Alkmena. I would never leave him alone. Such things happen only to the sons of servants. No, I want him to coo gently; I want him to be afraid of flies. Why, what's the matter with you?

Jupiter. Let's be serious, Alkmena. Is it true that you would prefer to kill yourself rather than to be unfaithful to your husband?

Alkmena. It's not nice of you to doubt what I say.

Jupiter. But it's very dangerous to kill oneself!

Alkmena. Not for me, and I assure you, dearest husband, there would be nothing tragic about my death. Who knows? Perhaps it will come about this evening if the god of war strikes you down later today. But I shall make sure that the spectators are impressed, not horrified, by the serenity of the scene. Surely there is a way for a corpse to smile and fold his hands in a tranquil fashion.

Jupiter. But your death could kill a son conceived the night before, as yet only half alive.

Alkmena. Then he would be no more than half dead. That would be half again better than what awaits him in the future!

Jupiter. It's easy for you to say all this without having thought about it.

Alkmena. Without having thought about it? What do you think a young woman thinks about? Gay and dimpled though she be, she is thinking of ways in which she can die without fuss or commotion if she is deceived or humiliated in love.

Jupiter [*he rises majestically*]. Listen carefully, dear Alkmena. You are a devout woman, and I see that you are perfectly capable of understanding the mysteries of the universe. I must speak to you——

Alkmena. No, no, dear Amphitryon! Now you are being too solemn. I know it's your way of being tender, but it only intimidates me.

Jupiter. Don't joke. I want to talk to you about the gods.

Alkmena. The gods!

Jupiter. It is time that I explain to you their relationship with humans. Men and their wives are permanently mort-gaged to the gods.

Alkmena. What silliness! You start talking about the gods the one moment of the day when humans, drunk with sunshine, starting out to work the fields or to fish, think only of humanity. And in any case, your army is waiting for you. There are only a few hours left if you want to kill your enemies before they breakfast. Leave now, dearest, so you can return to me all the sooner. And after all, my house is calling me—I have my morning inspection to make. If you stay, dear sir, I'll start talking in solemn fashion about my maids rather than the gods. I really think I must dismiss Nenetza. Aside from her mania for clean-ing only the black squares of the floors, she has yielded, as you would put it, to the gods—she is with child.

Jupiter. Alkmena! dear Alkmena! The gods appear pre-cisely when we least expect them.

Alkmena. Amphitryon, dear husband! Women disap-pear precisely when you think you've got them!

Jupiter. Their anger is terrible. They will neither be ordered around nor mocked!

Alkmena. But you're not that way, dearest, and that's why I love you. You'll accept a kiss blown from the hand across the room. Until this evening. Farewell.

Exit ALKMENA. *Enter* MERCURY.

Mercury. What happened, Jupiter? I expected to see you emerge from that bedroom in full glory, as you have from every other. Why did you let Alkmena leave like that? Why did you let her lecture you? And why wasn't she at all upset?

Jupiter. I can't pretend that all went well.

Mercury. What does that vertical furrow mean between your eyes? Is there a thunderbolt on the way? Does it an-nounce some disaster you are preparing for humanity?

Jupiter. This furrow? It's a wrinkle.

Mercury. Jupiter can't have a wrinkle. It must be a left-over from Amphitryon's body.

Jupiter. No, no, this wrinkle is mine. Now I know how men get them.

Mercury. But you seem tired, Jupiter. You're a little hunched.

Jupiter. A wrinkle is heavy to carry around.

Mercury. Are you finally experiencing that letdown that love brings about in men?

Jupiter. I think I'm in love!

Mercury. But you're often in love!

Jupiter. For the first time I held a human creature in my arms without seeing or hearing her—and, I understood her.

Mercury. What did you think about?

Jupiter. I thought that I was Amphitryon. It was Alkmena, rather than I, who was victorious. All night long I was unable to be anything other than her husband. Just now I had a chance to explain the creation of the world to her. I sounded like a schoolteacher, whereas with you my divine speech simply flows. Could I tell you about the creation?

Mercury. If you want to remake the world, all right, but not otherwise.

Jupiter. Mercury, humanity is not what the gods think it is! We believe that men are parodies of us. The spectacle of their pride is so amusing that we have made them believe that they are in conflict with us. We took great pains to impose the use of fire on them so that they would believe that they had stolen it from us. We went to great trouble to sketch convolutions in their recalcitrant brains so that they would invent weaving, cogged wheels, and olive oil, and imagine that they themselves won these accomplishments from us. Let me assure you that this conflict does exist and I'm its victim.

Mercury. You exaggerate Alkmena's power.

Jupiter. No, Alkmena, tender Alkmena, gentle Alkmena, possesses a nature more resistant to our laws than stone. It's she who is the true Prometheus.

Mercury. She just isn't very imaginative. It's imagination which opens the human brain to our influence.

Jupiter. Alkmena is open to nothing. Appearances, everything that gleams and glitters, leaves her unmoved. She has no imagination and perhaps not very much intelligence. That's just it; there's something limited but irreducible in her which remains out of reach and is the equivalent in human terms of our infinity. She is a prism through which the qualities shared by gods and men—courage, love, and devotion, passion—are refracted so that they become the distinctly human characteristics of constancy, sweetness, and devotion over which we have no power. She is the only woman whom I can stand to see dressed and veiled, whose absence is as potent as her presence, who is as attractive going about her household tasks as she is sitting down to dinner. Oh, the pleasure of eating with her— even breakfast—handing her the salt, honey, spices! Oh, the joy of touching her hand, even with a plate or spoon— that's all I can think about. In a word, I am in love with her, and I can assure you, Mercury, her son will be my favorite.

Mercury. The universe is already well aware of that!

Jupiter. The universe! I hope no one knows of my adventure!

Mercury. Everything in the world endowed with ears knows that Jupiter honored Alkmena with a visit today. Everything possessing a tongue repeats it. I announced it all at sunrise.

Jupiter. You betrayed me! Poor Alkmena!

Mercury. I acted just as I did about your other mistresses. This would be the first of your loves to remain a secret. You have no right to conceal the gift of your love.

Jupiter. What did you announce? That I had assumed the form of Amphitryon yesterday evening?

Mercury. Certainly not. That somewhat ungodlike ruse could be misinterpreted. Since your desire to spend a second night with Alkmena radiated from the whole palace, I announced that she would receive a visit from Jupiter this evening.

Jupiter. And to whom did you announce this?

Mercury. To the winds, first of all, and then to the waters, as I always do. Listen: the waves of air and sea speak of nothing else.

Jupiter. Is that all?

Mercury. I also told an old woman who was passing by below the palace.

Jupiter. The deaf concierge? We're lost.

Mercury. That's the way a human talks, Jupiter. You sound like a lover. Has Alkmena demanded that everything be kept secret until you carry her away from earth?

Jupiter. That's just the trouble! Alkmena doesn't know

anything. I tried a hundred times in the course of the night to make her understand who I was, and a hundred times she changed divine truth into human truth in the most humble, charming manner.

Mercury. Didn't she suspect anything?

Jupiter. Not once, and I don't want her to. What's that sound?

Mercury. That deaf woman has done her job. Thebes is preparing to celebrate your union with Alkmena. A procession is being organized and it seems to be coming toward us.

Jupiter. Don't let it reach the palace, turn them toward the sea, let them be swallowed up!

Mercury. Impossible, they're your priests.

Jupiter. They just jump at an occasion to worship me.

Mercury. You can't counter laws which you yourself have established. The entire universe knows that Jupiter will give Alkmena a child today. It's not a bad idea for Alkmena to know about it as well.

Jupiter. Alkmena won't be able to endure it!

Mercury. Let her suffer; it's worth it.

Jupiter. She won't suffer. There's no doubt about it, she will kill herself, and my son. Hercules will die with her. And I will once more be obliged, as I was with you, to open up my own thigh to provide shelter for the unborn infant. No thank you! Is the procession coming nearer?

Mercury. Slowly, but surely.

Jupiter. For the first time, Mercury, I have the impression that an honest god can be a dishonest man—— What are those songs?

Mercury. Those are the virgins, in ecstasy over the news, coming to congratulate Alkmena.

Jupiter. Are you sure you shouldn't have the priests swallowed up by the sea and give those virgins a touch of sun-stroke?

Mercury. What is it that you want, anyway?

Jupiter. What any man wants, alas! A thousand contrary desires. I want Alkmena to remain faithful to her husband and I want her to give herself to me with delight. I want her to be chaste to my touch and yet burning with desire when I look at her. I want her to be entirely ignorant of our intrigue and also to approve of it completely.

Mercury. I'm at a loss. I've carried out my job. The universe knows, as it was meant to, that you will spend a night with Alkmena——— Is there anything else I can do for you?

Jupiter. Yes. Let me sleep with her tonight.

Mercury. And with that famous moment of consent that you mentioned yesterday, no doubt?

Jupiter. Yes, Mercury. It's no longer a question of Hercules. That's over. It's a question of me. I want you to see Alkmena. Prepare her for my visit and depict my love to her——— Go to her on my behalf, let your godlike nature arouse her. I permit you to touch her. First arouse her nerves, then her pulse, then her pride. I can tell you I'm not going to leave this town until she receives me willingly for myself. And I've had enough of this humiliating livery! I shall come to her as a god.

Mercury. At last, Jupiter. That's the spirit! If you give up your disguise, I can assure you that within a minute or two I shall be able to convince her to wait for you at sundown. There she is now. Leave me alone with her.

Enter ALKMENA *on balcony.*

Alkmena. Darling!

Echo. Darling!

Jupiter. Is she calling someone?

Mercury. She's calling to her echo about Amphitryon. And you said that she wasn't a flirt. She never stops talking to that echo. Even her words have a mirror. Come on, Jupiter, she's approaching.

Jupiter. O chaste, pure vessel, so chaste and pure!——— Why are you smiling? Have you heard me say that before?

Mercury. Yes, Jupiter, under every balcony. There she is. Let's go.

Exit MERCURY *and* JUPITER. *Enter, below,* ALKMENA *and* ECCLISSE, *her nurse, coming from opposite sides.*

Alkmena. You seem very upset, Ecclisse.

Ecclisse. Here is some verbena, his favorite flower.

Alkmena. Whose favorite? I prefer roses.

Ecclisse. You'd dare decorate this room with roses on a day like this?

Alkmena. Why not?

Ecclisse. I've always heard that Jupiter hates roses. But perhaps you're right to treat gods as if they were ordinary men. That will make them prick up their ears. Shall I prepare the big red veil?

Alkmena. The big veil? Certainly not. The plain linen one.

Ecclisse. How clever you are, mistress. How right you are to make the palace seem homelike rather than to give it the atmosphere of a feast day. I have made some cakes and poured ambergris perfume into your bath.

Alkmena. That's good. That's my husband's favorite perfume.

Ecclisse. You know, your husband is going to be very proud and very happy, too.

Alkmena. What do you mean, Ecclisse?

Ecclisse. Dearest mistress, now you'll be famous through the centuries, and perhaps I shall be too, since I was your nurse. It was my milk that made you beautiful.

Alkmena. Has some good fortune come to Amphitryon?

Ecclisse. Something that will make him the happiest and most honored of princes.

Alkmena. Has he been victorious?

Ecclisse. Victorious, indeed! And over the greatest of the gods. Do you hear that?

Alkmena. What is that music—and those cries?

Ecclisse. But, dear mistress, all of Thebes knows the news. Everyone is rejoicing that, thanks to you, our town is favored above all.

Alkmena. Thanks to your master!

Ecclisse. Yes, of course. He, too, deserves some honor.

Alkmena. He alone!

Ecclisse. No, mistress, you. All Greece resounds with your glory. The priests tell me the cock's crow is a tone higher since this morning. Leda, the Queen of Sparta, whom Jupiter loved in the form of a swan, happens to be in Thebes. She wants to come and see you. Her advice might be useful—— Shall I tell her to come up?

Alkmena. Certainly——

Ecclisse. Ah, mistress, anybody could tell, even if they

hadn't see you every day in your bath as I have, that the gods would one day claim their due.

Alkmena. I don't understand you. Is Amphitryon a god?

Ecclisse. No, but his son will be a demigod. [*Shouting, music.*] Those are the virgins. They have outdistanced the priests. Don't show yourself, mistress. It's more dignified not to. Shall I speak to them? [*Talking to crowd outside.* ALKMENA *walks back and forth somewhat nervously.*] You're asking for the princess, my dears? Yes, yes, she's here! She's lying down now on her couch. She's gazing at an enormous gold sphere which all of a sudden is hanging from the ceiling. With her right hand she raises a bouquet of verbena to her face. With her left, she is offering a giant eagle, which has just come in the window, diamonds to peck at.

Alkmena. Stop your foolishness, Ecclisse. You can celebrate a victory without humbug.

Ecclisse. You want to know what she's wearing? No, she's not nude! She's wearing a tunic of the rare cloth called silk, bordered with a new color of red called madder. Her belt? And why wouldn't she be wearing a belt? Why are you laughing? Let me set you straight. Her belt is made of platinum and green jade. And you want to know whether she is preparing a meal for him, and what perfume she has on?

Alkmena. Have you finished yet, Ecclisse?

Ecclisse. They want to know what perfume you are wearing. [*A threatening gesture from* ALKMENA.] That's a secret, little ones, but this evening Thebes will be enveloped in it. You don't want her to become a star that's seen only twice a year? Yes, I'll warn her. And how will all this come to pass? Yes, I promise you, young maidens, that I will hide nothing from you. Farewell—— There they go, Alkmena. How delicious they look when they turn back to smile. Ah, what charming young girls!

Alkmena. You've gone quite wild.

Ecclisse. Yes, mistress, wild and crazy. What form will he take? Will he come by air, sea, or land? As a god, animal, or human? I couldn't chase away the birds today; at this very moment he may be one of them. I didn't dare run when that billy goat went after me. I let him butt me. He's out there in the antechamber, the dear creature, pawing the floor, and snorting. Maybe I should let him in? But who knows, maybe he's this wind that moves the curtains. I should have put up the bed curtains. Perhaps that's he, grazing the shoulder of your old nurse! I'm trembling. Ah, I'm in the wake of an immortal! Mistress, this is what makes Jupiter so skillful today—every part of his creation seems divine. Oh! Look what's coming in through the window!

Alkmena. Can't you see, it's a bee. Chase it!

Ecclisse. Certainly not! It's he! Don't move, mistress, I beg you. Hail, divine bee! We know who you are!

Alkmena. It's on me! Help!

Ecclisse. How beautiful you are, holding back that way! Oh, Jupiter is right to make you play this little game of being afraid. Nothing else would set off your purity and charm quite as well—— It's going to bite you!

Alkmena. But I don't want to be bitten.

Ecclisse. Oh, beloved bite! Let it bite you mistress! Let it land on your cheek. Look, it must be he, he's going for your breast! [ALKMENA *hits and crushes the bee. She kicks it away with her foot.*] Heavens! What have you done? What, no thunder and lightning? Wretched insect, to frighten us so.

Alkmena. Will you explain your conduct to me, Ecclisse?

Ecclisse. First of all, mistress, will you receive the delegations who have come to congratulate you?

Alkmena. I shall receive them with Amphitryon tomorrow.

Ecclisse. Yes, that's more natural. I'll be back, mistress. I'm going to look for Leda.

Exit ECCLISSE. ALKMENA, *somewhat agitated, walks to one end of the room. When she turns around, she sees* MERCURY *facing her.*

Mercury. Hail, Princess.

Alkmena. You must be a god to have come so audaciously but at the same time so discreetly.

Mercury. A god of ill repute, but a god.

Alkmena. Judging by your face, you are Mercury.

Mercury. Thank you. Most humans recognize me by the wings on my feet. You are either more clever or more skillful at flattery.

Alkmena. I am delighted to see a god.

Mercury. If you would like to touch one, I give you permission. I can see that gods interest you.

Alkmena. I spent my entire childhood imagining them and trying to catch their attention. At last, one of them has come! Here I am, caressing a bit of heaven! I love gods!

Mercury. All of them? Do your affections include me?

Alkmena. Earth asks to be loved for its individuals, the heavens must be loved all of a piece. But you, Mercury, have such a splendid reputation. You are supposed to be the god of eloquence. I saw who you were—at once.

Mercury. Because I was silent? Your face is so beautiful it seems to speak. Are you sure you have no favorite among the gods?

Alkmena. Of course, since I have a favorite among men.

Mercury. Who?

Alkmena. Must I tell you his name?

Mercury. Shall I run through the list of the gods according to their official rank, and you can stop me at your favorite?

Alkmena. Stop now. It is the first.

Mercury. Jupiter?

Alkmena. Jupiter.

Mercury. You astound me. Does his position of god among gods influence you to this degree? Doesn't his supreme idleness repel you? He's the foreman of our workshop, but he has no specialty; can it be that such idleness attracts you?

Alkmena. Divinity is his specialty. That counts for something.

Mercury. He doesn't understand the first thing about rhetoric, goldsmithing, or music of either the celestial or chamber variety. He's utterly without talent.

Alkmena. He is handsome, melancholy, and his august features are not marred by any of the tics which characterize blacksmiths or poets among the gods.

Mercury. He is handsome, there is no denying—and a lady's man.

Alkmena. You're disloyal to talk this way about him. Do you think that I don't understand the passionate impulses which hurl Jupiter into the arms of a mortal? You see, I've learned from my husband all about grafting—he's done wonderful things with cherries, you know. At school, too, we learned that hybrids of beauty and purity can result only from these visits to mortal women. Are you upset to hear me say this?

Mercury. You enchant me—— Then, the fate of Leda and Danae and all the others whom Jupiter loved and will love seems to you a happy one?

Alkmena. Infinitely happy.

Mercury. Enviable?

Alkmena. Very enviable.

Mercury. In short, you envy them?

Alkmena. I—envy them? Why do you ask?

Mercury. Can't you guess? Can't you guess why I've come, or the message I bring from my master?

Alkmena. Tell me.

Mercury. That he loves you—that Jupiter loves you.

Alkmena. Jupiter knows me? Jupiter deigns to know of my existence? I am the most fortunate of women.

Mercury. For days he has been watching you; he hasn't missed a single one of your gestures. Your entire form is inscribed on his mind.

Alkmena. For days?

Mercury. And nights. You grow pale?

Alkmena. That is true, but I should blush. Forgive me, Mercury. I'm distressed to think that I have not always been worthy of this attention. Why didn't you warn me?

Mercury. And what am I to tell him?

Alkmena. Tell him that henceforth I shall be worthy of his favor. There is already a silver altar dedicated to him in the palace. As soon as Amphitryon returns, we shall erect one in gold.

Mercury. It is not your altar that he wants.

Alkmena. Everything here belongs to him. Let him deign to choose something from among my favorite possessions.

Mercury. He has chosen, and he will come this evening at sundown to ask for it in person.

Alkmena. What is it?

Mercury. Your bed. Prepare yourself. I have just given my orders to the Night. She will need all day to amass the comets and shooting stars suitable to a heavenly wedding night. It won't be so much a night as an advance on your future immortality. I am happy to insert this scrap of eternity into your perishable days. It is my wedding present. You smile?

Alkmena. People smile at less.

Mercury. But why are you smiling?

Alkmena. Simply because you've mistaken me for another, Mercury. I am Alkmena and Amphitryon is my husband.

Mercury. Husbands are not included in the laws of destiny.

Alkmena. I am the simplest of Thebans. I did badly in school, and anyway I've forgotten everything I learned. People say I'm not very intelligent.

Mercury. I don't agree.

Alkmena. I want to point out to you that it is not your opinion that matters in this affair, but Jupiter's. And I'm simply not worthy of receiving Jupiter. He's seen me only in the light of his own brilliance. My own light is infinitely paler and more feeble.

Mercury. From heaven one can see your body lighting the Grecian night.

Alkmena. Yes. I have good powder, and creams. I manage to put up some kind of an appearance. But writing and thinking are beyond me.

Mercury. You talk very adequately. And, in any case, future poets will take it upon themselves to invent tonight's conversation.

Alkmena. Then they can invent the rest of it as well.

Mercury. Why are you so flippant? Do you think you can evade the gods and close your eyes to everything noble and beautiful which surpasses you? Don't you realize the seriousness of your role?

Alkmena. That is just what I have been trying to tell you! The role doesn't suit me. I live here in the most earthly of atmospheres which no god could stand for long.

Mercury. You're not thinking that a liaison is in question. It is a matter of a couple of hours.

Alkmena. You can't be sure of that. As I imagine Jupiter, I would not be surprised to find him constant. It is his interest in me which astonishes me.

Mercury. You have the best figure in the world.

Alkmena. Yes, I have a nice figure. Does he know that I tan very dark in summer?

Mercury. Your hands adorn the flowers in the gardens.

Alkmena. My hands are all right, but I have only two of them. And I have a tooth too many.

Mercury. Your walk is full of promise.

Alkmena. That doesn't mean anything. I'm not an experienced lover.

Mercury. Don't lie. Jupiter has watched you in this role, too.

Alkmena. One can pretend——

Mercury. Enough talk! No more coquetry! Alkmena, what do I see? Are those tears in your eyes? You are crying at a time when joy will rain down on men in your honor, for Jupiter has decided. He knows of your goodness; he knows you would prefer to see all mankind rejoice rather than to receive a shower of gold for yourself. A year of rejoicing begins tonight for Thebes. No more epidemics, no more famines, no more war!

Alkmena. That is all we needed.

Mercury. The children of the town who were to die this week—there are eight, if you want to know: four boys, four girls, your little friend Charissa among others—are going to be saved by tonight.

Alkmena. Charissa? That is blackmail.

Mercury. Health and happiness are the only blackmail the gods use. Do you understand? Listen! Those songs, that music, that merrymaking—it's all for you. All of Thebes knows that you will receive Jupiter tonight. The city is decked out in your honor. The sick, the poor, all those who will owe you life and happiness, Jupiter will cure them. He will overwhelm them with gifts as he passes through the city at sunset. There, you have been warned. Farewell, Alkmena.

Alkmena. Ah, so that was the victory! You are leaving, Mercury?

Mercury. I leave. I'll tell Jupiter that you are waiting for him.

Alkmena. You will be lying. I cannot await him.

Mercury. What are you saying?

Alkmena. I won't wait for him. I beg you, Mercury, turn Jupiter's favor away from me.

Mercury. I don't understand you.

Alkmena. I can't be Jupiter's mistress.

Mercury. Why?

Alkmena. He would despise me afterward.

Mercury. Don't be naïve.

Alkmena. I am impious. I blaspheme when I make love.

Mercury. You're lying. Is that all?

Alkmena. I'm tired. I'm sick.

Mercury. That is not true. Don't think you can put off a god in the same way you can put off a man.

Alkmena. But I love a man.

Mercury. What man?

Alkmena. My husband.

Mercury. Ah, you love your husband.

Alkmena. I love him.

Mercury. But, we counted on that. Jupiter's not a man. He doesn't choose his mistresses among unfaithful women. Anyway, don't pretend to be more ingenuous than you are. We know your dreams.

Alkmena. My dreams?

Mercury. We know that you dream. Sometimes, while they sleep in their husbands' arms, faithful women dream they are in the embrace of another man. They call him Jupiter.

Alkmena. My husband can be my Jupiter. Jupiter cannot be my husband.

Mercury. You really are stubborn. Don't force me to be blunt and to show you what's behind what you call candor. You are sufficiently cynical as it is.

Alkmena. If I was surprised naked, I would have to fight with my body and my bare limbs. You don't leave me any choice of words.

Mercury. Well, then, I won't mince words. Jupiter doesn't insist absolutely upon entering your bed as a man——

Alkmena. You may have seen that I don't accept women in bed either.

Mercury. We have noticed certain natural spectacles, certain fragrances, certain beings which gently agitate you in both body and soul. Often, even in Amphitryon's arms, these objects and beings inspire you with a tumult of apprehension. You love to swim. Jupiter could become the water that envelops and impels you. Or, if you think that your infidelity will be less marked if you receive the favors of the master of the gods from a plant or animal, say so, and he will grant you your wish. What is your favorite feline?

Alkmena. Mercury, leave me alone.

Mercury. One thing more, and I'll be gone. A child will be born of this evening's encounter, Alkmena.

Alkmena. He has a name, I suppose.

Mercury. He does—Hercules.

Alkmena. Poor little girl, she'll never be born.

Mercury. It's a boy, and he will be born. All the monsters who still lay waste to the earth, all the fragments of chaos which still hinder the work of creation, Hercules will destroy and dissipate. Your union with Jupiter has been established from the beginning of time.

Alkmena. And what will happen if I refuse?

Mercury. Hercules must be born.

Alkmena. And if I kill myself?

Mercury. Jupiter will restore you to life. This child must be born.

Alkmena. A child of adultery—never. He will die, child of heaven though he be.

Mercury. The patience of the gods has its limits, Alkmena. You despise their courtesy. So much the worse for you. After all, we don't need your consent. Perhaps you should know that yesterday——

ECCLISSE *enters hurriedly.*

Ecclisse. Mistress——

Alkmena. What is it?

Mercury. It must be Amphitryon.

Ecclisse. No, my lord. Queen Leda has arrived at the palace. Perhaps I should send her away?

Alkmena. Leda? No! Tell her to wait.

Mercury. Receive her, Alkmena, she may give you some useful advice. As for me, I'm going, and I'll report our conversation to Jupiter.

Alkmena. You'll tell him my reply?

Mercury. Do you want to see your town struck by the plague or destroyed by fire? Your husband, vanquished and fallen? I am going to tell him that you await him.

Alkmena. You will be lying.

Mercury. It's with the morning's lies that women make the evening's truth. Until this evening, Alkmena.

[MERCURY *disappears.*

Alkmena. Ecclisse, what does she look like?

Ecclisse. Her dress? Silver, bordered with swan's-down, but very tasteful——

Alkmena. I meant her face. Hard? proud?

Ecclisse. Noble and tranquil.

Alkmena. Run, then. Tell her to come quickly. I have an idea, a marvelous idea! Leda will save me.

Exit ECCLISSE.

Leda [*enters*]. Is this an indiscreet visit, Alkmena?

Alkmena. On the contrary, Leda. I've been longing for you to come.

Leda. In this the bedroom which history will remember?

Alkmena. It's my bedroom.

Leda. The sea and the mountains—you've arranged things beautifully.

Alkmena. And the sky above all——

Leda. Perhaps he's a little too familiar with the sky—— Is it to be this evening?

Alkmena. That is what they say.

Leda. How did you manage? Did you pray every day and reveal to him your suffering and nostalgia?

Alkmena. No, I prayed to show my gratitude and happiness.

Leda. That's the best way of calling yourself to his attention—— Have you seen him?

Alkmena. No. Did he send you?

Leda. I was just passing through Thebes, I heard the news, and I've come to see you.

Alkmena. Are you sure you're not hoping to see him again?

Leda. But I never saw him! Surely you've heard the circumstances of my affair?

Alkmena. Is the legend true, Leda? Was he a real swan?

Leda. Ah! So you're interested! Yes, up to a point, a cloud of a bird, a gust of swan.

Alkmena. Was it real down?

Leda. To tell you the truth, Alkmena, I'd just as soon

that he wouldn't assume the same form with you. I don't mean to be jealous, but permit me this little distinction. There are so many other birds, and some far more rare.

Alkmena. But very few as noble as swans. They have such a distant air about them.

Leda. That is quite true.

Alkmena. To me they don't appear more stupid than geese or eagles, and they at least sing.

Leda. Yes, they do sing.

Alkmena. No one hears them, but they sing. Did he sing? Did he speak?

Leda. Well——he spoke to me in a well-articulated warble. I couldn't understand what he said, but the syntax was so pure that I could guess which were the verbs and which were the pronouns.

Alkmena. Is it true that the joints of his wings creaked harmoniously?

Leda. Perfectly true, like a grasshopper's, only less metallic. With my fingers I touched the roots of his wings. It was like a harp of feathers!

Alkmena. Had you been told of his choice?

Leda. It was summer. Great clouds of swans were coursing high up among the stars. They were so beautiful I couldn't take my eyes off them. My husband joked with me and said I looked well under the sign of the swan.

Alkmena. Your husband joked about it?

Leda. My husband doesn't believe in the gods. He tells me my affair was a fantasy, or else he makes puns about it. It's an advantage, you know.

Alkmena. Was he a little rough? Were you surprised?

Leda. Assaulted, gently assaulted! Suddenly caressed by something other than these imprisoned serpents we have for fingers, these stumps of wings we have for arms, swept up by a movement which was not earthly, but astral—the sea-swell of the spheres! In short, a beautiful voyage. But you will know better than I very shortly.

Alkmena. And how did he leave you?

Leda. He left me lying there. He rose straight to the zenith. He graced me for several seconds with superhuman sight which permitted me to watch him go as far as the zenith of the zenith. There I lost him.

Alkmena. And since, nothing of him?

Leda. A few favors—and his priests are very polite. Sometimes a shadow of a swan lingers on me in my bath—no soap erases it. The branches of a certain pear tree bend in witness as I pass. Of course, I could never endure a liaison, even with a god. A second visit, yes, perhaps. But he neglected this point of etiquette.

Alkmena. Oh, that could be remedied! And have you been happy since?

Leda. Happy? Alas, no! But sanctified, at least. You will see how this surprise will relax you. It will be a life-long tonic.

Alkmena. But I'm not tense, and besides I am not going to see him.

Leda. Ah, but you will feel him. And, in the future, your husband's embrace will seem new and fresh.

Alkmena. Leda, you who know Jupiter, do you think one could make him change his mind?

Leda. But I don't know him. I knew him only as a bird.

Alkmena. But to judge by his behavior as a bird, what is his character as a god?

Leda. A logical mind, and very little knowledge of women—but he is open to suggestion and grateful for a helping hand. Why do you ask?

Alkmena. I've decided to refuse Jupiter's favors. I beg you to save me!

Leda. Save you from glory?

Alkmena. First of all, I'm unworthy of such glory. Now you are not only the most beautiful of queens, but the most intelligent. Who else could have understood the syntax of bird calls? And didn't you invent writing as well?

Leda. That's quite useless with the gods; they'll never learn to read!

Alkmena. You know astronomy. You know where your zenith is and your nadir. I confuse them. You're already placed in the universe like a star. One has only to see you to understand that you are one of those women that are made all the more attractive by learning. You're a living statue already, a perfect model of all of those in marble which will someday grace every public garden.

Leda. And you have nothing but youth and beauty. What are you driving at, my dear?

Alkmena. I shall kill myself, rather than submit to Jupiter's love. I love my husband.

Leda. Just so. And you will never be able to love anyone but him once you leave Jupiter's bed. No man or god will dare touch you.

Alkmena. I would then be forced to love my husband. I would not love him of my own free will. He would never forgive me.

Leda. Your eye might begin to wander later on. Why not begin with a god?

Alkmena. Save me, Leda! Revenge yourself on Jupiter who only embraced you once and thinks he can console you with the obeisance of a pear tree!

Leda. How can I take revenge on a poor white swan?

Alkmena. With a black one. I will explain. Take my place.

Leda. Your place?

Alkmena. That door leads to my room. Go in there— put on my veils, spray my perfume about. Jupiter will be deceived, and to his advantage. Isn't this the kind of service one friend does for another?

Leda. Without saying too much about it—yes, often, dear creature.

Alkmena. Why do you smile?

Leda. After all, Alkmena, perhaps I should listen to you. The more I see you, the more I hear you, the more I begin to be persuaded that celestial contact might be fatal to your special charm. I will help you.

Alkmena. Oh, Leda, Leda.

Leda. I want very much to save you, dear Alkmena. But listen, there is one condition.

Alkmena. Condition?

Leda. You must admit that I have the right to specify an incarnation that won't be repulsive to me.

Alkmena. Oh, yes——

Leda. In what form will Jupiter come?

Alkmena. I don't know.

Leda. You can know.

Alkmena. How?

Leda. He will take the shape of what you desire and dream of.

Alkmena. But my desires are satisfied.

Leda. I hope that you don't like serpents. I have a horror of them. If that's the case, don't count on me—unless it's a beautiful serpent, covered with rings.

Alkmena. No animal, no vegetable haunts me—

Leda. I refuse the minerals, too. But, Alkmena, you must have one weakness?

Alkmena. Not one. I love my husband.

Leda. But that must be it! There can be no doubt. That's the way you will be conquered. You've never loved anyone but your husband?

Alkmena. That is right.

Leda. Why didn't we think of this before? Jupiter will carry out the simplest of ruses. What he loves in you, I perceive as I begin to know you, is your humanity. What intrigues him is to know you as a human being, in your own surroundings, among your true joys. In order to get to you, he has only one course, to assume the shape of your husband. Your swan will be Amphitryon! Jupiter will await your husband's first absence to enter your chamber and deceive you.

Alkmena. You terrify me. Amphitryon is away now!

Leda. Away from Thebes?

Alkmena. He left yesterday for the war.

Leda. When will he return? An army can't decently wage a war in less than two days, can it?

Alkmena. I'm afraid.

Leda. Before this evening, Alkmena, Jupiter will make his way into the palace looking so like your husband that you will give yourself to him without a moment's hesitation.

Alkmena. I will recognize him.

Leda. For once a man will be of divine workmanship. You will be deceived.

Alkmena. That is just the point. He will be more perfect than Amphitryon, more noble, and more intelligent. I shall hate him at first sight.

Leda. And I tell you that with me he was a simply enormous swan and I couldn't distinguish him from the little swans I see every day on my own river.

Enter ECCLISSE.

Ecclisse. News, mistress, unexpected news!

Leda. Amphitryon is here!

Ecclisse. How did you know? Yes, the prince will reach the palace in a minute. From the ramparts I saw his horse leap the moats.

Alkmena. No rider ever jumped them before!

Ecclisse. He sailed across!

Leda. Is he alone?

Ecclisse. Alone, but one senses that there is an invisible squadron surrounding him. He is radiant. He doesn't look worn out as he usually does returning from war. He makes the morning sun pale by comparison. He's a mass of light in the form of a man. What should I do, mistress? Jupiter is at hand and my master will risk the wrath of the gods. I thought I heard a thunderclap when he started up toward the palace——

Alkmena. Be off with you, Ecclisse!

Exit ECCLISSE.

Leda. Now are you convinced? It's Jupiter, Jupiter, the sham Amphitryon.

Alkmena. Very well, then, he will find the sham Alkmena. In all the future tragedies of the gods, this will be remembered, thanks to you, Leda, as a little divertissement on behalf of women. Let us revenge ourselves!

Leda. What does your husband look like? Have you his portrait?

Alkmena. Oh yes. Here.

Leda. He is not bad at all. His eyes are a little enigmatic, like those of statues. I would adore statues if only they could talk and be responsive. Is he dark? His hair is not curly, I hope?

Alkmena. Straight hair, Leda, like a raven's wing.

Leda. A military bearing? Rough, red skin?

Alkmena. Certainly not. Muscular, but supple.

Leda. You will never hold it against me that I will take from you the image of the body you love?

Alkmena. I promise you I will not.

Leda. You will never hold it against me that I take from you a god whom you do not love?

Alkmena. Quick—he's coming. Save me.

Leda. The little room is in there?

Alkmena. Yes—quickly.

Leda. Are there steps going down? I have a horror of slipping in the dark.

Alkmena. No, a smooth level floor.

Leda. I hope it isn't a cold marble couch?

Alkmena. There is a thick wool rug. You won't weaken at the last minute?

Leda. I know how to keep a promise. I'm a very conscientious friend. Here he comes. Have a little fun with him before sending him into me. Avenge yourself with the false Amphitryon for the unhappiness which the real one will cause you some day——

Exit LEDA. *Enter* AMPHITRYON.

Voice of a Servant [*off*]. Your horses, my lord. What should I do with them? They're worn out!

Amphitryon. Don't bother me about my horses. I'll be off again in an instant.

Alkmena. He doesn't want to be bothered about his horses. It's not Amphitryon.

AMPHITRYON *approaches her.*

Amphitryon. Here I am!

Alkmena. You and no other, I see.

Amphitryon. Aren't you going to kiss me, darling?

Alkmena. Not yet, please. It's too light here. Later, in our bedroom.

Amphitryon. Right away! The thought of this minute hurled me toward you like an arrow!

Alkmena. It makes you scale mountains, leap rivers, and climb the heavens! No, no, come this way into the sunlight so that I can look at you. You're not afraid to let your wife see your face, are you? She knows all its perfections and imperfections.

Amphitryon. Here it is, dear, the best I can do!

Alkmena. Yes, it's the best you can do. An ordinary wife would be taken in. Everything is here. Those two sad wrinkles which frame your smile, that comical hollow which catches your tears, that sign of age, where some bird has put his foot right there at the corner of your temples. Jupiter's eagle, no doubt?

Amphitryon. A crow, dearest. Those are crow's-feet. Usually you kiss them.

Alkmena. Yes, all this belongs to my husband. But where's that scratch he gave himself yesterday? Strange, husband, to come back from war with one nick less.

Amphitryon. There's nothing like air for a wound.

Alkmena. The air of combat—yes, it's well known. Let's see your eyes. Oh, no, dear Amphitryon. When you set out, your eyes were gay and open. Whence that serious look in your right eye, the gleam of hypocrisy in the left?

Amphitryon. Husband and wife should not look too sharply into one another's eyes. Come along——

Alkmena. Wait. There's a shadow in your eyes which I've never seen there before. I don't know what it is about you this evening, my love, but when I look at you, I grow dizzy. I seem to know the past and I can foretell the future. I can guess at hidden knowledge.

Amphitryon. That's always the way it is before making love, dear. I feel the same way, too. It will pass.

Alkmena. What is this extraordinarily wide forehead thinking of?

Amphitryon. Of the beautiful Alkmena, always true to herself.

Alkmena. And what is this face thinking of, which grows larger as I look at it?

Amphitryon. Of kissing your lips.

Alkmena. Why my lips? You never mentioned my lips in the past.

Amphitryon. Of biting your neck.

Alkmena. Have you gone crazy? In the past you never dared name any of my features.

Amphitryon. I reproached myself for it last night, and now I'm going to name them all. I decided to while I was reviewing my troops, and now they must all reply as I call them off: eyelids, throat, neck, teeth. Your lips!

Alkmena. You can have my hand.

Amphitryon. What's wrong? Have I irritated you? Did I say something wrong?

Alkmena. Where did you sleep last night?

Amphitryon. In a bramble patch with a bundle of vines as a pillow, which I burned when I awakened—— I must be off again, in an hour, dearest. We're going into battle this morning—— Come—— What are you doing?

Alkmena. I have the right to caress your hair, don't I? It's never shone so.

Amphitryon. That must be the wind.

Alkmena. Yes, the wind is your slave. And what a cranium you have all of a sudden! I've never seen it so large!

Amphitryon. Intelligence, Alkmena——

Alkmena. Intelligence is your daughter——

Amphitryon. And these are my eyebrows, if you must know—this is my occipital bone, and this is my jugular vein. Dear Alkmena, why do you tremble so, touching me? You seem a fiancée, not a wife. What makes you so withdrawn with your husband all of a sudden? Now you, too, seem strange to me. And everything that I shall discover today will be new to me——

Alkmena. I'm sure of that——

Amphitryon. Don't you want a present? Is there nothing you wish for?

Alkmena. Before we go into our bedroom, I want you to kiss my hair ever so lightly.

Amphitryon [*takes her in his arms and kisses her on the neck*]. There you are!

Alkmena. What are you doing? Kiss me from a distance, on the hair, I told you.

Amphitryon [*kissing her on the cheek*]. There!

Alkmena. Don't you understand? Do you think I'm bald?

Amphitryon [*kisses her on the lips*]. There—— And now let me carry you off.

Alkmena. Wait a minute! Follow me in a minute, as soon as I call you.

Exit ALKMENA. AMPHITRYON *remains alone.*

Amphitryon. What a charming wife! How sweet life is when it slips by thus without jealousy or risk. How sweet this domestic happiness, untouched by intrigue or lust. I can return to the palace at dawn or dusk to find it exactly as I left it—tranquil. May I come in, Alkmena? She doesn't answer. I know her—that means she is ready. How delicate —she summons me with her silence, and what a silence! How it resounds! Yes, yes, here I am, darling——

When he enters the bedroom, ALKMENA *returns stealthily, looks after him with a smile, holds aside the drapery, and returns to the middle of the stage.*

Alkmena. There, now, the trick worked! He is in her arms. I don't want to hear anything more about the wickedness of the world. A child's game renders it harmless. I don't want to hear any more about destiny—it's nothing more than a by-product of human weakness. The trickery of men and the desires of the gods cannot withstand the will of a faithful wife. Isn't that what you think, Echo, you who always gave me the best advice? What have I to fear from man or god, I who am loyal and true? Nothing, do I? Nothing.

Echo. Everything, everything!

Alkmena. What's that?

Echo. Nothing, nothing.

Curtain

ACT THREE

Terrace near the palace. SOSIE, TRUMPETER, ECCLISSE.

TRUMPETER. What is the subject of your proclamation this evening?

Sosie. Women.

Trumpeter. Bravo! The perils of women?

Sosie. The natural fidelity of wives in wartime, that's the subject of the proclamation. What's more, it may even be true this time, since the war only lasted a day.

Trumpeter. Read it, quickly! [*He sounds his trumpet.*]

Sosie. O Thebans, among other advantages, war——

Ecclisse. Silence!

Sosie. Why silence? The war is over, Ecclisse. You have here two conquerors. The army is a quarter of an hour's march behind us.

Ecclisse. Silence, I tell you. Listen!

Sosie. Listen to your silence, that's new.

Ecclisse. I'm not the one doing the talking today, it's heaven that's talking. A heavenly voice has told the Thebans of the exploits of an unknown hero.

Sosie. Unknown? Do you mean little Hercules? The son Alkmena will conceive tonight by Jupiter?

Ecclisse. You've heard.

Sosie. The whole army knows. Ask the trumpeter.

Trumpeter. And I want you to know that we all rejoice. Soldiers of every rank attribute our rapid victory to this event. Not one man killed, madam, and even the horses were wounded in the left leg. Only Amphitryon is still uninformed, but thanks to these celestial pronouncements he will soon know.

Ecclisse. Amphitryon could have heard the pronouncements on the plain.

Trumpeter. Not a word was lost where we were with the crowd below the palace. Remarkable! A struggle between your future master and a monster with a bull's head had us worried for a minute. Hercules won, but it was a close thing—— Listen, there it is again!

Celestial voice. O Thebans, the minotaur is no sooner

killed than a dragon comes to lurk at the gates of your town, a dragon with thirty heads who feeds on human flesh, your flesh, except for his one herbivorous head. [*Shouts of dismay from the crowd.*] But Hercules, the son whom Alkmena will conceive tonight by Jupiter, will shoot the thirty heads with thirty arrows, shot from a single bow.

Cheering from the crowd.

Trumpeter. I wonder why he killed the herbivorous head.

Sosie. Look at Alkmena up on her balcony. She's not missing a single word. How clever Jupiter is! He knows how our queen longs for children and so he describes Hercules in order to win her.

Ecclisse. My poor mistress. The whole idea oppresses her. This giant of a son seems to be all around her.

Trumpeter. I would have Hercules himself speak instead of Jupiter. That would touch Alkmena more deeply.

Sosie. Quiet! There's the voice!

Celestial voice. From my father Jupiter I shall inherit my smooth skin and curly hair.

Shouts from the crowd.

Ecclisse. The gods took you up on your idea, trumpeter.

Trumpeter. Yes, but they were a little slow.

Celestial voice. From my mother, Alkmena, I shall inherit a gentle, faithful expression in my eyes.

Ecclisse. There's your mother, little Hercules. Do you see her?

Celestial voice. I see her and I admire her.

Shouts from the crowd.

Sosie. Why did your mistress close her window so brusquely? She shouldn't turn her back on a celestial voice! And by the way, Ecclisse, why does she look so melancholy? And why does the palace look so dreary? All the festival banners should be floating in the breeze. But I heard that your mistress saw Leda to ask her advice. I hear they spent the day laughing together. Is that true?

Ecclisse. It's true. But she left scarcely an hour ago. Immediately after her departure the voices announced that Jupiter would come at sundown.

Sosie. Did the priests confirm the announcement?

Ecclisse. They are just leaving.

Sosie. Then is Alkmena getting ready?

Ecclisse. I've no idea.

Trumpeter. Madam, certain rather disturbing rumors are circulating in Thebes concerning you and your mistress. It is said that Alkmena is childish enough, coquettish enough, to pretend not to appreciate Jupiter's favor, and that she dreams of nothing less than preventing the birth of the little hero.

Sosie. Yes, and they say that you are to help her in this infanticide.

Ecclisse. How can anyone say such things about me! Oh, how I am longing for this child! Remember that I'm the one who will be his first opponent; with me he'll learn how to save the world. For ten years I'll be the hydra, the minotaur! I must learn the noises they make so that I can accustom him to them.

Sosie. Calm yourself. Tell us about Alkmena. It's unseemly for Thebes to offer the gods a morose, reluctant mistress. Is it true that she is looking for a way to frustrate Jupiter's plan?

Ecclisse. I fear so.

Sosie. She doesn't realize that if she did so Thebes would be lost; there would be a plague and rioting within our city! Amphitryon would be stoned by the crowd. Faithful women are all alike. They think only of their fidelity and never of their husbands.

Trumpeter. Rest assured, Sosie, she will not succeed. Jupiter will not be diverted from his project; the essential characteristic of divinity is stubbornness. If man were sufficiently obstinate he too would be a god. Think of the scholars who pry divine knowledge from the elements simply through persistence. Jupiter is persistent. He will discover the secret of Alkmena. Besides, everything is all set for his coming. You'd think there was going to be an eclipse. All the little boys in Thebes have burned their fingers smoking bits of glass so that they can look at him as he passes, without being blinded.

Sosie. Have you alerted the musicians and kitchen staff?

Ecclisse. There is wine from Samos and cakes.

Sosie. There's nothing like a nurse to appreciate adultery!

You don't seem to understand that it's not a question of some clandestine rendezvous but of a marriage, a real marriage. And where's the crowd? Jupiter demands a crowd for every amorous exploit. How many people do you expect to assemble at this late hour?

Ecclisse. I was just going into town to collect all the poor, the sick, and the crippled. My mistress wants them to assemble along Jupiter's path so that he will be touched and softened.

Trumpeter. Hunchbacks and clubfeet to cheer Jupiter! Show him imperfections he knows nothing about! Why that would exasperate him! You mustn't do it!

Ecclisse. But I have no other course. My mistress ordered me to.

Sosie. She's wrong. The trumpeter is right.

Trumpeter. It's sacrilegious to show our creator where he bungled. He loves the world only because he thinks it's perfect. If he sees that we are bandy-legged and one-armed, suffering from jaundice and kidney stones, he'll be furious with us—all the more because he claims to have made us in his own image. There's nothing worse than a bad mirror.

Ecclisse. But he himself, through the celestial proclamation, asked for every miserable wretch in Thebes to come forth.

Trumpeter. And they will. I heard the proclamation and I made it my business to spread the word. But these unfortunates should give him a lofty idea of human misfortune. Don't be anxious, Sosie. Everything will be ready. Just now I assembled a special group of paralytics.

Ecclisse. How can paralytics climb up here?

Trumpeter. They made it with no trouble, and you'll see them. Come in, my dears, come in. Come show your poor limbs to the master of the gods.

Enter young dancers.

Ecclisse. But these are dancers.

Trumpeter. No, paralytics—or at least that's what we'll tell Jupiter they are. To him they will seem weaklings. And I also have, over there, behind the bushes, a dozen singers. We'll tell him they are mutes. With a few giants posing as midgets, we'll have a crowd of unfortunates which will not make Jupiter blush at his creation. He will be so pleased with himself that he will fulfill your mistress' desires and the wishes of the Thebans. From which direction will he come?

Ecclisse. His back will be to the sun, so the priests say. Today sunset will be doubly bright.

Trumpeter. Put the bakers here so that the light will strike their face. We'll tell him that they are lepers.

A dancer. But, learned sir, what shall *we* do?

Sosie. Dance. You don't know how to do anything else, I hope.

Dancer. Which dance? The symbolic one, where we strip?

Sosie. Too energetic. Don't forget that to Jupiter you're cripples.

Another dancer. Oh, it's for Jupiter. We could do our trout dance with those zigzags like a bolt of lightning. That would flatter him.

Trumpeter. Don't delude yourself. The gods see dancers from above, not from below. They don't care for dance as much as men do. Jupiter prefers to watch people swim.

Dancer. Well, there's our wave dance. We lie on our backs and wave our legs in the air.

Trumpeter. Tell me, Sosie. Who's that warrior climbing up the hill? Isn't it Amphitryon?

Ecclisse. Yes, it is Amphitryon! I am afraid.

Sosie. I'm not worried. He's a man of sound judgment and devotion. He will help persuade his wife.

Dancer. Look how he is running.

Trumpeter. I understand his haste. Many husbands want to wear out their wife so that she'll be no more than a lifeless body in the arms of a god—— Come on, my dears. It's time for us to begin the music. Well, it's thanks to the two of us that the ceremony will be worthy of the guests. We're just in time—— Sosie, your proclamation! [*He sounds the trumpet.*]

Sosie. O Thebans. Among other advantages, war clothes the body of a woman in steel armor without a chink for the hand of desire to slip through——

Enter AMPHITRYON. *He dismisses* SOSIE *and the* TRUM-PETER *with a gesture.*

Amphitryon. Is your mistress here, Ecclisse?

Ecclisse. Yes, my lord.
Amphitryon. Is she in her room?
Ecclisse. Yes, my lord.
Amphitryon. I'll wait for her.

The CELESTIAL VOICE *resounds after the silence.*

Celestial voice. Women—the son Alkmena will conceive this evening by Jupiter knows that they are all unfaithful, fond of honors, with a soft spot in their hearts for glory. [*Shouting from the crowd.*] He seduces them, wears them out, abandons them, insults their husbands outrageously. Through them he knows mortality——

Shouts from crowd. Enter ALKMENA.

Alkmena. What shall we do, Amphitryon?
Amphitryon. What shall we do, Alkmena?
Alkmena. All is not lost since he has allowed you to arrive before him.
Amphitryon. When is he to come?
Alkmena. In a few minutes, alas—at sundown. I don't dare look over there in the west. You who see eagles before they see you—don't you see anything in the sky?
Amphitryon. A star that seems to waver.
Alkmena. He must be passing. Have you a plan?
Amphitryon. I have my voice, my eloquence, Alkmena! I will persuade Jupiter, convince him!
Alkmena. Poor darling! You've never convinced anyone but me in the whole world, and you didn't speak to do that. That's what I fear, a conversation between you and Jupiter. You'd be the loser, and you'd give me to Mercury as well.
Amphitryon. Well, then, Alkmena, we're lost.
Alkmena. Let us trust in his goodness—— Here, where we receive distinguished guests, let us wait for him. I'm under the impression that he didn't know of our love. From the heights of Olympus he must see us thus beside each other, on our threshold. Let the vision of us as a couple begin to destroy his image of an isolated woman. Take me in your arms! Hold me tightly, here in broad daylight, so that he can see that a couple forms a single being. You still don't see anything in the sky?

Amphitryon. The Zodiac is trembling. He must have bumped into it. Shall I give you my arm?

Alkmena. No, nothing so ordinary, so artificial. Leave a space between us, sweet—that gentle doorway which children, cats, and birds love to enter between husband and wife.

Shouting and music are heard.

Amphitryon. There is the signal from the priests. He can't be far off now! Shall we say farewell in his presence, or now, Alkmena? We must think of everything!

Celestial voice. Announcing the Farewells of Alkmena and Amphitryon!

Amphitryon. Did you hear that?

Alkmena. Yes.

Celestial voice. The Farewells of Alkmena and Amphitryon.

Amphitryon. Aren't you afraid?

Alkmena. Haven't you ever felt, dearest, at those moments when life seems suddenly full and spacious, a strange voice within you giving a name to what you feel? The day we met and the day we first went swimming in the sea, didn't you hear a voice saying: The Engagement of Amphitryon! Alkmena's First Swim! No doubt the proximity of the gods has made the air so resonant today that we can actually hear what usually speaks mutely within us. Let us say farewell.

Amphitryon. To be frank, I'm not upset, Alkmena. From the moment I first met you, I knew that I would someday have to say farewell, not in parting, but as a new vow of what I feel. Destiny obliges me to say farewell today. This may be the last day of our life, and it would be appropriate if it were. For it is always when we are most happy and when nothing threatens our bliss that I feel the need to bid you farewell, to pour out my heart in new tenderness.

Alkmena. New tenderness? Tell me!

Amphitryon. I knew that I had one more secret to tell this face on which I shall never see a wrinkle, these eyes where I shall never see a tear, these eyelids which will never lose a lash.

Alkmena. Don't go into details, dearest. Let my limbs be nameless, and die unsung.

Amphitryon. Do you really think that we are going to die?

Alkmena. No! Jupiter will not kill us. To punish our obstinacy, it is more likely that he will change us into animals of two different species. He will alter all the tastes and pleasures we have in common. There are stories of love between a nightingale and a toad, a willow tree and a fish; we shall resemble these strange couples, and forever be apart. I'll stop so I won't give him any more ideas. I can't even bear to see you eat with a spoon if I'm eating with a fork; what pleasure will be left for me if you breathe through gills and I through leaves, or if you croak and I trill? What will there be left for me to enjoy in life?

Amphitryon. I shall join you, I shall remain beside you.

Alkmena. Beside me? Perhaps my presence will only bring you suffering. Perhaps we shall be face to face tomorrow at dawn, you exactly as you are, whereas I shall be deprived of that virginity which a wife must always preserve for her husband. Can you imagine living with a wife who has been dishonored, even if by a god? Can you imagine a third name on our lips, unsayable, which would make our meals and our kisses taste of gall? I cannot. How would you look at me when the thunder rumbles, when the sky is filled with lightning? Even the beauty of everything around us would remind us of our shame. I would rather be changed into the most humble of beings and remain pure. You are so conscientious that I would surely recognize you if you were a fish or a tree by the way you responded to the wind, seized your prey, or swam.

Amphitryon. There's Capricorn rising, Alkmena. He's approaching.

Alkmena. Farewell, Amphitryon. I would have liked to grow old with you, to watch you become stooped, to see whether it's true that old couples grow to look more alike. I would have enjoyed the pleasures of staying at home and looking back on our life. Let us pretend to be old for a minute, Amphitryon. Imagine that we have long years of marriage behind us, rather than twelve months. Did you love me, dear old husband?

Amphitryon. All my life!

Alkmena. Do you remember, about the time of our silver wedding, that young girl who was both bold and timid whom your exploits and the very sight of you ravished, you monster!

Amphitryon. You have always been younger than any sixteen-year-old.

Alkmena. When I was fifty and cried or laughed nervously without any reason, urging you, I don't know why, to certain other women, under the pretext that our love would thereby be freshened, you said nothing, you did nothing, you did not obey, did you?

Amphitryon. No. I wanted you to be proud of us both when we grew old.

Alkmena. What a splendid old age! Let death come!

Amphitryon. How good our memory is of this distant time! And this morning, Alkmena, when I returned at dawn from the battlefield to embrace you, you remember?

Alkmena. At dawn? At dusk you mean?

Amphitryon. Dawn or dusk, what difference is it now! Maybe it was noon. The only thing I remember is that my horse leaped the moat and that later in the morning I won in battle. But what's wrong, dearest? Why are you so pale?

Alkmena. I beg you, Amphitryon. Tell me if you came at evening or in the morning.

Amphitryon. Of course I'll tell you, dearest. Why not?

Alkmena. You came at night, didn't you?

Amphitryon. It was night in our room, completely black. You're right! Let death come!

Celestial voice. Let death come.

Enter MERCURY *and* JUPITER.

Jupiter. Let death come, you say? It's only Jupiter.

Mercury. Let me present Alkmena, my lord, the recalcitrant Alkmena.

Jupiter. Why is that man with her?

Mercury. That's her husband, Amphitryon.

Jupiter. Amphitryon, the victor of the great battle of Corinth?

Mercury. You're anticipating. The battle of Corinth is five years from now. But that's he.

Jupiter. Who told him to come here? What does he intend to do?

Amphitryon. My lord——

Mercury. No doubt he has come to offer you his wife himself. Didn't you see him from the sky preparing her, kissing her, caressing her, arousing her so that your night would be the supreme success you desire? Thank you, Prince.

Amphitryon. Mercury is wrong, my lord.

Jupiter. Ah, Mercury is wrong? You don't seem convinced that it is ordained that I must lie with your wife tonight and take your place. As for me, I am convinced.

Amphitryon. My lord, I am not!

Mercury. There's no time left for talk, Jupiter. The sun is going down. If the gods begin to converse with humans and engage in disputes, the good days are over.

Amphitryon. I have come to defend Alkmena against you, my lord, or else to die.

Jupiter. Listen to me, Amphitryon. As one man to another. You know my power. You realize that I can enter your bed invisibly even when you're there. With nothing more than the grass beneath our feet, I can make a potion which will make your wife fall in love with me and make you glad to have me as a rival. There can be no real conflict between us; alas, your protest is only a matter of form, as if you were a heretic or a schismatic. There's no doubt that I shall have Alkmena; the question is how. Are you going to enter into combat with the gods over this one short night, this pure formality?

Amphitryon. I cannot give away Alkmena. I prefer that other formality, death.

Jupiter. You must understand that I wish you well. I don't love Alkmena alone. If that were the case, I would have arranged to be her lover without consulting you. I love you as a couple. You are like a pair of beautiful carved figureheads on a galley looking ahead to a new era. I stand between you as a friend.

Amphitryon. You are our friend already, and we venerate you. I refuse to let you have Alkmena.

Jupiter. Then you will have to pay the price. On with the festivities, Mercury. Assemble the entire town. Since he forces us to make known the truth, reveal what happened yesterday evening and this morning. We have divine means at our disposal to convince this couple.

Amphitryon. Miracles do not convince a general.

Jupiter. Are those your last words? You're determined to fight with me?

Amphitryon. If necessary, yes.

Jupiter. I believe that you're a sufficiently intelligent general not to risk yourself unless you're as well armed as I. That's the ABC of tactics.

Amphitryon. I have a weapon as good as any of yours.

Jupiter. What's that?

Amphitryon. I have Alkmena.

Jupiter. Very well, then, let's go to it. I await your weapon without flinching. I even beg you to leave me alone with her. Come here, Alkmena. Disappear, you two!

MERCURY *and* AMPHITRYON *disappear.*

Alkmena. Alone at last!

Jupiter. Well said! This is the hour in which you'll belong to me.

Alkmena. Then it's my last hour.

Jupiter. Stop this blackmail. It's unworthy of us. Yes, here we are, face to face for the first time—I knowing your virtue, and you knowing my longing—alone at last!

Alkmena. Legend says you are often alone with someone in this way, doesn't it?

Jupiter. But rarely so much in love, Alkmena. Never so weak. From no other woman have I stood such disdain.

Alkmena. Does the term *in love* exist among the gods? I thought that they were merely adjusting the mechanism of the world when they came from time to time to nibble the face of a beautiful mortal.

Jupiter. "Adjust" is harsh. Let's say that destiny impels them.

Alkmena. Doesn't it seem repulsive to apply the laws of destiny to one so little fitted for it? All this dark hair with this skimpy blonde head!

Jupiter. For the first time destiny has a color. How delightful! Destiny has no hold on you, you're an eel in its hands.

Alkmena. And a plaything in yours. Oh, Jupiter, truly, do I please you?

Jupiter. If "please" means more than pleasure—a young doe aroused, an almond tree in flower—then, Alkmena, you please me.

Alkmena. That's my only hope. If I should displease you ever so little, you would not hesitate to take me by force in order to avenge yourself.

Jupiter. Do I please you?

Alkmena. Do you doubt it? Would I feel so strongly that I was deceiving my husband with a god who repelled me? That would be a disaster for my body, but my honor would be preserved.

Jupiter. Is it because you love me that you won't have me? Is it because you belong to me that you resist?

Alkmena. That's the essence of love.

Jupiter. You force Olympus to speak a very precious language this evening.

Alkmena. It will do him no harm. It seems that the most simple word in your language, no more than one word, could destroy the world, so brutal is your tongue.

Jupiter. Thebes is not really in any danger today.

Alkmena. Then why should Alkmena be? Why must you torture me, why must you break apart a perfect couple, why must you have an instant of happiness and leave ruins behind you?

Jupiter. That's the essence of love——

Alkmena. And, if I offered you something better than love? You can enjoy love with other women. But I would like to forge a softer and more powerful link between us; alone among women I can offer it to you. And I now do so.

Jupiter. What is it?

Alkmena. Friendship!

Jupiter. Friendship! What is this word? Explain it to me. This is the first time I've heard it.

Alkmena. Really! Oh, then, I'm delighted! I won't hesitate any longer! I offer you my friendship. It will be yours, completely virginal——

Jupiter. What does that mean? Is it a word much used on earth?

Alkmena. It's used.

Jupiter. Friendship—— It is true that up so high we miss certain aspects of human life—— Go on, tell me—— When people hide as we are hidden now and take gold pieces from the seams of their ragged clothing to count them and fondle them, is that friendship?

Alkmena. No, that's avarice.

Jupiter. What about those who stand naked in the full moon staring at it and running their hands over their bodies as if they were washing themselves in moonlight, are they friends?

Alkmena. No, they're moonstruck.

Jupiter. Make yourself clear! What about those who instead of loving the woman herself concentrate on one of her gloves or her shoes and wear out the suede or the kidskin with kisses? Are they friends?

Alkmena. No, they are perverse.

Jupiter. Then explain to me this friendship. It's a passion?

Alkmena. A wild passion!

Jupiter. What is its object?

Alkmena. It unites the most unlikely people and makes them equal.

Jupiter. I think I understand! Sometimes from our observatory we see creatures pair off and we don't understand what draws them to each other. A cabinet minister pays a daily visit to a gardener, a certain lion has a poodle in his cage, a sailor has a professor as a friend, and an ocelot a wild boar. And it's true they seem completely equal; together they face daily routine and make a common front against death. We were beginning to think that such creatures were drawn together by some secret substance in their bodies.

Alkmena. That may be. In any case, that's friendship.

Jupiter. I can still see that ocelot. He ran circles around the boar, his dear friend. Then he would hide in an olive tree, and when the boar snuffled at its roots he would drop, velvet-pawed, on its bristled back.

Alkmena. Yes, ocelots make good friends.

Jupiter. The cabinet minister used to walk in the garden with the gardener. He talked about grafting and slugs, the gardener about parliamentary debates and taxes. Then, when each had had his say, they stopped at the end of the garden path, having traced the furrow of their friendship to its limit, stroked their beards, and exchanged a wink in parting.

Alkmena. True friends.

Jupiter. And what shall we do if I become your friend?

Alkmena. First of all, I'll think about you rather than believe in you. And my thought will be voluntary, heartfelt, whereas my belief was a habit which I owed to my ancestors. My prayers will no longer be prayers but conversation.

Jupiter. Won't that be too much work for you?

Alkmena. Oh, no, the friendship of the master of the gods, the fellowship of a being who can do anything, destroy everything, and create everything, is the very least that will satisfy a woman. That's why women usually don't have any friends.

Jupiter. And what shall I do?

Alkmena. On days when I've had my fill of the company of men, you will appear, silently, and sit down very calmly on the foot of my divan. You will not stroke the tail or the claws of the leopard skin covering it—that would be love—and after a bit, suddenly, you will disappear. But you will have been there. Do you understand?

Jupiter. I believe I do. Ask me questions. Tell me on what occasion you would ask for my help and I will try to tell you what a good friend would do in that case.

Alkmena. Excellent. Are you ready?

Jupiter. Ready!

Alkmena. My husband is away?

Jupiter. I detach a comet to guide him. I give you second sight so you can see him in the distance and a secret voice to speak to him at a distance.

Alkmena. Is that all?

Jupiter. Oh, forgive me! I bring him back to you.

Alkmena. What would you do when dull women or boring relations come to call?

Jupiter. I unleash a plague which makes their eyes start out of their sockets. I afflict them with liver complaints and trouble them with colic. The ceiling falls in on them, the floor skids out from under them—— Won't that do?

Alkmena. It's too much or else not enough.

Jupiter. Oh, forgive me once again. I send them away——

Alkmena. If I have a sick child?

Jupiter. The universe is plunged in sadness. The flowers lose their fragrance. The animals hang their heads.

Alkmena. Wouldn't you cure him?

Jupiter. Obviously! How stupid I am.

Alkmena. That's what the gods always forget. They pity the sick, they detest the wicked, but they forget to cure or punish. But by and large you've understood. I'll pass you, but without honors.

Jupiter. Dear Alkmena——

Alkmena. Don't smile that way, Jupiter, don't be cruel! Have you never yielded to a single one of your creatures?

Jupiter. I've never had the chance.

Alkmena. You do now. Will you let it slip by?

Jupiter. Get up, Alkmena. It's time for you to receive your reward. Ever since this morning I have admired your courage and obstinacy; I have liked the way you have mingled loyalty and trickery, sincerity and falsehood. You have touched my heart, and, if you can find a way to justify your refusal to the Thebans, I will not force this night on you.

Alkmena. Why tell the Thebans? I am delighted, you can imagine, and Amphitryon will be delighted to have the whole world think I am your mistress. People will envy us but we will be glad to suffer for you.

Jupiter. Let me take you in my arms, Alkmena. Let us say farewell.

Alkmena. In the arms of a friend, Jupiter, of course!

Celestial voice. The Farewell of Alkmena and her lover Jupiter.

Alkmena. Did you hear that?

Jupiter. I heard it.

Alkmena. My lover Jupiter.

Jupiter. Lover can mean friend as well; a celestial voice can use a flowery style.

Alkmena. I'm anxious, Jupiter. Suddenly that word arouses all sorts of fears in me.

Jupiter. Calm yourself.

Celestial voice. The Farewell of Jupiter and his mistress Alkmena.

Jupiter. It's some joke of Mercury's. I'll straighten it out. But what's wrong, Alkmena? Why are you so pale? Must I tell you once again I accept your friendship?

Alkmena. Without qualifications?

Jupiter. Without qualifications.

Alkmena. You're very quick to accept it! And you seem very satisfied!

Jupiter. I am satisfied.

Alkmena. Are you satisfied not to have been my lover?

Jupiter. That's not what I mean.

Alkmena. And that's not what I think. Jupiter, now that you're my friend, be frank. Are you sure you've never been my lover!

Jupiter. Why do you ask?

Alkmena. You were playing a while ago when you talked with Amphitryon. There was no real battle between his love and your longing. You were playing a game. You had already decided to relinquish me. My knowledge of men leads me to believe that that's because you've already possessed me.

Jupiter. Already? What do you mean by already?

Alkmena. Are you sure that you never appeared in a dream or took the form of Amphitryon?

Jupiter. Absolutely sure.

Alkmena. Perhaps you've forgotten. It's not surprising with so many affairs——

Jupiter. Alkmena!

Alkmena. Then I'm not one of your great loves. Obviously I wouldn't have done it a second time, but to have slept beside Jupiter for one night, that would have been something for a little housewife like me to remember. Too bad.

Jupiter. Dear Alkmena, you're trying to trap me!

Alkmena. Trap you? Then you can be caught?

Jupiter. I've seen what you've gone through, Alkmena, all your suffering and plotting. I see that you were ready to kill yourself if I had been your lover. I never was.

Alkmena. Take me in your arms.

Jupiter. Gladly, little Alkmena. Is that nice?

Alkmena. Yes.

Jupiter. Yes, who?

Alkmena. Yes, Jupiter, darling. It sounds natural, doesn't it?

Jupiter. You said it very naturally.

Alkmena. Why did I say it just like that, of my own accord? That's what intrigues me. And this ease, this con-

fidence which I feel beside you, where does it come from?
I feel as if you were the source of this ease.

Jupiter. Well, yes, we understand each other very well.

Alkmena. No. We don't agree at all about many things.
Your creation, to begin with, and the way you dress, for
another; but our bodies agree. Our two bodies are still at-
tracted to each other as if they had been magnetized.
When did this occur? Admit what happened.

Jupiter. Never, I tell you.

Alkmena. Then why am I so troubled?

Jupiter. You're troubled because, in spite of myself, in
your arms I feel myself tempted to take the form of
Amphitryon. Or else, perhaps, you're beginning to love
me.

Alkmena. No, this is not a beginning. Are you sure it
wasn't you the night of the great fire in Thebes who came
to my bed, still hot from the flames?

Jupiter. And it was not I that night your husband returned all wet from sea water from saving the drowning
child——

Alkmena. See! You know about it!

Jupiter. But I know everything about you, don't I? Alas,
it was your husband that night. What soft hair!

Alkmena. It seems to me this is not the first time that
you have arranged this lock of hair, bending over me this
way. Was it at dawn or dusk that you came and took me?

Jupiter. You know very well, it was dawn. Do you think
I failed to understand your trick with Leda? I accepted
Leda to please you.

Alkmena. O master of the gods, can you give forgetfulness?

Jupiter. What would you like to forget?

Alkmena. Today. Of course I want to believe that everything happened as it should and that everyone played his
part loyally, but there is something ambiguous about the
day which disturbs me. I'm not a woman who can bear a
single cloud of the unexplained in my life. My entire
body rejoices in that hour when I knew you, but my soul
is made uneasy by it. Isn't that the contrary to what I
should feel? Give my husband and me the chance to forget today, your friendship aside.

Jupiter. Let it be as you wish. Let me take you in my

arms once again. This time be as gentle as you know how.

Alkmena. Yes, since I shall forget everything.

Jupiter. Indeed I must embrace you, for it is only with a kiss that I can give you forgetfulness.

Alkmena. Are you going to kiss Amphitryon on the lips as well?

Jupiter. Since you are going to forget everything, Alkmena, don't you want me to show you what awaits you in the future?

Alkmena. Heaven preserve me from that.

Jupiter. It will be a happy one, believe me.

Alkmena. I know what a happy future is like. My beloved husband will live and die. My beloved son will be born, live, and die. I shall live and die.

Jupiter. Why don't you want to be immortal?

Alkmena. I detest adventures, and immortality is an adventure.

Jupiter. Alkmena, dear friend, I want you to participate if only for an instant in the life of the gods. Since you will forget everything, don't you want to glimpse the true nature of the world?

Alkmena. No, Jupiter, I'm not curious.

Jupiter. Don't you want to see the void, that succession of voids, which is infinity? If you think such a void will strike terror in your heart, I will fill it with your favorite flower, a rose or a zinnia, so that infinity will be marked for a moment by your emblem.

Alkmena. No, no.

Jupiter. Let me exercise my divinity for you and your husband today. Don't you wish to see humanity at its labors, from its birth to its final day?

Alkmena. No.

Jupiter. For the last time I question you, dear obstinate woman! Don't you want to know, since you're going to forget, the illusions your happiness and your virtue are based on?

Alkmena. No.

Jupiter. And don't you want to know what I really am to you, Alkmena? And don't you want to know what this stomach, this dear stomach, conceals?

Alkmena. Make haste!

Jupiter. Then, forget everything except this kiss. [*He kisses her.*]

Alkmena [*coming to herself*]. What kiss?

Jupiter. Oh, don't worry about the kiss! I was careful to put it just this side of forgetfulness.

Enter MERCURY.

Mercury. All of Thebes is below, Jupiter, waiting for you to show yourself in the arms of Alkmena.

Alkmena. Come over here, Jupiter. Everyone will see us and rejoice.

Mercury. They want you to speak a few words, Jupiter. Don't hesitate to speak to them in a very loud voice. They are standing sideways so that they won't risk damaging their ears.

Jupiter [*very loudly*]. At last, dear Alkmena, we meet——

Alkmena [*very low*]. Yes, we must part, dear Jupiter.

Jupiter. Our night begins, fortunate for all the world.

Alkmena. Our day ends, a day that I was beginning to love.

Jupiter. Before these magnificent, proud Thebans——

Alkmena. These poor fellows, they applaud what they know is my error and would, if they knew, insult my virtue——

Jupiter. I welcome you with a kiss for the first time.

Alkmena. And I for a third time, in eternal farewell.

They walk the length of the balustrade. Then ALKMENA *leads* JUPITER *to a small door.*

Jupiter. And now?

Alkmena. And now that the legend is suitably established in a manner appropriate to the gods, let us complete the story with compromise, in a manner appropriate to humanity. No one can see us from here. Let us remove ourselves from the influence of destiny. Amphitryon, are you there?

Enter AMPHITRYON *through the little door.*

Amphitryon. Here I am, Alkmena.

Alkmena. Thanks, Jupiter, dearest. He wants to return me to you himself, intact.

Amphitryon. Only a god could be so considerate!

Alkmena. He wanted to test us. All he asks is that we have a son.

Amphitryon. In nine months, my lord, we shall have one!

Alkmena. And we promise you to call him Hercules since you like that name. He will be a good little boy.

Jupiter. Yes, I can see him now. Farewell, then, Alkmena, be happy. And you, Mercury, master of revels, before we leave, prove our friendship by giving them the reward which a couple just reunited deserves.

Mercury. A couple just reunited? That's easy! To witness their delight I call on all of you, the gods, and you, Leda, who have some news coming to you, and you, good people, who have all day been the subalterns of love and war, groom, warrior, trumpeter! Open wide your eyes and let there be music and thunder around this bed to drown out their cries.

All the people evoked by MERCURY *appear.*

Alkmena. Oh, Jupiter, make him stop. For Alkmena's sake!

Jupiter. Alkmena and more Alkmena! There's nothing but Alkmena today! Then it's Mercury's mistake! Let theirs be the most quiet, the most private of reunions. Let's disappear, gods and supernumeraries, to our zeniths and our cellars. And you, spectators, withdraw without a word, pretending the most complete indifference. For one supreme instant let Alkmena and her husband stand alone in a circle of light. Let my arm have no other power than to point out their happiness. And on this couple who have never known and will never know adultery, who will never taste an illicit kiss, you, curtain of the night, enclose with velvet this little island of fidelity. Fall!

Curtain.

ELECTRA

A Play in Two Acts

◄§§►

CAST OF CHARACTERS

(IN ORDER OF APPEARANCE)

ORESTES

THE EUMENIDES, *first as three little girls, later as twelve-year-olds, then as fifteen-year-olds, still later the same age as Electra.*

GARDENER

JUDGE

AGATHA THEOCATHOCLES, *his young wife*

AEGISTHUS

BEGGAR

CLYTEMNESTRA

ELECTRA

YOUNG MAN

CAPTAIN

NARSES' WIFE

SERVANT

PAGE

MESSENGER

Villagers, soldiers, servants, attendants, beggars

SCENE—In front of Agamemnon's palace in ARGOS.

ELECTRA

ACT ONE

A stranger, ORESTES, *enters, escorted by three* LITTLE
GIRLS (THE EUMENIDES). *At the same time the* GARDENER
*enters from the other side of the stage, dressed in his best
and accompanied by wedding guests from the village.*

FIRST LITTLE GIRL. Look how handsome the gardener is!
  Second little girl. No wonder! It's his wedding day.
  Third little girl. Here you are, sir. This is Agamemnon's
palace.
  Orestes. What a strange façade! Are you sure there's
nothing wrong with it?
  First little girl. That depends on what you mean by
"wrong." The right wing isn't really there. You think you
see it, but it's a mirage. Just like the gardener over there
who's coming to talk to you. He's not really coming over.
He won't be able to say a word.
  Second little girl. Or else he'll bray like a donkey, or
miaow like a cat.
  Gardener. The building is all right, stranger. Don't listen
to these liars. You're fooled because the right wing is constructed of limestone, which sweats at certain times of the
year. When this happens, the townspeople say that the
palace is weeping. The left wing is built of our marble
from Argos which—no one has ever known why—suddenly begins to glow as if the sun were shining on it. Sometimes it even happens at night. Then people say that the
palace is laughing. Just now the palace is laughing and
weeping at the same time.
  First little girl. That way it can be sure not to make a
mistake.
  Second little girl. It's a perfect palace for a widow.
  First little girl. Or else it's like a childhood memory of
a palace.
  Orestes. I didn't remember that the façade was so sensitive——

159

Gardener. You've visited the palace before?

First little girl. He was only a child.

Second little girl. Twenty years ago.

Third little girl. He hadn't yet learned to walk——

Gardener. Still, it's not easy to forget once one has seen it.

Orestes. All I remember of Agamemnon's palace is a mosaic. When I was naughty they put me down on a diamond of tigers, and when I was good on a hexagon of flowers. And I used to crawl from one to the other, I remember—past some birds.

First little girl. And past a capricorn.

Orestes. How did you know, little one?

Gardener. Did your family live in Argos?

Orestes. And I remember bare feet, lots of them. No faces—they were high in the sky—but bare feet. They wore gold anklets which I grabbed for through the fringes that half concealed them. Some ankles were joined by chains—these were the ankles of slaves. But I remember best two small white feet, the smallest and whitest. Their step was always measured and circumspect as if also restrained by a chain—an invisible one. I'm sure they were Electra's. I must have kissed them, don't you think? A baby kisses everything he touches.

Second little girl. If you did, it's the only kiss Electra ever received.

Gardener. No doubt of that.

First little girl. Are you jealous, gardener?

Orestes. Does Electra still live in the palace?

Second little girl. She still does. But not for long.

Orestes. That's her window, isn't it—the one with the jasmine?

Gardener. No. That's the room where Atreus, the first king of Argos, killed his brother's sons.

First little girl. The meal at which he served their hearts took place in the room next door. I would love to know how they tasted.

Third little girl. Did he dice them first or did he cook them whole?

Second little girl. Cassandra was strangled in the watchtower.

Third little girl. They had thrown a net over her and

stabbed her, but she screamed like a madwoman—— I
would like to have seen her, veiled that way.

First little girl. As you see, all this took place in the
laughing wing.

Orestes. The one with the roses?

Gardener. Stranger, don't try to find any connection between the various windows and the flowers decorating
them. I'm the palace gardener. I choose the flowers according to whim. After all, a flower is a flower.

Second little girl. Not at all. There are flowers and
flowers. Phlox doesn't suit Thyestes at all.

Third little girl. Or mignonette Cassandra.

Gardener. Will they never be quiet! The window with
the roses, stranger, is the window of the bath where our
king, Agamemnon, Electra's father, slipped, the day he
returned home from the war, and killed himself by falling
on his sword.

First little girl. He took his bath after he died. Two
minutes after. Not before.

Gardener. Up there, that's Electra's window.

Orestes. Why is it so high? It's practically under the
eaves.

Gardener. Because from that floor she can see her father's tomb.

Orestes. But why in such an aerie?

Gardener. Because that room used to belong to little
Orestes, her brother, whom her mother banished when he
was two years old. We've never heard from him since.

Second little girl. Listen, sisters, listen! They're talking
about little Orestes.

Gardener. Move along, won't you! Get going! Can't you
leave us alone? You buzz like flies.

First little girl. We can't move along. We're with the
stranger.

Gardener. You know these little girls?

Orestes. I ran into them at the gates of the town. They
followed me.

Second little girl. We followed him because we think
he's nice.

Third little girl. He's a good deal handsomer than you,
gardener.

First little girl. He doesn't have caterpillars crawling out of his beard.

Second little girl. Or beetles out of his nose.

Third little girl. I suppose that, if flowers are to have any fragrance, the gardener has to stink.

Orestes. Where are your manners, children? Tell us, what is your business in life?

First little girl. It's our job not to be polite.

Second little girl. We lie. We slander. We insult people.

First little girl. But our specialty is reciting.

Orestes. What do you recite?

First little girl. We don't know beforehand. We invent as we go along. But it's always good, very good.

Second little girl. The king of Mycenae, whose sister-in-law we insulted, told us that what we said was very, very good.

Third little girl. If there's anything bad to be said, we say it.

Gardener. Don't listen to them, stranger. No one knows who they are. They've been going about the town for the last two days, apparently without friends or family! If you ask them who they are, they claim to be called the little Eumenides. And what is so terrifying is that they grow taller and fill out before your very eyes—— Yesterday they were years younger than they are today—— Come here, you!

Second little girl. For a bridegroom he's awfully rough!

Gardener. Look at her—— You can see her eyelashes growing. Look at her bosom. If you've ever watched mushrooms grow the way I have, then you'll know what to look for—— They're growing now—as fast as toadstools.

Second little girl. The poisonous ones grow the fastest.

Third little girl [*to the first*]. Is your bosom growing?

First little girl. Shall we recite? Yes or no?

Orestes. Let them recite, gardener.

First little girl. Let's recite the one about Clytemnestra, Electra's mother. Are you ready?

Second little girl. We're ready.

First little girl. Queen Clytemnestra has a sallow complexion. She wears rouge.

Second little girl. She's sallow because she can't sleep.

Third little girl. She can't sleep because she's afraid.

First little girl. What is Queen Clytemnestra afraid of?
Second little girl. Of everything.
First little girl. What's everything?
Second little girl. Silence. Silences.
Third little girl. Noise. Noises.
First little girl. The idea that it will soon be midnight. That spiders, spinning their threads, will soon foretell misfortune instead of happiness.
Second little girl. Everything red, because red is the color of blood.
First little girl. Queen Clytemnestra is sallow. She wears blood.
Gardener. What nonsense!
Second little girl. Nice, isn't it?
First little girl. It's very poetic, isn't it, the way we repeat the beginning at the end?
Orestes. Most interesting.
First little girl. Since you're interested in Electra, we could do one about her. Ready, sisters? Let's recite one about her as she was at our age.
Second little girl. Fine! Ready then!
Third little girl. We've been ready since day before yesterday when we weren't yet born!
First little girl. Electra thinks it's fun to make Orestes fall out of his mother's arms.
Second little girl. Electra waxes the steps to the throne so that her uncle, Aegisthus, the regent, slips on the marble!
Third little girl. Electra plans to spit in the face of her little brother Orestes if ever he returns.
First little girl. That bit isn't true. But it sounds good.
Second little girl. She's been accumulating spittle—bitter spittle—in her mouth for nineteen years.
Third little girl. She thinks about the slugs in your garden, sir, to make her mouth water more.
Gardener. That's enough now, you dirty little vipers!
Second little girl. Look! Look! The bridegroom's angry.
Orestes. He has a right to be. Get going!
Gardener. And don't come back!
First little girl. We'll be back tomorrow.
Gardener. Just try! The palace is closed to girls of your age!

First little girl. Tomorrow we'll be full grown!

Second little girl. Tomorrow will be the day after Electra's marriage to the gardener. We'll be full grown.

Orestes. What are they saying?

First little girl. You didn't defend us, stranger; you'll be sorry!

Gardener. Hideous little creatures! Like three little Fates! Pretty horrible, destiny, when it takes the form of a child.

Second little girl. Here's destiny's tail, gardener. Watch it grow!

First little girl. Come, sisters. Let's leave them in front of their filthy old palace.

Exit the little EUMENIDES, *from whom the wedding guests draw back in terror. Enter the* JUDGE *and his young wife,* AGATHA THEOCATHOCLES.

Orestes. What were those little girls saying? Are you, the gardener, about to marry Electra?

Gardener. She will be my wife an hour from now.

Agatha. He's not going to marry her. We've come to stop him.

Judge. Gardener, I'm your distant cousin as well as an associate justice of the tribunal. I am, therefore, doubly authorized to advise you to return to your radishes and your squashes. Do not marry Electra.

Gardener. But Aegisthus has ordered me to marry her.

Orestes. Have I gone mad? If Agamemnon were alive, Electra's wedding would be the most splendid ceremony in all Greece; and here is Aegisthus marrying her off to the gardener! And his family is protesting, although you'd think they would be honored. Electra isn't ugly or a hunchback, is she?

Gardener. Electra is the most beautiful girl in Argos.

Agatha. Well, she's not bad.

Judge. And she's straight as straight can be, like plants that grow in the dark without twisting and turning to follow the sun.

Orestes. Is she backward, then, or simple-minded?

Judge. She's intelligence itself.

Agatha. It's her memory that's most exceptional. They're not always the same thing. Take me: I can't remember a thing. Except your birthday, darling. I never forget that.

Orestes. Then what has she done, what has she said, for her to be treated in this way?

Judge. She hasn't done anything. She hasn't said anything. It's just that she's there.

Agatha. Yes, she's there.

Orestes. But she has a right to be. It's her father's palace. It's not her fault that he's dead.

Gardener. Never would I have dared dream of marrying Electra, but since Aegisthus has ordered me to, I don't see what there is to fear.

Judge. There's everything to fear—she's the kind of woman who can't leave well enough alone.

Agatha. And it's not as if you were the only one involved! The family has everything to fear as well.

Gardener. I don't understand.

Judge. Let me elucidate: life can be very agreeable, can't it?

Agatha. Very agreeable—infinitely agreeable.

Judge. Don't interrupt me, darling, especially to repeat what I've already said—— Life can be very agreeable. Things tend to work out for the best in life. A wounded spirit heals faster than a stomach ulcer and grief disappears sooner than a sty in your eye. But if you select at random two groups of people, each containing the same dose of crime, falsehood, vice, adultery——

Agatha. Adultery is an awfully strong word, darling——

Judge. Don't interrupt me, especially to contradict me. Why does life flow by calmly, smoothly in one group, with the living forgetting the dead and getting along with one another, whereas in the other group it's hell?—— It's simply that in the second there's a woman who can't let well enough alone.

Orestes. It's simply that the second group has a conscience.

Agatha. I want to go back to your word *adultery.* I still think it's a very strong word.

Judge. Hush, Agatha. A conscience! That's what you think! If the guilty don't forget their sins, if the vanquished don't forget their defeats, and the victors their victories, if the air is charged with hatred, quarreling, and imprecations, it's not the fault of the conscience of most people who are always inclined to forgive and forget, but the fault of ten or fifteen women who can't leave well enough alone.

Orestes. I'm completely in agreement. Ten or fifteen women who can't leave well enough alone have saved the world from self-interest.

Judge. They've saved it from happiness! I know Electra's game! Let's say she is everything you say she is, the soul of justice, generosity, and duty. But it is justice, generosity, duty, and not self-interest and lack of principle, that ruin the state, the individual, and the best families.

Agatha. Absolutely, darling—— But why?—— I know you told me, but I've forgotten!

Judge. Because these three virtues contain the only substance which is truly fatal to humanity—implacability. Happiness has never been the lot of those who are implacable. A happy family signifies a localized surrender. An era of happiness means complete capitulation.

Orestes. Did you surrender the first time you were rebuked?

Judge. No, alas! Others would have been quicker. That's why I'm only an associate justice today.

Gardener. In what way is Electra implacable? She visits her father's tomb every night, but that's all, isn't it?

Judge. Yes, I've followed her. Followed her, the embodiment of innocence, along the very same route by the river where my job had taken me one night on the track of our most dangerous murderer. Horrible it was, too, to follow her. They both stopped at the same spots: the yew tree, the bridge, the milestone have the same significance for the criminal and the innocent. But, strangely enough, the murderer made the night seem pure, reassuring, unambiguous. The evil in the night was isolated in him just as the risk of a broken tooth is isolated in the pit of a fruit—cut it out and you have nothing to worry about. On the other hand, Electra mingled day with night and made even the light of the full moon seem ambiguous. You've seen fishermen set out their bait in the evening for the next day. That's what she was doing all along that dark stream. And that's what she does every evening—lures everything which, if it weren't for her, would have left this pleasant, easygoing earth: all the old rusty, blood-stained bits of

confession and remorse, the bones of murdered men, in-
formers' filth—— It won't be long now before the traps
will be teeming—— The fisherman will have only to come
by.

Orestes. But he's bound to come, sooner or later.

Judge. Not so! Not so!

Agatha [*very much taken with the young stranger*]. Not
so!

Judge. Even this child sees the weakness in your argument. Each day the worst of our faults, our deficiencies,
our crimes, the truth of our lives, is stifled under a triple
layer of forgetfulness, death, and the ordinary course of
justice. It's foolish not to rely on this process. It's hideous
to be in a country where some solitary righter of wrongs
has roused the half-sleeping phantoms of the murdered,
where perjury and even ordinary shortcomings are never
forgiven, where ghost and avenger forever loom. When the
sleep of the guilty continues, after the term of punishment
prescribed by law, to be more troubled than the sleep
of the innocent, society is compromised. When I see
Electra, I feel the sins of childhood stirring in me once
more.

Agatha. I feel my future sins. Not that I'll ever commit
them, darling. You know that. Especially what you insist
on calling adultery—— But they're already tormenting me.

Gardener. I'm of somewhat the same mind as Electra.
I'm none too fond of the wicked. And I'm fond of the
truth.

Judge. I suppose you think you know the truth about our
family since you're so eager to publicize it! No question
that we're a well-ordered, respected family doing very well
for ourselves—you won't deny that you're the most lowly
member—but I know from experience that it's risky to
test such appearances very far. It won't be ten days, if
Electra becomes our cousin, before its discovered—I'm in-
venting at random—that as a young unwed mother our old
aunt strangled her baby. Then someone will tell her old
husband and he'll be so rabid that nothing will calm him
down until he hears how his grandfather was solicited as a
young boy. Take little Agatha, she is the soul of gaiety and
she can't sleep any more. You're the only one not to see
what Aegisthus is up to. He wants to palm off on the Theo-

cathocles family everything that might one day put the Atrides in an unfortunate light.

Orestes. What have the Atrides to fear?

Judge. Nothing. Nothing that I know of. But they're like every happy family, every powerful couple, every satisfied individual. They have the most formidable enemy in the world to fear, which will consume them completely, gnaw them to the bone: Electra's ally—total justice.

Gardener. Electra adores my garden. If she's a little high-strung, the flowers will do her good.

Agatha. She won't do the flowers any good.

Judge. No doubt of that! You'll see what they're really like, your fuchsias and geraniums. You'll see them cease to be amiable symbols and become deceitful and ungrateful. Electra in a garden is the equivalent of justice and memory among flowers, that is, of hatred.

Gardener. Electra is devout. The dead are all for her.

Judge. The dead! Oh! I can imagine what they'll say when they hear Electra is coming. I can see them, the murdered already half mingled with the murderers, the shades of those who have been robbed or duped gently entwined with the shades of thieves, rival families parted and freed of each other; I see them all stirring and saying to each other, "Good God, here's Electra coming. And we were so peaceful!"

Agatha. There's Electra now.

Gardener. No. Not yet. It's Aegisthus. Leave us, stranger. Aegisthus isn't very fond of meeting men he doesn't know.

Judge. You go along, too, Agatha. He's only too fond of women he does know.

Agatha [*most interested in the stranger's handsome face*]. May I show you the way, handsome stranger?

Exit AGATHA *and* ORESTES. *Enter* AEGISTHUS, *hailed by the guests, while servants install his throne and set a stool by a column.*

Aegisthus. What's that stool for? Why are you putting it there?

Servant. It's for the beggar, my lord.

Aegisthus. What beggar?

Servant. Or the god, if you prefer. For the beggar who has been wandering about the town for the last few days.

No one has ever seen a beggar who looked more like a beggar; therefore people are saying he must be a god. Everyone lets him come and go as he pleases. He's prowling about the palace now.

Aegisthus. Does he change grain into gold in the houses he visits? Does he get the serving girls with child?

Servant. He does no harm of any kind.

Aegisthus. A strange sort of god he must be—— And the priests haven't been able to decide whether he's Jupiter or a beggar?

Servant. The priests have requested that no one put this question to them.

Aegisthus. Shall we leave the stool, my friends?

Judge. I believe that in the long run it's cheaper to honor a beggar than to humiliate a god.

Aegisthus. Leave the stool. But if he appears, warn us. We need to be in strictly human company for about a quarter of an hour. But don't offend him. He may be the emissary of the gods to Electra's marriage—a marriage to which the gods invite themselves, whereas our judge considers it a blot on his family.

Judge. My lord——

Aegisthus. Don't protest. I've heard everything. The acoustics of the palace are remarkable; everything that's said echoes through the entire place. The architect, it would appear, wanted to listen to the council debating on what his fee and his percentage should be.

Judge. My lord——

Aegisthus. Silence. I know everything you're going to tell me in favor of your fine, upstanding family, in favor of your worthy sister-in-law the infanticide, your respected uncle the satyr, and your slandering nephew the informer.

Judge. My lord——

Aegisthus. The officer who wears the king's plume into battle to divert the enemy puts it on with more enthusiasm—— You're wasting your time—the gardener will marry Electra——

Servant. The beggar is here, my lord.

Aegisthus. Detain him a moment. Offer him something to drink. Wine is equally suitable for a beggar or a god.

Servant. God or beggar, he is already drunk.

Aegisthus. Then let him come in; he won't understand

us even though we're just about to mention the gods. It might even be amusing to discuss them in his presence. Your theory concerning Electra is reasonably pertinent, judge, but it's very limited—that is to say, bourgeois. In my capacity as regent, allow me to raise your thinking to a conceptual level—— Do you believe in the gods, Judge?

During this speech the BEGGAR *enters, conducted by the* SERVANT, *and, greeting everyone with elaborate gestures, settles himself on the stool. He remains distracted throughout the first part of the scene, looking about.*

Judge. Do you, my lord?

Aegisthus. My dear Judge, I have often asked myself whether I believed in the gods. I have asked myself this question because it's the only problem a statesman must have thought through for himself. I believe in the gods. Or rather I believe that I believe in the gods. But I don't believe that they are great brooding presences watching over us; I believe they are completely absent-minded. Between space and time, always flirting with each other, between the void and the pull of gravity, always at war with one another, there exist giants of indifference, the gods. Far from being ceaselessly occupied with humanity— that supreme, mobile mold on the earth's surface—I imagine that they have attained such a level of serenity and ubiquity that only beatitude remains to them, that is to say, unconsciousness. They are as unconscious at the top of the scale of being as the atom is at the bottom. The difference is that their unconsciousness is dazzling, omnisci .it, chiseled in a thousand facets; like diamonds they are lackluster unless they catch a light; they respond only to signals, but without understanding them.

The BEGGAR, *settled on his stool at last, feels called upon to applaud.*

Beggar. Well-spoken. Bravo.

Aegisthus. Thank you—— Moreover, Judge, it's indisputable that now and then something intervenes in the life of man which is so fortuitous and on such a scale that it seems to be the result of a superhuman interest or justice. These events can be recognized as superhuman or divine because they are inexact, rough jobs. The plague does indeed strike when a town has sinned out of folly or impiety, but it strikes the neighboring town, which is particularly holy. War is unleashed when a people grows degenerate and vile, but it devours the last of the just, the last of the brave, and spares the cowards. Or else, whatever sin is being punished and whether or not it has in fact been committed, the same country or the same family always pays, whether innocent or guilty. I knew a certain mother of seven children who was in the habit of always spanking the same one—she was a divine mother. For this is precisely how the gods behave—as if they were blind, content when they boxed or spanked to strike the same cheek or the same buttock. On the whole it's amazing, if one considers how bewildered they must be, waking out of a state of beatitude, that their blows are not wider of the mark. At least when the wife of a just man rather than the wife of a perjurer is hit on the head by a shutter which has been knocked off in a high wind, and when pilgrims rather than robber bands are dogged by accidents, at least it's usually humanity who receives the blows. I say usually. Sometimes one sees crows or deer felled by inexplicable epidemics: it's possible that a blow destined for man struck too high or too low. But whatever the case, it must be a chief of state's first concern to be continually vigilant lest the gods be shaken out of their lethargy. He must see that the only harm they do is in their sleep, snoring and thundering.

Beggar. Bravo! You make it crystal clear! I understand perfectly.

Aegisthus. I'm delighted.

Beggar. What you say is truth itself. For example, take someone like me who does a lot of traveling. There are times when every hundred feet you find a dead hedgehog. Dozens of them, males and females, cross the roads at night and get crushed—— You know what the roads are like the evening after a fair—— You'll tell me they're idiots, that they should be able to find a mate on their own side of the ditch. I can't help it: for hedgehogs love is first of all a matter of crossing the road—— What the devil was I going to say?—— I've lost track—— Go ahead—it will come back to me——

Aegisthus. No doubt! What's he trying to say?

Judge. Could we talk about Electra, my lord?

Aegisthus. What did you think we were talking about? Our charming little Agatha? We were speaking of no one but Electra, Judge, and of my obligation, with the happiness of all of you in mind, to remove her from the royal family. Why, since I have become regent, while other towns are consumed by dissension, and their citizens by moral crises, are we the only ones to be at peace with others and with ourselves? Why do riches flood into our city? Why is it that in Argos alone the price of raw materials is the highest it's ever been, and the price of finished articles the lowest? Why, when we're exporting more cattle, is the price of butter dropping? Why do storms bypass our vineyards, heresies our temples, hoof and mouth disease our stables? Because I have waged war without cease here in our city against those who signal to the gods.

Judge. What do you call signaling the gods, Aegisthus?

Beggar. There, now! I've found it!

Aegisthus. Found what?

Beggar. What I was going to say, the point of my story. I was talking about the way hedgehogs die——

Aegisthus. One minute, please. We're talking about the gods.

Beggar. What? There's an order of precedence? Gods first, hedgehogs second?—— I'm not sure I'll be able to remember——

Aegisthus. There's one way, and only one, of signaling, Judge, and that consists of separating oneself from the crowd, climing up to a high place, and waving a lantern or a flag. One betrays the earth in the very same way one betrays a besieged fortress—with signals. A philosopher signals from his terrace, a poet or a desperate man from his balcony or his swimming pool. If, for the last ten years, the gods haven't succeeded in interfering with our lives, it's because I've seen to it that the promontories are empty and the fair grounds crowded; because I've forced dreamers, painters, and chemists to marry; because to avoid the development of differing moral strains among our people —which cannot help but give men a different coloration in the eyes of the gods—I have always pretended to attribute enormous importance to misdemeanors and ludicrously little to crimes. Nothing serves better to keep the gods immobile than to treat a murderer and a thief who snitches a loaf of bread in the same way. I must admit that in this matter the courts have given me ample backing. And every time I've been obliged to crack down, no one up there has noticed. None of my sanctions has been a vivid enough target to enable the gods to adjust their aim in vengeance. I never exile. I kill. Exiles have the same tendency to crawl up steep places as the dung beetle. And I never publicize my punishments. Whereas our poor neighbors betray themselves by erecting their gallows on hill tops, I crucify men in the bottom of valleys. And now that's all I have to say about Electra——

Gardener. What did you say about her?

Aegisthus. That there is at present only one person in Argos who signals the gods, and that's Electra—— [*To the* BEGGAR, *who is making a stir among the wedding guests.*] What's going on?

Beggar. Nothing's going on but it would be a good idea for me to tell you my story now—— Five minutes from now, at the rate you're going, it won't make sense any more. I just want to confirm what you're saying. Among the hedgehogs which have been crushed, you see dozens which seem to have died a hedgehog's death. Their muzzles have been flattened by a horse's hoof, their spines crushed by a wheel—they're smashed hedgehogs and nothing more. Hedgehog original sin brought on their death—that is, the desire to cross main and local roads on the pretext that slugs and partridge eggs taste better on the other side, in reality to make love, hedgehog fashion! That's their business. No one gives them a second thought. And then suddenly you find one, a little young one, lying there not quite like the others, far less dirty, his little paws extended, his little jaws firmly closed, far more dignified. When you see him, you get the idea that he didn't die a hedgehog's death but that he died for someone else, for you. His glazed little eye is your eye, his quills your beard. I always pick them up, especially since they're the youngest and the most tender to eat. Over a year old, a hedgehog won't sacrifice himself for man—— You can see I've understood what you said. The gods made a mistake, they wanted to strike a perjurer or a thief, and they killed a hedgehog— a young——

Aegisthus. Yes, you understood.

Beggar. And what is true for hedgehogs is true for other species.

Judge. Of course! Of course!

Beggar. What do you mean, of course? It's completely false. Consider the marten. You may be a judge, but you're not going to pretend to me that you've ever seen a marten die for you?

Aegisthus. You don't mind if we go on talking about Electra?

Beggar. Go ahead! Go ahead! And, in any case, looked at the other way around, I must admit that when you see the bodies of men who have died, many seem to have died for cattle, for pigs, for tortoises, and not many for men. A man who looks as if he had died for other men—that's hard to find, I can tell you. Or even for himself—— Are we going to see her?

Aegisthus. See whom?

Beggar. Electra—— I would very much like to see her before she's killed.

Aegisthus. Electra killed? Who's talking about killing Electra?

Beggar. You.

Judge. There's never been any question of killing Electra!

Beggar. I have one talent. I don't understand what people say. I've never been educated. I see men as they are rather than as they say they are—— You want to kill Electra.

Judge. You don't understand at all, stranger. This man is Aegisthus, Agamemnon's cousin, and Electra is his beloved niece.

Beggar. Are there two Electras? The one he has been talking about who is going to ruin everything, and a second one, who is his beloved niece?

Judge. No, there's only one.

Beggar. Then he wants to kill her. There's no doubt of that. He wants to kill his beloved niece.

Judge. I assure you that you don't understand!

Beggar. I get around a lot, you know. I used to know a family called Narses—— Knew her a great deal better than him, actually. She was ill, kept swallowing air—— Yes, I knew her a lot better than I did him—— No comparison——

Gardener. He's been drinking. He's a beggar.

Judge. He repeats himself, he's a god.

Beggar. Not at all. I was just getting ready to tell you that someone gave them a little she-wolf. They loved that little wolf cub. But there comes one day when, all of a sudden, at noon, little wolf cubs turn into big wolves. They were not wise enough to foresee the day. Two minutes before noon she was licking them fondly. One minute after noon she was at their throats. I didn't mind about him!

Aegisthus. And then?

Beggar. I was passing by at the time. I killed the wolf. She was beginning to eat Narses' cheeks. She didn't turn up her nose at them. Narses' wife escaped. Thank you, she's just fine. You'll be seeing her. She's coming to fetch me later on.

Aegisthus. Where's the connection?

Beggar. Don't expect to see the queen of the Amazons. There's nothing like varicose veins to age a woman.

Judge. He asked you where's the connection?

Beggar. The connection? It's just that I imagine that this man, since he's chief of state, must be more intelligent than Narses. You can't imagine what a stupid man Narses was. I could never teach him to smoke a cigar except by the lighted end—— And as for knots! It's vital to know how to tie knots in life—— If you make a loop where you're supposed to make a knot and vice versa, you're lost. Your change slips out, or you catch cold, or you strangle yourself; your boat slips its mooring or batters against the wharf, or you can't get your shoes off—I mean if you're the kind that takes them off—— And don't forget snares —remember Narses was a poacher——

Judge. We're asking you where the connection is.

Beggar. Here is the connection. If this man distrusts his niece, if he knows that one of these days, all of a sudden, she's going to make one of her signals, as he puts it, begin biting people, turn the town topsy-turvy, make the price of butter climb, bring on war, etc., etc., he shouldn't hesitate. He should kill her before she becomes herself, what she truly is. When will this happen?

Judge. What do you mean?

Beggar. What day and at what hour will she become what she truly is? When will she become a wolf? When will she become Electra?

Judge. But nothing indicates that she will become a wolf, does it?

Beggar [*pointing to* AEGISTHUS]. Oh, yes! He thinks so. He says so.

Gardener. Electra is the sweetest of women.

Beggar. Narses' wolf was the sweetest of wolves.

Judge. It has no meaning, your phrase "Becomes truly herself."

Beggar. My phrase has no meaning? What do you understand of life if you don't understand that? On May 29 when all of a sudden you see ploughed fields alive with thousands of little yellow, red, or green balls hopping about and chirping, fighting over every bit of thistledown and rejecting every bit of dandelion floss, aren't the goldfinches becoming truly themselves? And on the fourteenth of June when in the backwaters of a stream you see two reeds—always the same ones—quiver although there is no wind or current, quiver without stopping until the fifteenth of June—and remember, no bubbles rise to the surface such as a tench or a carp would send up—isn't that a pike becoming what he truly is? And don't judges like you become what you are the day of your first death sentence, when the condemned man leaves the box, beside himself, and for the first time you savor the taste of blood? In nature, everything becomes what it truly is. Even the king himself. And I would even go so far as to say, although you might not believe me, that the chief question now is whether the king will come out in Aegisthus before the true Electra comes out in Electra. He's got to know exactly the day she will emerge so that he can kill her the day before, at the bottom of a valley as he puts it, or down in the smallest valley, the most handy and least visible, that is in her bathtub——

Judge. What a monster he is!

Aegisthus. You're forgetting about the marriage, beggar——

Beggar. That's true. I'm forgetting about the marriage. Still, as a way of killing someone it's not as sure as death. All the more with a girl like her, a sensitive late-bloomer and all of that—she's sure to become herself the minute a man takes her in his arms for the first time—— You're about to marry her off?

Aegisthus. This very instant, right here.

Beggar. Not to the king of another city, I hope?

Aegisthus. Of course not. To the gardener.

Judge. To this gardener.

Beggar. And she has agreed? I would never come into my own in the arms of a gardener. But every man to his own taste. I became myself on Corfu, in the bakery on the square with the fountain and the plane trees. You should have seen me that day! I was weighing the hands of the baker's wife, one in one pan of scales, one in the other. I couldn't get them to balance. I made up the difference in the right pan with flour and in the left with oatmeal—— Where does the gardener live?

Gardener. Outside the ramparts.

Beggar. In the village?

Gardener. No. My house is set apart from any other.

Beggar [*to* AEGISTHUS]. Bravo! I understand your plan. It's not a bad idea. It's not hard to kill a gardener's wife. Much easier than a princess in her palace.

Gardener. I beg you, whoever you may be——

Beggar. It's a lot quicker to bury someone in compost than in marble, isn't it?

Gardener. What are you suggesting? And in any case, remember she won't be out of my sight for a minute.

Beggar. Bend over to pull up a leek. Pull a second time because the roots are caught by a clod. Death has come and gone!

Judge. Stranger, I don't know whether you fully realize where you are. You're in Agamemnon's palace, in the presence of Agamemnon's family.

Beggar. I see what I see; I see that this man is afraid, that he lives with fear, fear of Electra.

Aegisthus. My dear guest, let's not misunderstand each other. I don't pretend that Electra doesn't make me uneasy. I sense that trouble and misfortune will abound in the Atrides family from the day that she becomes truly herself, as you put it. And everyone will suffer, for no citizen escapes what happens to the royal family. For this reason I'm transferring her to a family which is formless, invisible to the gods, within which her eyes and her gestures will lose their phosphorescence, so that they will cause nothing more than localized, private, bourgeois damage—to the Theocathocles.

Beggar. Good idea. Good idea. Just so long as the family is more than usually anonymous.

Aegisthus. They are, and I shall see that they remain so. I shall see to it that no Theocathocles becomes known for his ability or courage. As for daring and genius, I don't have to worry—they can take care of that on their own.

Beggar. Beware. Little Agatha isn't bad. Beauty can signal, too.

Judge. I beg you to leave Agatha out of the discussion.

Beggar. It's true one can always destroy her beauty with vitriol.

Judge. My lord——

Aegisthus. Objection sustained.

Judge. But I'm looking at the situation from destiny's point of view, Aegisthus!—— After all, what Electra's got is not an illness. Even so you think that it can be transmitted?

Beggar. Yes. Like hunger among the poor.

Judge. It's hard for me to believe that destiny would settle for our obscure little clan instead of a royal family, and be willing to become the destiny of the Theocathocles after being the destiny of the Atrides.

Beggar. Don't worry. The royal cancer doesn't turn up its nose at a bourgeois.

Aegisthus. Judge, if you don't want the entrance of Electra into your family to bring with it disgrace to those of its members who are magistrates, see that you don't say another word. In a third-class family, destiny will do only third-class damage. Speaking purely personally, I'm most distressed because of the high esteem in which I hold the Theocathocles; but the royal family cannot afford to take any further risks, nor can the city, or the state.

Beggar. And you can go ahead and kill her, just a tiny bit, if the occasion presents itself.

Aegisthus. I have spoken—— You may fetch Clytemnestra and Electra. They are waiting.

Beggar. It's high time. I don't want to sound difficult, but what our conversation needed was a woman.

Aegisthus. There are two coming, and they both talk.

Beggar. And argue with each other, I hope.

Aegisthus. Where you come from, do people like it when women argue?

Beggar. They love it. This afternoon I was in a house where an argument was going on. Nothing lofty like this— no comparison. They weren't discussing a royal murder plot as you are; they were arguing whether chicken should be served with or without the liver when there are guests for dinner. And the neck, of course. The women were in a rage. They had to be separated. Come to think about it, it was a pretty vehement discussion in its own way—— Blood flowed.

Enter CLYTEMNESTRA, ELECTRA, *and attendants.*

Judge. Here they both are.

Clytemnestra. "Both" is saying a lot. Electra is never more absent than when she's present.

Electra. No. Today I'm here.

Aegisthus. Good! Let's make the most of it. You know why your mother has brought you here?

Electra. Out of habit, I believe. She has already surrendered one daughter as a sacrifice.

Clytemnestra. There's Electra for you. She never says a word that isn't perfidious or insinuating.

Electra. Pardon me, Mother. It's so easy to sound that way if one is an Atrides.

Beggar. What does she mean? Is she going to get mad at her mother?

Gardener. It would be the first time anyone has ever seen Electra get angry.

Beggar. That would make it all the more interesting.

Aegisthus. Electra, your mother has told you of our decision. For a long time we've been worrying about you. I don't know whether you're aware that anyone who saw you lately would think that you were sleepwalking in broad daylight. Everyone in the palace and the city whispers your name for fear that if you were awakened you would fall to the ground.

Beggar [as loud as possible]. Electra!

Aegisthus. What are you doing?

Beggar. Oh, I beg your pardon. That was a joke. Excuse me. But you are the one who is afraid, not she. She's not a sleepwalker.

Aegisthus. I beg you——

Beggar. In any case, my experiment worked. You're the one who faltered. Imagine what you would have done if all of a sudden I had shouted: Aegisthus!

Judge. Let our regent speak.

Beggar. I'll shout Aegisthus later on when no one will be expecting it.

Aegisthus. You must be cured, Electra, whatever remedy may be necessary.

Electra. The cure is simple. Bring the dead back to life.

Aegisthus. You are not the only one to mourn your father. But he would never have wanted your mourning to be an offense to the living. We put the dead in an awkward position if we keep them bound to our lives. We rob them of whatever liberty they may have.

Electra. Of course death has given him liberty—liberty to remind me that he is no longer alive.

Aegisthus. Do you really believe that he likes to see you weep for him not in the manner of a daughter but as a wife?

Electra. I am my father's widow for lack of any other.

Clytemnestra. Electra!

Aegisthus. Widow or not, today we're celebrating your marriage.

Electra. Yes, I know of your plot.

Clytemnestra. Plot? Is it a plot to want to marry a twenty-one-year-old daughter? At your age I was already carrying the two of you in my arms, you and Orestes.

Electra. You didn't carry us safely. You let Orestes fall on the marble floor.

Clytemnestra. What could I do? You pushed him.

Electra. That's not true. I didn't push Orestes.

Clytemnestra. How can you tell? You were only fifteen months old.

Electra. I didn't push Orestes! Beyond the reach of memory I can recall it. O Orestes, wherever you may be, hear me! I didn't push you!

Aegisthus. That's enough, Electra.

Beggar. They're really going at it this time. It would be interesting if the little one became truly herself right here in front of us.

Electra. She's lying, Orestes, she's lying!

Aegisthus. I beg you, Electra.

Clytemnestra. She pushed him. Of course, at her age she didn't know what she was doing, but she pushed him.

Electra. With all my strength I held on to him. By his little blue tunic. By his arm. By the end of his fingers. By the air he fell through. By his shadow. I sobbed when I saw him on the ground with a red mark on his forehead!

Clytemnestra. You laughed; your body shook with laughter. And just between us, his tunic was mauve.

Electra. It was blue. I know Orestes' tunic was blue. When it was drying on the line, you couldn't see it against the sky.

Aegisthus. Can I put in a word? Haven't you had time in the last twenty years to settle this argument?

Electra. For the last twenty years I've been waiting for a chance. Now I have it.

Clytemnestra. Why can't she understand that with the best will in the world she may still be wrong?

Beggar. They're both talking with the best will in the world. That's what the truth means.

Judge. Princess, I implore you! What interest does the question have now?

Clytemnestra. None, I agree.

Electra. What interest? If I pushed Orestes I would prefer to be dead. I would prefer to kill myself—— My life would lose all sense!

Aegisthus. Will we have to silence you by force? Are you as mad as she is, Queen?

Clytemnestra. Listen, Electra. Let's not quarrel. I'll tell you exactly how it happened. I was carrying him on my right arm.

Electra. No, on your left!

Aegisthus. Will you stop, Clytemnestra. Yes or no?

Clytemnestra. I'll stop. But a right arm is a right arm, and not a left, and a mauve tunic is mauve and not blue.

Electra. It was blue. As blue as Orestes' forehead was red.

Clytemnestra. That much is true. His forehead was red. You even touched the wound with your finger; you danced around his little body as he lay there; you laughed as you tasted the blood——

Electra. I! I wanted to dash my head against the step which had wounded him! I couldn't stop trembling for a week.

Aegisthus. Silence!

Electra. I'm still trembling!

Beggar. Narses' wife kept her child strapped to herself with a sling. A loose one, not tight. Often the child would be askew, but he never fell.

Aegisthus. That's enough. We will soon see how Electra carries her children—— For you agree, don't you? You agree to be married?

Electra. I agree.

Aegisthus. I must advise you that suitors are not flocking to you.

Beggar. They say——

Aegisthus. What do they say?

Beggar. They say that you secretly threatened to kill all the princes who were eligible to marry Electra—— That's what they say in the city.

Electra. That's just as well. I want no prince.

Clytemnestra. What about a gardener? Do you want a gardener?

Electra. I know you both have been planning to marry me to my father's gardener. I am willing.

Clytemnestra. You're not going to marry a gardener.

Aegisthus. We have agreed, Queen. We have given our word.

Clytemnestra. I take it back. It was an evil word. If Electra is ill, we shall take care of her. I am no longer willing to give my daughter to a gardener.

Electra. Too late, Mother. You have already given me.

Clytemnestra. You dare aspire to Electra, gardener?

Gardener. I am unworthy, Queen, but Aegisthus commands the marriage.

Aegisthus. I command it. And here are the rings. Take your wife.

Clytemnestra. You are risking your life, gardener, if you persist!

Beggar. Then don't persist. I like to see soldiers die, not gardeners.

Clytemnestra. Does that man always have to put in a word? Marry Electra, gardener, and you are a dead man.

Beggar. It's your business. But come back to the garden a year after the gardener's death. Then you'll see. You'll see what's happened to the escarole after a year of widowhood. Escarole doesn't get the care of a king's widow.

Clytemnestra. The garden is not going to suffer in the slightest. Come, Electra.

Gardener. Queen, you can refuse me Electra, but it's not fair to speak ill of a garden one does not know.

Clytemnestra. I do know it: barren land scattered with sewage.

Gardener. Barren land? The best tended garden of Argos!

Judge. If he begins to tell you about his garden, we'll never be finished.

Aegisthus. No need to describe it.

Gardener. The queen has provoked me. I shall reply. My garden is my dowry, my honor!

Aegisthus. What difference does it make! That's enough quarreling!

Gardener. Barren land! It covers ten acres of hillside, my garden, and six in the valley. No! No! I won't keep quiet! Not an inch is barren, is it, Electra? On the terraces I have garlic and tomatoes. On the slopes, grapevines and my peach trees. At the bottom of the valley I have vegetables, strawberries, and raspberries. In every rock fall there is a fig tree, clinging to stones which warm the figs.

Aegisthus. Fine. Let your figs ripen and take your wife.

Clytemnestra. Imagine daring to talk about that garden. It's completely dried out. I have seen it from the road— it looks like a bare skull. You shall not have Electra.

Gardener. Dried out! There is a spring which never dries up even in the dog days of summer, and from it flows a stream off which I have cut two trenches, one through the valley bottom and the other through sheer rock. Just try to find a skull that looks like that! And as for sewage, I have the best soil in all Argos! Right now in the early spring the whole place is carpeted with hyacinth and narcissus. I have never seen Electra smile, but it was in my garden that I saw on her face what came closest to a smile!

Clytemnestra. See if she is smiling now.

Gardener. That's what I call Electra's smile.

Clytemnestra. Smiling at your dirty hands, your black nails——

Electra. Dear gardener——

Gardener. My black nails? See if my nails are black! Don't believe her, Electra. You're out of luck today, your Majesty. I whitewashed my house this morning so that there would be no trace of field mice or grasshoppers, and as a result my nails are not black as you wanted them to be but rimmed with white.

Aegisthus. That's enough, gardener.

Gardener. I know, I know it's enough. And my hands are dirty. Look. Are these hands dirty? I made a special point of washing them after I took down the onions and the mushrooms I had hanging from the rafters. I didn't want their smell to disturb Electra's sleep—— I shall sleep in the shed, Electra, from where I shall watch over you, in case an owl swoops in or the mill gate opens or a fox steals a hen from the barnyard. I have finished——

Electra. Thank you, gardener.

Clytemnestra. And thus will live Electra, daughter of Clytemnestra and the king of kings, watching her husband go to and fro among his garden beds, imprisoned in the barrel hoop from which are suspended his water buckets.

Aegisthus. And there she can mourn the dead as she wishes. Plan to sow her everlastings tomorrow.

Gardener. And there she will escape anguish, torment, and, perhaps, drama. I know very little about human beings, Queen, but I know the seasons. Now is the moment —but it won't last long—to transplant misfortune in our city. You're not grafting the Atrides onto our poor family but onto the seasons, the meadows, the winds. It's my impression they won't lose anything by that.

Beggar. Allow yourself to be persuaded, Queen. Don't you see that there is in Aegisthus a sort of hatred which impels him to kill Electra, that is to give her to the earth? But by mistake he is giving her to a garden where things live and grow. She stands to win from his mistake. She stands to win her life—— [AEGISTHUS *has risen.*] What? I was wrong to say what I did?

Aegisthus [*to* ELECTRA *and the* GARDENER]. Approach, both of you!

Clytemnestra. Electra, I beg you——

Electra. It was you who wished it, Mother!

Clytemnestra. I no longer want it. You can see very well that I no longer want it.

Electra. Why do you no longer want it? Are you afraid? It's too late.

Clytemnestra. What must I say to recall to you who I am, who you are?

Electra. You must tell me that I didn't push Orestes.

Clytemnestra. Stupid girl!

Aegisthus. Are they back to that again?

Beggar. Yes, yes, they are going to start all over.

Clytemnestra. And unjust! And obstinate! Let Orestes fall! I never break anything! I never let a glass or a ring fall! I'm so steady that birds light on my arms. Things take off from me, they don't fall—— That's just what I said to myself when he lost his balance. Why, oh, why would ill luck have it that his sister was near him!

Aegisthus. They are insane!

Electra. And I said to myself as soon as I saw him fall: if she's a real mother, the least she can do is bend to break his fall. She will squat or arch her body to make a slope so that she can catch him on her thighs or her knees. Let's see if they catch him, if they understand that that's their job, those regal thighs and knees! I'm none too sure, but let's see.

Clytemnestra. Be quiet.

Electra. Or else she'll bend back, so that little Orestes slips down her as a child does from a tree where he has been hunting for birds' nests. Or else she will fall, so that he falls only on her. It's not too late; there are so many things a mother can do to save her son. She can still become a curve, a shell, a maternal slope, a cradle. But she remained as she was, rigid and upright, and he fell straight, the full height of his mother!

Aegisthus. Your objection is sustained, Clytemnestra. Let us depart!

Clytemnestra. Just let her try to remember what she saw and what she didn't see when she was fifteen months old! That's the point!

Aegisthus. No one listens to her, no one believes her, except you!

Electra. There are so many ways to keep a child from falling, I can think of a thousand more, and she did nothing!

Clytemnestra. If I had moved the slightest bit, you would have fallen, too.

Electra. That's exactly what I mean. You stopped to reason, to calculate. You acted like a nurse, not a mother!

Clytemnestra. My little Electra——

Electra. I'm not your little Electra. You had to rub up against your two children in order to arouse your mother love. And then it was too late.

Clytemnestra. I implore you——

Electra. That's right! Spread out your arms. That's what you did! Look, everyone! That's just what you did!

Clytemnestra. Let us depart, Aegisthus——

[*Exit* CLYTEMNESTRA.

Beggar. I have the impression that the mother is afraid, too.

Aegisthus [*to the* BEGGAR]. What did you say there?

Beggar. Me? I didn't say anything. I never say anything—— On an empty stomach I do a lot of talking. On an empty stomach I monopolize the conversation. But today I had a little something to drink——

Exit AEGISTHUS. *Enter* AGATHA *and* ORESTES.

Agatha. At last! Aegisthus is gone. Off with you, gardener!

Gardener. What do you mean?

Agatha. Off with you, and be quick about it. This man is going to take your place.

Gardener. My place is beside Electra!

Orestes. Yes, it is I she is going to marry.

Electra. Let go of my hand!

Orestes. Never again while I live!

Agatha. Look at him, at least, Electra! Before escaping from the embrace of a man, one should at least see what he looks like! I assure you that its to your advantage to do so.

Electra. Help me, gardener! Help me!

Orestes. I will make no attempt to justify myself to you,

gardener. But look at me full in the face. You are an expert at identifying strains and species. Look into my eyes and tell me what species I am. That's right. Look carefully with your poor peasant eyes. With that look of humble folk which is a mixture of devotion, bleariness, and fear, with the pale, sterile eyes of the poor which no longer weep from either harsh weather or misfortune, look carefully and see if I can evade you. Fine—— Give me your ring—— Thank you——

Electra. Agatha! Cousin! Help me! I swear that I won't say a word about your assignations or your quarrels! I swear I won't!

Agatha [*leading away the* GARDENER]. Come—— The Theocathocles are saved. Let the Atrides make out as best they can.

Exit AGATHA *and the* GARDENER.

Beggar. She's running, like a little wood louse running back under its stone at the first sign of day.

Orestes. Now don't put up a fight.

Electra. I'll fight to the death.

Orestes. Is that what you think? In a little while you'll take me in your arms of your own accord.

Electra. Don't be insulting.

Orestes. In a minute you will kiss me.

Electra. Shame on you for taking advantage of two infamous deeds!

Orestes. Just see how I trust you—I'm letting you go——

Electra. I never want to see you again! Farewell!

Orestes. No! I shall say one word and you will come back, sweet and docile.

Electra. You're lying——

Orestes. One word and you will be sobbing in my arms. A single word—— My name——

Electra. In the whole world there is only one word which could draw me to a human being.

Orestes. That's the one. It's my own.

Electra. You are Orestes!

Orestes. Oh, ungrateful sister, who recognizes me only by my name!

Enter CLYTEMNESTRA.

Clytemnestra. Electra!

Electra. Yes, Mother!

Clytemnestra. Return to the palace where you belong. Leave the gardener. Come with me.

Electra. The gardener is no longer here, Mother.

Clytemnestra. Where is he?

Electra. He has given me to this man.

Clytemnestra. To what man?

Electra. To this man here, who is now my husband.

Clytemnestra. This is no time to joke. Come.

Electra. What do you mean "come"? This man is holding my hand.

Clytemnestra. Hurry up.

Electra. You know, Mother, how a filly is hobbled to keep her from cantering about? This man has hobbled me in the same way.

Clytemnestra. I'm ordering you this time. You must be in your room by nightfall. Come.

Electra. But that's just the point. How can I abandon my husband on the eve of my wedding night?

Clytemnestra. What are you doing here? Who are you?

Electra. He won't answer. This evening my husband's lips belong to me with all they have to say.

Clytemnestra. Where have you come from? Who was your father?

Electra. Don't worry, he comes of good family.

Clytemnestra. Why are you looking at me that way? What is there in your eyes that seems to defy me? And your mother, who was she?

Electra. He never saw her.

Clytemnestra. She is dead?

Electra. Perhaps that's what you see in his eyes, the fact that he has never seen his mother. He is handsome, isn't he?

Clytemnestra. Yes—— He looks like you.

Electra. Don't you think it's a good sign, Mother, that our first hour of marriage has made us resemble each other as old couples do?

Clytemnestra. Who are you?

Electra. What does it matter to you! Never has a man been less yours!

Clytemnestra. Whoever he is, whoever you are, stranger,

don't fall in with her whim. It would be better if you helped me with her. We shall see tomorrow if you are worthy of Electra. I shall try to convince Aegisthus—but I've never known a night to seem less propitious. Leave this man, Electra.

Electra. Too late. He is holding me in his arms.

Clytemnestra. You can break iron when you want.

Electra. Iron, yes; this iron, no.

Clytemnestra. What has he said against your mother for you to accept him in this manner?

Electra. We haven't yet had time to speak of either my mother or his. Leave us and we shall begin.

Orestes. Electra!

Electra. That is all he can say. When I take my hand away from his mouth, he keeps repeating my name. You can't get anything else out of him. Kiss me, husband, now that your lips are freed!

Clytemnestra. How shameful! So this madness was Electra's secret!

Electra. Kiss me in front of my mother!

Clytemnestra. Farewell. And yet I did not think you were the kind of girl who would give herself to the first passer-by.

Electra. Nor did I. But I did not know what it was like to be kissed for the first time.

Exit CLYTEMNESTRA.

Orestes. Why do you hate our mother so violently, Electra?

Electra. Don't mention her—her above all else. Let's imagine for a minute, just to be happy, that we were brought into the world without a mother. Not a word.

Orestes. I have so much to tell you.

Electra. Your presence tells me everything. Be quiet. Don't look me in the eyes. Your words and your glance are too piercing, they wound me. I often used to wish, if ever I found you once again, to come upon you while you slept. It's more than I can stand to rediscover all at once your eyes, your voice—the very life of Orestes. I would have liked you to be dead at first and then slowly come to life, so that I could get used to you gradually. But my brother has been reborn like the son, a brute of gold as he dawns.

Or else I would like to be blind, and bring my brother back into the world with the tips of my fingers—— What a joy to be blind for a sister who regains her brother! For twenty years my hands have touched nothing that was not base and mediocre, and here they are touching a brother! A brother in whom everything is true. There could have been, inserted in this head or in this body, fragments that were suspect, fragments that were false. By some marvelous chance everything is fraternal in Orestes, everything is Orestes!

Orestes. You're smothering me.

Electra. I'm not smothering you. I'm not killing you—— I'm caressing you. I'm bringing you back to life. From that mass which I was too dazzled to take in, I'm carving you in full detail. Now I'm sculpting my brother's hand with his handsome, finely modeled thumb. Now I'm forming my brother's chest, and now it comes to life in my hands and swells and respires, giving my brother the breath of life. Now I'm making his ear. You want me to make it small, don't you—curled on the edge like the hem of a handkerchief and diaphanous as the wing of a bat?—— One last little touch and the ear is done. I'll make them both alike. What a success, these ears! And now I'm making my brother's lips, soft and dry, and now I fasten them, all quivering with life, to his face. Take your life from me, Orestes, and not from your mother!

Orestes. Why do you hate her?—— Stop!

Electra. What's wrong? Why are you pushing me away? That's the ingratitude of children for you! You've hardly finished making them, and they break away and escape.

Orestes. Someone is watching us from the staircase.

Electra. It's she, I'm sure it's she. As usual, she is jealous and afraid.

Beggar. Yes, yes, it's she all right.

Electra. She knows that we are here, re-creating ourselves in our own image, freeing ourselves from her. She knows that my caress will enfold you, wash away every trace of her, orphan you from her—— Oh, brother, who will ever do the same for me!

Orestes. How can you speak thus about the woman who brought you into the world! I am less hard on her, no matter how harsh she was with me!

Electra. That's precisely what I can't bear about her—the fact that she brought me into the world. That's my shame. Because of her there's something equivocal about the way I came into the world. She was nothing more than an accomplice at my conception. I love only the part my father had in it. I love the way he stripped off his fine wedding garments and lay down to beget me in full abandon of body and mind. I love the black circles of a father-to-be around his eyes. I love the way his body trembled with surprise the day I was born, that little quiver, hardly perceptible, which nevertheless did far more to propel me into the world than my mother's labor. I was born of his deep wedding night sleep, of his nine months' thinness, of the solace he found with other women while my mother carried me, of his paternal smile after my birth. Whatever part my mother had in my birth, I detest.

Orestes. Why do you hate women so vehemently?

Electra. I don't hate women—I hate my mother. And I don't hate men—I hate Aegisthus.

Orestes. But why do you hate them?

Electra. I don't yet know. I know only that I feel the same hatred for both of them. That's why I feel as if I were being crushed under a great weight. I can't tell you how many times I have tried to convince myself that I hated each of them with a separate hate. Hatred, like grief, is easier to bear if it is divided between two objects. If you grieve over two things, one balances the other. I tried to persuade myself that I hated my mother because she had let you fall when you were a baby, and Aegisthus because he had stolen the throne from you. But I didn't succeed. The fact was that I pitied this great queen, the most powerful in the world, who, like an ordinary, frightened, shaky old peasant woman, all of a sudden let her child slip. I pitied Aegisthus, cruel tyrant though he is, for he is destined to die one day by your hand. As I thought of my mother and Aegisthus, they became pitiful; the specific causes of hatred were washed away, but as soon as I felt docile and predisposed toward them, a stronger wave of hatred engulfed me. I hate them with a hatred which seems to come from outside me.

Orestes. I am here. It will cease.

Electra. Do you think so? I used to think that your re-

turn would free me from this hatred. I thought your absence was the cause of my suffering. I was prepared to be
completely tender with everyone, even with them, when
you returned. I was wrong. I am still suffering this evening, and it is because you are here. My hatred greets you
with a smile—it is the very love I feel for you. It caresses
you as a hound licks the hand which unleashes him before the hunt. You've given me a glimpse and a whiff of
my hatred, and now I'm off after my quarry, on its
scent—— Who's there? Is it she?

Beggar. No! No! You forget what time it is. She has
gone up to her room. She is undressing.

Electra. She is undressing. Before her mirror, contem-
plating Clytemnestra at leisure, our mother undresses. Our
mother whom I love because she is so beautiful, whom I
pity because she is beginning to age, whom I admire for
her regal appearance and voice—— Our mother whom I
hate.

Orestes. Electra, my darling sister! Calm yourself, I beg
you.

Electra. Shall I be off, then, and follow the scent?

Orestes. Calm yourself.

Electra. Me? I'm perfectly calm. Me? I'm perfectly
sweet. I'm sweet to my mother, so sweet—— My sweetness is the hatred which swells within me, which is destroying me.

Orestes. Now it's your turn to be quiet. Let's leave
hatred till tomorrow. This evening let me taste, if only for
an hour, the sweetness of a life I never knew which nonetheless I am rediscovering.

Electra. All right, an hour, then.

Orestes. The palace is so beautiful in the moonlight. My
palace—— In this light all the power of our family seems
to emanate from it—my power. Let me lie in your arms
and imagine how much happiness might have been stored
within these walls by more judicious, sensible men. Oh,
Electra, how many names in our family were at the outset
sweet and tender, intended to be happy names!

Electra. Yes, I know: Medea, Phaedra.

Orestes. Even those, why not?

Electra. Electra—— Orestes——

Orestes. Isn't there still a chance for them? I have come to save them.

Electra. Quiet! There she is!

Orestes. Who?

Electra. She who bears the name of happiness: Clytemnestra.

Enter CLYTEMNESTRA.

Clytemnestra. Electra?

Electra. Mother?

Clytemnestra. Who is this?

Electra. Guess.

Clytemnestra. Let me see his face.

Electra. If you can't see it from a distance, you won't see it better close to.

Clytemnestra. Let us make peace, Electra. If you really want this man for your husband, I am willing. Why do you smile? Wasn't I the one who wanted you to have a husband?

Electra. Not at all. You wanted me to be a wife.

Clytemnestra. What is the difference?

Electra. You wanted me to be married like you. You didn't want to be perpetually confronted with your worst enemy.

Clytemnestra. My daughter?

Electra. Chastity.

Orestes. Electra——

Electra. Leave me alone—leave me alone—— I have found the scent.

Clytemnestra. Chastity! This girl who is gnawed by desire talks to us of chastity! This girl who at the age of two couldn't look at a boy without blushing. If you must know, it was because you wanted to kiss Orestes that you threw him out of my arms!

Electra. Then I was right. Then I have something to be proud of. It was worth it.

There is noise. People can be seen through the windows of the palace. AEGISTHUS *appears, leaning over a balcony.*

Aegisthus. Are you there, Queen?

Beggar. Yes. She is here.

Aegisthus. Important news, Queen. Orestes is not dead. He escaped. He is headed for Argos.

Clytemnestra. Orestes!

Aegisthus. I have dispatched my best soldiers to meet him. I have stationed my most trusted guards around the walls. You have nothing to say?

Clytemnestra. Orestes is returning?

Aegisthus. He is returning to take over his father's throne, to put an end to my regency, to end your rule as queen—— His agents are organizing an uprising in the city. But don't be concerned. I shall see that order is maintained. Who is down there with you?

Clytemnestra. Electra.

Aegisthus. And her gardener?

Beggar. And her gardener.

Aegisthus. Then you're no longer trying to keep them apart? You see now that my fears were justified! You agree with me now, don't you?

Clytemnestra. No. I don't care any more.

Aegisthus. Don't let them leave the palace. I have given orders for the gates to remain closed until the soldiers return. Those two in particular are not to leave—— Do you hear me, gardener?

Electra. We won't go out.

Aegisthus. And you, Queen, come back upstairs. Return to your room. It is late and the council meets at dawn. I bid you a good night.

Electra. Thank you, Aegisthus.

Aegisthus. I was speaking to the queen, Electra. This is no time to mock. Come upstairs, Queen!

Clytemnestra. Until tomorrow, Electra.

Electra. Until tomorrow, Mother.

Clytemnestra [*starts to go and then turns back*]. Until tomorrow, husband of my daughter.

CLYTEMNESTRA *climbs the staircase slowly, and exits.*

Beggar. It can happen in the best families! Anything can!

Electra. What was that?

Beggar. Nothing! No one said a word. Can you imagine anyone saying a word at a moment like this?

Orestes. Tell me, Electra! Tell me!

Electra. Tell you what?

Orestes. Your hatred. The reasons for your hatred. You know why now. Just then, when you were speaking with Clytemnestra, you almost fainted in my arms. From joy or from horror, I couldn't tell.

Electra. From both joy and horror. Are you strong or weak, Orestes?

Orestes. Tell me your secret and then I will be able to tell you.

Electra. I haven't yet unraveled my secret. I've only found the beginning of the thread. But don't worry. It will all unravel—— Look out. There she is.

Enter CLYTEMNESTRA.

Clytemnestra. So it's you, Orestes?

Orestes. Yes, Mother, it is I.

Clytemnestra. Is it sweet to see your mother after so many years?

Orestes. Both sweet and sad to see a mother who drove me away.

Clytemnestra. You don't come very close to see what she looks like.

Orestes. She is as I imagined her.

Clytemnestra. So is my son. Handsome. Regal. And yet I approach him.

Orestes. I keep my distance. At a distance my mother is a most excellent one.

Clytemnestra. She might not be so excellent close to?

Orestes. Or maternal—— That's why I am staying where I am.

Clytemnestra. You don't need anything more than the mirage of a mother?

Orestes. I have had far less until today. And to a mirage I can say what I would never say to my true mother.

Clytemnestra. That would be better than nothing. What have you to tell?

Orestes. Everything I shall never tell you. Everything which, if I said it to you, would be a lie.

Clytemnestra. That you love me?

Orestes. Yes.

Clytemnestra. That you respect me?

Orestes. Yes.

Clytemnestra. That you admire me?

Orestes. In that alone, mirage and mother can share.

Clytemnestra. I feel just the opposite. I care nothing for the mirage of my son. But if my son himself should live and breathe before me, if he should speak to me, I would faint.

Orestes. You would revive again the moment you thought of hurting him.

Clytemnestra. Why are you so harsh? Yet you don't look as if you were cruel. Your voice is gentle, isn't it?

Orestes. Yes. In every way I resemble the son I could have been. You too resemble the admirable mother you could have been. If I were not your son, I would be fooled.

Electra. Why do you both go on talking? What do you hope to gain, Mother, playing the coquette as only a mother can! You have had a glimpse of what you both might have been, mother and son. The moment is past; be content with the ray of light you have had and return to the dark night of hatred and menace in which you live.

Clytemnestra. Why so soon? How do you know that a minute of maternal love is sufficient for Orestes?

Electra. You have no right in your life to more than a minute of filial love. You have had it now—and more. Don't carry on! Go——

Clytemnestra. Very well. Farewell——

Enter the EUMENIDES, *now twelve or thirteen years old.*

First of the Eumenides. Farewell, my true son.

Orestes. Farewell.

Second of the Eumenides. Farewell, mirage of a mother.

Electra. No need to say farewell. You will see each other again.

ELECTRA *and* ORESTES *go to sleep. The* BEGGAR *remains on stage.*

First of the Eumenides. They are asleep. Now it's our turn to play Clytemnestra and Orestes. But not the way they play it. Let's play the real way!

Beggar [*to himself*]. What I would like to know is who pushed or didn't push——

Second of the Eumenides. Leave us alone, you! Let us play!

The three little EUMENIDES *assume the positions of the actors in the previous scene and parody it, wearing masks.*

First of the Eumenides. So it's you, Orestes?

Second of the Eumenides. Yes, Mother, it is I.

First of the Eumenides. You have come to kill me, and to kill Aegisthus?

Second of the Eumenides. That's the first I've heard of it.

First of the Eumenides. But not to kill your sister—— Have you ever killed, my little Orestes?

Second of the Eumenides. The kind of thing one kills when one is virtuous—a doe—— And I carried virtue even further—I took pity and I killed her faun, too, so that he wouldn't be orphaned—— Kill my mother? Never! That would be parricide.

First of the Eumenides. Did you kill them with this sword?

Second of the Eumenides. Yes, it cuts iron. You can imagine what it did to the faun! It went right through him before he felt a thing.

First of the Eumenides. Don't think that I'm actually thinking of anything of the kind, or that I'm trying to influence you—but if a sword like yours were to kill your sister, life would be more peaceful, wouldn't it?

Second of the Eumenides. You want me to kill my sister?

First of the Eumenides. Of course not. That would be fratricide. It would be perfect if the sword could kill her by itself. If it drew itself out of its scabbard like this, and killed her all by itself. Then I could marry Aegisthus in peace. We would ask you to return. Aegisthus is getting old. It wouldn't be long before you succeeded him. You would be King Orestes.

Second of the Eumenides. A sword doesn't kill by itself. There's got to be a murderer.

First of the Eumenides. Of course. I should have realized. But sometimes swords do kill by themselves. People who go around righting wrongs are the bane of civilization. And they don't improve the older they get, I'm sure you realize. Whereas criminals, without exception, become virtuous with age, they, without exception, become criminal.

No! They really do. I tell you this is a good opportunity for a sword that can make its own decisions, which can get about by itself, which can kill on its own. As for you, we could marry you to Alkmena's younger daughter, the one with the nice teeth and the pretty smile. You would be Orestes, the husband.

Second of the Eumenides. I don't want to kill either my sister whom I love, or my mother whom I detest.

First of the Eumenides. I know, I know. In a word, you are weak and you are a man of principle.

Third of the Eumenides. Why do you both go on talking? Since the moon is shining and the nightingale singing on this dark night of hatred and menace, take your hand from the hilt of your sword, Orestes, and see what it will have the brains to do by itself!

First of the Eumenides. That's right, leave it alone—— It's moving, friends—— It's moving!

Second of the Eumenides. So it is, no question. It's a sword that can think—— It's thinking so hard that it's half out of its scabbard!

Orestes [*in his sleep*]. Electra!

Beggar. Off with you, you filthy little creatures, or you'll wake them up!

Electra [*in her sleep*]. Orestes!

Exit the EUMENIDES. ELECTRA *and* ORESTES *remain asleep.*

Beggar. I would still like to get to the bottom of this business of who pushed or didn't push Orestes. For, depending on who did or did not push, Electra is lying or telling the truth; she may remember pushing him—in which case she's lying consciously, or she may not remember what she did. I don't believe she pushed him. Just look at her: they're lying two inches off the ground and she's clutching her brother as if they were on the edge of an abyss. He may dream he's falling, of course, but that's not her fault. The queen, on the other hand, looks as if she might have done it: she looks like those bakers' wives who don't even bend over to pick up their change, or like those griffin bitches which smother the best puppy in their litter while they sleep. Then they lick him, the way the queen was just licking Orestes—but it takes more than saliva to make a child. I can just see what happened. It's all per-

fectly clear if you suppose that the queen was wearing a
diamond brooch and that a white cat went by. She's holding Electra on her right arm because the little girl is getting
pretty heavy; she's holding the baby on her left, a little
away from her body, so that he won't scratch himself on
the brooch or press it into her skin—it's the kind of pin
a queen wears, not a nurse. And then the child sees the
white cat. All that living, moving white fur—it's pretty
wonderful, a white cat. He arches his back so that he can
go on following it with his eyes and then he starts to
slip—— And she's a woman who always tends to favor her
own sex. All she had to do to keep hold of the child when
she saw him about to topple out of her arms was to free
her right arm by letting little Electra slide down to the
floor. To hell with what happened to little Electra—let the
poor little thing break her neck, provided that the son of
the king of kings was safe and sound! But she favors her
own sex. To her a woman matters as much as a man because she is one; the belly as much as the loins because she
is a belly; she wouldn't for a minute dream of harming a
daughter with a belly to save a son with loins, and so she
kept hold of Electra. Now Electra is quite another story.
She has become truly herself in her brother's arms. And
she was right. She couldn't have made a better choice.
Fraternity is the distinctive quality of humans. Animals
know only love—cats, parrots, etc.—brotherhood with their
own kind means no more than a coat of the same fur. To
find true brothers, they have to strike up with men, to love
them. When a duckling leaves the flock and comes over to
watch us humans while we're eating or puttering, what's
gleaming in that tender little eye uptilted in his duck's
cheek, if not that we men and women are his brothers?
I've picked up these little ducks. Nothing would have been
easier than to have strangled them. That's how brotherly
they were, coming up and trying to understand what I was
doing, as I cut myself some bread and cheese and added a
bit of onion. Brother to ducks, that's our true title. And
you can be sure that that little russet and blue head which
they plunge into the mud to dabble for tadpoles and sala-
manders is the very picture of cleanliness, tenderness, and
intelligence when they cock it in your direction. Needless
to say, the head is uneatable except for the brain——

What I want to do is to teach them to weep, those ducks! So Electra did not push Orestes—which means that everything she says is correct, everything she claims, incontestable. She is the truth without any residue, lamp oil without sludge, light without a wick. So that if she kills all peace and happiness around her, as it seems she is going to, it's because she's in the right! If some fine day a young girl feels a trace of anguish in her heart, if, during the most splendid century or most splendid feast day, she catches a whiff of noxious gas escaping, she must find its source immediately. Young girls are the chatelaines of truth; they must see that it is protected, that the guilty lead the life of the guilty, even if the world rocks on its foundations, even if generations are shattered, even if thousands of innocents die. Look at these two innocents. The fruit of their union will be the rebirth for all time of a crime which is too far in the past to be subject to punishment under the law— a crime, the punishment of which will be an even worse crime. How right they are to sleep while they still can! Let us leave them. I think I'll stretch my legs. I'll be back to wake them. I always sneeze three times when the moon reaches its zenith, and it's unsanitary to muffle a sneeze in one's hands. But you who remain, be still and quiet! It's Electra's first rest! It's Orestes' last!

Curtain.

The GARDENER *appears before the curtain.*

Gardener. The play will go on without me. That's why I am free to come and tell you what the play cannot tell you itself. In a story like this, they're not about to stop killing each other, to interrupt their biting and gnashing of teeth and come tell you that there's only one goal worth pursuing in life, namely, love. In fact, a parricide would disgrace himself if he stopped with his dagger in mid-air and spoke to you in praise of love. It would seem artificial. Many people would not believe him. But abandoned and desolate as I am, I don't really see how I can do otherwise! I'm impartial, of course. I shall never bring myself to marry anyone but Electra, and Electra will never be mine. I was made to live with a woman night and day, and I shall always live alone—made to give myself without res-

pite at any time or place, and I shall always hold myself
back. This is my one and only wedding night and I am
spending it here all alone—thank you for being here. The
orange syrup I prepared for Electra—I had to drink it
myself. There's only a drop left; it's been a long wedding
night. Who would doubt what I say! The trouble is that
I always find myself saying somewhat the opposite of what
I mean. But I really would give up if today, with my heart
so heavy and this bitter taste in my mouth—you know,
when you come down to it, oranges are bitter—I'd give up
if I managed to forget that I wanted to speak to you of
Joy. Yes, of Joy and Love. I've come to tell you that they
are preferable to Sourness and Hatred. They make a far
better motto to be carved over an entrance or printed on a
scarf or formed out of dwarf begonias in a garden bed. It
goes without saying that life is a failure, but all the same
it's a fine thing, life, very fine. It goes without saying that
nothing ever happens as it should, nothing ever works out,
but you've got to admit that now and again something
works out just fine—— Not for me—— But no! For me
too!—— If my own longing to love everything and everyone has been the result of my great misfortune, I can
scarcely imagine how much those who have suffered less
must long to love. What love must those men feel who
marry women they don't care for? What joy those who are
abandoned by a wife they adore after they have had her in
their house no more than an hour? What delight those
whose children are very ugly? Obviously it hasn't been
much fun here in the garden tonight. I won't be quick to
forget such a high old time. Now and then I tried to pretend that Electra was here. "Come in, Electra!" I said.
"Are you cold, Electra?" I asked. But it was no good. No
one was fooled, not even the dog—not to mention me.
He promised us a bride, thought the dog, and here he
brings us a word. My master married a word; he put on his
white tunic—the one my paws leave marks on so that he
won't let me jump up and lick him—all in order to marry
a word. He gives orange syrup to a word. He calls me a
fool for barking at shadows—and, after all, it's all right
for a shadow to have no substance—and here he is trying
to embrace a word. Not that I went to bed—sleeping with
a word is more than I can do. You can talk to a word, but

that's all! But if you'd been sitting the way I was, in this
garden where everything goes a little astray at night with
the moon gleaming on the sundial and the blind screech
owl trying to drink from the cement walk rather than from
the stream, you would have understood, that is to say, the
truth. You would have understood that your parents were
being born on the day they died, that you became rich the
day you were ruined, that your child was showing gratitude
the day he seemed most ungrateful, that the world was
rushing to embrace you the day you felt most abandoned.
That's just what happened to me here in these quiet,
empty outskirts of the city. These petrified trees, these
immovable hills came hurtling toward me. And all this has
to do with this play. You certainly couldn't say that what
Electra feels for Clytemnestra is the essence of love. But
look more closely and you'll realize that what Electra
wants is a mother. She would make a mother for herself out
of the first person to come along. She was going to marry
me because she sensed that I was the only man, absolutely
the only one, who could be a sort of mother. But no, on
second thought, I'm not the only one. There are men
who would be delighted to carry a child nine months, if
that's what it took to have a daughter. All men, in fact.
Nine months is a bit long, but a week, a day, there isn't
a man who wouldn't be proud. It may be that in trying to
find a mother within her mother she will have to cut open
her breast. But don't worry. With royalty this is never as
gory as you would think—kings practice pure science. They
succeed with experiments which never work for the humble
—they achieve pure hatred, pure wrath. It's always purity
they're after. That's what Tragedy is all about, with its
incests and parricides: purity—innocence, in effect. I don't
know whether you are like me, but in tragedies the phar-
aoh's wife who commits suicide speaks to me of hope, the
treasonous general speaks to me of good faith, the duke
who commits murder, of tenderness. Cruelty is a work of
love—sorry, I mean Tragedy is a work of love. That's why
I am sure that if I called on heaven this morning to signal
its approval, it would do so; there's a miracle up there
ready and waiting, an inscription or an echo repeating my
motto: Joy and Love. If you wish, I'll ask God for a sign.
Sure as I'm standing here before you, a voice from up there

would answer me—God has all his thunder, his loud-speakers, and his amplifiers ready if I ask for them—shouting at my behest: Joy and Love. But I advise you not to ask me to call on him. First of all it's unseemly. It's not a gardener's place to ask God for a storm, even of tenderness. And then, it's so useless. We're all perfectly aware that right now, or yesterday, or tomorrow, or forever, the gods are up there, however many they may be—and even if there's only one of them, and even if he's absent—they're up there ready to shout: Joy and Love. It's so much more dignified to take the gods at their word—that's a euphemism, word—without obliging them to underline anything, to pitch in, to become one another's creditors and debtors. For my part it's always been silence which I've found convincing. Yes, I even ask them not to shout Joy and Love. If they absolutely must, let them shout it. But I implore them, I implore you, God, as a proof of your affection, of your voice, of your shouting, to be silent, to create a second of silence—— It's so much more convincing. Listen—— Thank you.

ACT TWO

Same setting. A little before daybreak. ELECTRA *is still seated holding the sleeping* ORESTES. *The* BEGGAR *is also onstage. A cock crows. There is the sound of a distant trumpet.*

BEGGAR. Not far off now, is it, Electra?

Electra. No. Not far off.

Beggar. The day.

Electra. Light. I was thinking of the light.

Beggar. Won't you be satisfied if the faces of liars are dazzling in the sunshine? If adulterers and murderers go about under the bright blue sky? That's what day means. That's good enough, isn't it?

Electra. No. I want their faces to be black at noon, their hands red. That's what I mean by light. I want their eyes to rot away and their mouths to breathe forth the plague.

Beggar. Be sure to think of everything while you're at it. A cock crows.

Electra. There's the cock—— Shall I awaken him?

Beggar. If you wish. I would let him have another five minutes.

Electra. Five minutes of nothingness—a poor gift.

Beggar. One never knows. I've heard of an insect that lives only five minutes. It's young, adult, and senile all in five minutes; it exhausts all the possible experiences of childhood and adolescence; it's gone in the knee and suffers from cataract; it contracts unions both legitimate and morganatic. Just in the instant I've been talking it's reached measles and puberty.

Electra. We'll wait for it to die. I'll concede you that much.

Beggar. Thank you. See how soundly he sleeps, that brother of yours.

Electra. He went right to sleep. He slipped from me into sleep just as he slipped from me and fell in real life.

Beggar. He's smiling in his sleep. That's his real life.

Electra. Tell me anything, beggar, except that it's Orestes' real life to smile!

204

Beggar. To split with laughter, to love, to dress in fine clothes, to be happy. I had only to see him to guess that it was so. He'd be happy as a lark, Orestes would, if life had been kind to him.

Electra. He's been unlucky.

Beggar. Yes, he hasn't had much luck. All the more reason not to hurry and wake him.

Electra. I agree. Since Orestes was made to split with laughter, to dress in fine clothes, to be happy as a lark, and since he will awaken to horror without end, I'll let him have five minutes more.

Beggar. That way—since you have the choice—you can fix it so that for once the morning and the truth begin the day together. That's what I would do in your place. Yoke them together; they're a fitting team for a young girl—it would please me to see you do so. The truth of men's lives is tied too closely to their routines; it comes out any old time—at nine in the morning when workers say they're going to strike, at six in the evening when a woman admits where she's been all afternoon, etc. Those are bad times for the truth to come out—there's never enough light to see it by. If only the truth could come out the way animals start from their lairs. That's what I'm used to, animals. They know how to start out right. When the rabbit leaps in the heather just at sunrise, when the plover hops on his stilts, when the bear cub tumbles from his rocky cave, I assure you they're making a start for the truth. If they don't reach it, it's because it's not their job to reach it. A mere nothing distracts them, a gudgeon, a bee. But do as they do, Electra, set out at dawn!

Electra. Happy kingdom in which falsehood amounts to no more than a gudgeon and a bee! But they're stirring already, those animals of yours!

Beggar. No. Those are the animals of the night going home. The screech owls. The rats. The truth of the night is returning to its den. But listen, you would know it, the last two are the nightingales—there goes the truth of the nightingales.

Enter AGATHA *and the* YOUNG MAN.

Agatha. You understand, my darling, don't you?

Young man. Yes. I have an answer for anything he may say.

Agatha. If he meets you on the stairs?

Young man. I was on my way to see the doctor who lives upstairs.

Agatha. You've already forgotten! He's a veterinary. You're on your way to buy a dog—— And if he finds me in your arms?

Young man. I carried you home. You sprained your ankle on the street.

Agatha. And if he finds us in the kitchen?

Young man. I'll pretend I'm drunk. I don't know where I am; I break all the glasses.

Agatha. Just one is enough, darling! One of the little ones. The big ones are crystal. And if we're in the bedroom, but fully clothed?

Young man. He's just the man I'm looking for; I want to talk over a matter of state with him. I'm forced to corner him in his bedroom, he's that hard to see.

Agatha. What if we're in the bedroom, but undressed?

Young man. I took you by surprise; you're resisting my advances; you're the soul of perfidy—you've been leading me on for six months and then, when the time comes, you treat me as a thief! Whore!

Agatha. Oh, my darling.

Young man. A real whore!

Agatha. I heard you! That's enough! It's almost daybreak, dearest, and you've been mine scarcely an hour. How much longer will he be willing to go on believing that I'm a sleepwalker and that it's less dangerous to let me wander around in the woods than on the roof tops. Dear heart, there must be some lie we could tell which would permit me to have you in our bed at night so that I could lie there between the two of you.

Young man. Think hard. You'll find one.

Agatha. A lie so perfect that it would allow you to talk to each other about the elections or the races, across your little Agatha—— So perfect that he wouldn't suspect a thing! That's exactly what we need!

Young man. As simple as that!

Agatha. Alas! Why is he so vain? Why is he such a light sleeper? Why does he adore me?

Young man. That's the age-old refrain. Why did you marry him? Why did you love him?

Agatha. Me? Liar! I have never loved anyone but you!

Young man. Anyone but me! Think whose arms I found you in day before yesterday!

Agatha. I'd just sprained my ankle. The man you're talking about was carrying me home.

Young man. Seems to me I've heard something about a sprained ankle before.

Agatha. You don't know what you're talking about. You don't understand: it was that accident which gave me the idea for us to use!

Young man. When I pass him on the stairs, he never has a dog with him, or a cat, I assure you.

Agatha. He's a horseman. He can't take his horse upstairs to the veterinary.

Young man. He always comes out of your apartment.

Agatha. Why are you forcing me to betray a state secret? He comes to consult my husband. There are rumors of a plot brewing in the city. I beg you, don't tell a soul. He would be dismissed if you did. I'd be out on my ear.

Young man. One evening he was in quite a hurry; his scarf was thrown on and his tunic was half open.

Agatha. I can imagine. That's the day he tried to kiss me. I fixed him!

Young man. He's very strong! Are you sure you didn't let him kiss you? I was waiting downstairs. He was up with you two hours.

Agatha. He was with me two hours, but I didn't let him kiss me.

Young man. Then he kissed you without your permission. Admit it, Agatha, or I'm leaving!

Agatha. Is that the way to repay my frankness, forcing me to confess? Yes, he kissed me—once—on the forehead.

Young man. Well? Wasn't it horrible?

Agatha. Horrible? Ghastly!

Young man. It doesn't seem to have caused you any suffering.

Agatha. None at all—— Suffering, did you say? I thought I was going to die. Kiss me, darling. Now you know everything, darling, and, to tell you the truth, I'm glad you do. Don't you prefer everything to be open and aboveboard between us?

Young man. Yes. I prefer anything and everything to a lie.

Agatha. What a sweet way to tell me you prefer me above everything, my love.

Exit AGATHA *and the* YOUNG MAN.

Beggar. The dawn of such a day deserves a song in its praise—at the very least!

Electra. Is the insect dead, beggar?

Beggar. Dead and returned to dust. By now its great-grandsons are old men with gout.

Electra. Orestes!

Beggar. See, he's no longer asleep. He has opened his eyes.

Electra. Say something, Orestes! What are you thinking about?

Enter the EUMENIDES, *now age fifteen.*

First of the Eumenides. Orestes, you still have a moment more! Don't listen to your sister!

Second of the Eumenides. Don't listen to her! We've just found out what life is like, and it's marvelous!

Third of the Eumenides. We found out just by chance, as we grew in the night.

Second of the Eumenides. Love, that's the best part—but we're not going to tell you about that!

First of the Eumenides. And she's going to poison everything with her venom.

Third of the Eumenides. With the venom of truth, the only one for which there is no antidote.

First of the Eumenides. We know what you're thinking, and you're right. It's magnificent to be a king, Orestes! Think of the young girls in the royal park feeding bread to the swans, wearing medallions pinned to their dresses, which they received from King Orestes whom they kiss on the sly. Think of leaving for war with all the women watching you from the roof tops, with the sky like the sail of a ship, and a white horse prancing to the fanfare of trumpets. Think of returning from war—your face would no longer seem that of a king but of a god, just because you'd been a little cold, a little hungry, a little afraid, a little compassionate. If the truth is going to spoil all this, let it perish!

Second of the Eumenides. You're right. It's magnificent, Orestes, love! We've heard that lovers never leave each other! It seems that as soon as they're separated they come running back to each other and clasp hands. Wherever they go, they come face to face with each other. The world is round for lovers. I'm already bumping into the man I love, and I haven't met him yet. This is what Electra wants to take from you with this truth of hers, and from us, too. We want to love. Flee from Electra.

Electra. Orestes!

Orestes. I have awakened, sister.

Electra. Awake from this waking: don't listen to these girls.

Orestes. Oh, Electra, are you sure they aren't right? Is it not the grossest arrogance for a man in my situation to try to retrace his own steps? Why not take the first path and follow where it leads? Trust in me. This is one of those moments when I am on the track of that special quarry called happiness.

Electra. Alas, that's not the game we're after today.

Orestes. Never again to be separated, that's all that counts! Let's flee from this palace. We'll go to Thessaly. You'll see my house there, covered with roses and jasmine.

Electra. You saved me from the gardener, darling Orestes. Don't give me to the flowers a second time.

Orestes. Please believe me. Let's slip from the embrace of the octopus which soon will be tightening its tentacles about us. Rejoice that we awakened before it! Come with me!

First of the Eumenides. It has awakened! You can see it in her eyes!

Third of the Eumenides. You're right. It's marvelous, Orestes, the spring. You see the backs of the animals cropping the new grass over the tops of hedgerows which haven't yet sprouted. Nothing but their backs—only the donkey lifts his head and looks at you. It would look pretty funny, the head of that donkey, if you had assassinated your uncle. You'd feel funny with a donkey looking at you and you with your hands red with your uncle's blood.

Orestes. What's she saying?

Third of the Eumenides. Let me tell you about the springtime! Those butterballs of yellow foam which fleck the streams among the cress leaves in the spring—you will see how they can comfort the heart of those who have killed their mothers. Just try spreading butter on your bread that day with a knife, even if it's not the knife that killed your mother, and you'll see.

Orestes. Help me, Electra!

Electra. Then you're like all other men, Orestes! They give way to the least flattery; they're won by the slightest charm. Help you? I know what you want to hear me say.

Orestes. Then say it to me.

Electra. That men are good when all is said and done, and life is good!

Orestes. Isn't it true?

Electra. That it's not so bad a fate to be young, handsome, and a prince—to have a sister who is young and a princess. That one should be content to leave men to their vain and lowly pursuits. That one should enjoy the beauties of the world without bursting the pimples on the face of humanity!

Orestes. And that's not what you're telling me?

Electra. No. I'm telling you that our mother has a lover.

Orestes. You're lying! That's impossible!

First of the Eumenides. She's a widow. That's reason enough.

Electra. I tell you that our father was killed!

Orestes. Killed? Agamemnon!

Electra. Stabbed by assassins.

Second of the Eumenides. Seven years ago. It's ancient history.

Orestes. You knew all this and you let me sleep all night!

Electra. No, I received all this from the night. Strewn on the face of the night were these facts. Now I know what prophetesses do. They hold their brothers to their heart for an entire night.

Orestes. Our father, killed! Who told you so?

Electra. He, himself.

Orestes. He spoke to you before he died?

Electra. He spoke to me when he was already dead, the very day of the murder. It has taken seven years for me to understand what he said.

Orestes. He appeared to you?

Electra. No. I saw his corpse during the night, just as it was on the day of the murder. Written in a fold of his clothes, ever so luminously, I read the words: I am not the fold of death, I am the fold of murder. And on his shoe was a buckle which said: I am not the buckle of accident, but the buckle of crime. And there was in his closed eyelid a wrinkle which said: I did not see death, I saw regicide.

Orestes. What about our mother? Who told you about her?

Electra. She, herself. Just as he did.

Orestes. She confessed?

Electra. No. I saw her dead. Her future corpse gave her away. No doubt about that. Her eyebrows were the eyebrows of a dead woman who has had a lover.

Orestes. Who is this lover? Who is this assassin?

Electra. I'm awakening you so that we can find them. Let's hope they are the same man. Then you will have only one blow to strike.

Orestes. I'm afraid you'd better go along, girls. My sister awakens me to the prospect of a prostitute queen and a murdered king. My parents.

First of the Eumenides. That's not bad for a start. Don't feel you have to add anything.

Electra. Forgive me, Orestes.

Second of the Eumenides. Now she's asking his forgiveness.

Third of the Eumenides. I ruin your life, and I ask your forgiveness.

Beggar. She's wrong to ask his forgiveness. That's exactly the kind of awakening our wives and our sisters always have in store for us. You'd almost think that's what they were made for.

Electra. They're made only for that. In the morning when a man sees only regal purple and gold through his swollen lids, it's his wife, or his sister-in-law, or his mother-in-law, who hands him, along with his morning coffee and his pitcher of hot water, hatred for injustice and disdain for all the lesser forms of happiness.

Orestes. Forgive me, Electra!

Second of the Eumenides. Now it's his turn to ask forgiveness! Beautiful manners they've got in that family.

First of the Eumenides. They don't take off their hats when they greet each other—they take off their whole head.

Electra. Women are there waiting for men to wake up. And men, even if they have slept only five minutes, have reclothed themselves in the armor of happiness fashioned out of a satisfaction with life, indifference, generosity, and a good appetite. A spot of sunlight reconciles them to all the bloodstains in the world. The song of a bird, with all the lies. But women lie there, all of them, ravaged by insomnia, contending with jealousy, envy, love, memory— that is, with the truth. Have you awakened, Orestes?

First of the Eumenides. We'll be as old as he is an hour from now! Let's hope we're not like him!

Orestes. I believe I am awakening.

Enter CLYTEMNESTRA.

Beggar. Your mother is coming, my children.

Orestes. Where is my sword?

Electra. Bravo. That's what I call a good awakening. Here is your sword. Here is your hatred. Here is your strength.

Clytemnestra. Their mother appears and they become like statues.

Electra. Or rather orphans.

Clytemnestra. I shall no longer listen to an insolent daughter!

Electra. Then listen to a son.

Orestes. Who is he, Mother? Confess!

Clytemnestra. What sort of children are you, to make a scene every time we meet? Leave me alone or I shall cry for help!

Electra. Whom will you call? Him?

Orestes. You're putting up quite a struggle, Mother.

Beggar. Careful, Orestes. An innocent quarry struggles just as hard as a guilty one.

Clytemnestra. Quarry? What sort of quarry am I for my children? Tell me, Orestes, tell me.

Orestes. I don't dare!

Clytemnestra. Electra, then. She will dare.

Electra. Who is he, Mother?

Clytemnestra. Whom, or what, are you talking about?

Orestes. Mother, is it true that you have a——

Electra. No need to be specific, Orestes. Simply ask her who he is. Buried in her there is a name. Whatever your question, if you press hard enough for an answer, out the name will come——

Orestes. Mother, is it true that you have a lover?

Clytemnestra. Is that your question as well, Electra?

Electra. You could put it that way.

Clytemnestra. My son and my daughter ask me if I have a lover?

Electra. Your husband can no longer ask you himself.

Clytemnestra. The gods would blush to hear you.

Electra. That would astonish me. For some time now their blushes have been few and far between.

Clytemnestra. I have no lover. But be careful what you do. All the evil in the world is the fault of the self-styled pure in heart, a result of their eagerness to unearth secrets and expose them to the light of the sun.

Electra. What the sun putrefies does not offend me.

Clytemnestra. I have no lover. I cannot take a lover, even if I want to. But be careful. The curious have not been lucky in our family: investigating a theft they discovered a sacrilege; looking into a love affair they ran up against incest. You will not discover that I have a lover, since I have none, but you'll stumble on something which will be fatal for your sisters and yourselves.

Electra. Who is your lover?

Orestes. At least listen to her, Electra!

Clytemnestra. I have no lover. But just tell me, what would be so criminal about it if I did?

Orestes. Oh, Mother, you are the queen!

Clytemnestra. The world is still young, and the day is just born. But it would take us from now till dusk to name all the queens who have had lovers.

Orestes. Go on fighting, I beg you, Mother. Convince

us. If this struggle gives us back a queen, may she be
blessed. All will be well with us once again!

Electra. Don't you see that you are giving her the
weapons she needs, Orestes?

Clytemnestra. All right. Leave me alone with Electra,
will you?

Orestes. Must I, sister?

Electra. Yes. Yes. Wait there, under the arch. And as
soon as I shout "Orestes," come running. Come running
as fast as you can. Because I shall know everything.

Exit ORESTES.

Clytemnestra. Help me, Electra!

Electra. Help you do what? Tell the truth or lie?

Clytemnestra. Protect me.

Electra. This is the first time you have ever turned to
your daughter, Mother. You must be afraid.

Clytemnestra. I am afraid of Orestes.

Electra. You are lying. You are not afraid of Orestes.
You see what he is like: passionate, changeable, weak. He
still dreams that the Atrides can be happy. It is I whom
you fear; it is for my benefit that you still play this game.
The sense of it escapes me. You have a lover, don't you?
Who is he?

Clytemnestra. He knows nothing. He's not involved.

Electra. He doesn't know he is your lover?

Clytemnestra. Give up this role of judge, Electra. Cease
your interrogation. After all, you are my daughter.

Electra. After all. Precisely—after all. That's why I am
interrogating you.

Clytemnestra. Then cease to be my daughter. Cease
hating me. Content yourself with being what I long for
you to be: a woman. Take up my cause, it is your own.
Defend yourself by defending me.

Electra. I am not a member of the sisterhood of women.
It would take someone other than you to enroll me.

Clytemnestra. You are wrong. Our bodies, our condition
are the same; we are companions in misfortune. If you
betray me, you will be the first to feel Orestes' hatred. A
scandal never breaks on those who are involved. What do
you hope to win for yourself? If you besmirch all women

by besmirching me, you will defile yourself in the eyes of Orestes insofar as you resemble me.

Electra. In no way do I resemble you. For years I have been looking in my mirror to be sure that I don't look like you. Every polished slab of marble, the pools of all the palace fountains—they have all cried out to me, just as your face itself does: Electra's nose bears no resemblance to Clytemnestra's nose. My forehead is mine. My mouth is mine. And I have no lover.

Clytemnestra. Listen to me! I have no lover. I am in love.

Electra. Don't try to trick me. You throw love at my feet the way drivers pursued by wolves throw them a dog. Dogs are not my food.

Clytemnestra. We are women, Electra. We have a right to love.

Electra. One has many rights within the sisterhood of women, but the entrance fee is high: one must admit that women are weak, base, and prone to falsehood. But if one pays the fee, one has the right to be weak, base, and prone to falsehood. The trouble is that women are strong, loyal, and noble. In other words, you are mistaken: you have no right to love anyone but my father. Did you love him? On your wedding night, did you love him?

Clytemnestra. What are you driving at? You want to hear me say that your birth owed nothing to love, that you were coldly conceived. Set your mind at rest. Not everyone can be like your aunt Leda, and just lay an egg. But not once did you speak within me. From the very first minute of your existence we were indifferent to each other. You didn't even make me suffer while I was giving birth to you. You were thin, reticent. You kept your lips pinched shut. You pinched them obstinately shut for a whole year for one reason only—for fear that your first word would be your mother's name. Neither you nor I cried the day you were born. Never have you and I wept together.

Electra. Now is not the time for me to start.

Clytemnestra. You will soon weep—you can be sure of that—and perhaps on my shoulder.

Electra. Eyes can cry all by themselves. That's what they are there for.

Clytemnestra. Yes—even yours which look like two stones. One day they will be drowned in tears.

Electra. May that day come—— But why, if you don't want me to pursue you, are you throwing me coldness instead of love?

Clytemnestra. So that you will understand that I have a right to love. So that you will know that everything in my life has been as harsh to me as my daughter the day she was born. From the time I was married, I never had a moment of solitude or privacy. I never went into the forest except on the day of a procession. I could never rest. Even my body had no repose. By day it was covered with golden robes, and at night by a king. Everything, plants, animals, animate or inanimate, was permeated with suspicion. Often when I saw the lindens by the palace—sullen, silent trees, smelling of the tea nursemaids make from their flowers— I said to myself: they're looking at me the way Electra did the day she was born. Never has a queen experienced the lot of queens as I have—the absence of her husband, the suspicion of her sons, the hatred of her daughters—— What is left for me?

Electra. What is left to others: to wait.

Clytemnestra. Wait for what? Waiting is horrible.

Electra. Perhaps you are waiting for her who holds you at this moment.

Clytemnestra. Can you tell me for whom you are waiting?

Electra. I am waiting no longer—but for ten years I awaited my father. Waiting is the only happiness I have ever known in this world.

Clytemnestra. It's happiness suitable for a virgin. It's a solitary happiness.

Electra. You think so? Except for you and the other human beings in the palace, everything waited with me for my father, everything was my accomplice. It began in the morning, Mother, when I took my first stroll under the lindens that hate you so. They were waiting for my father, trying in vain to suppress their sense of expectancy, vexed to have to live from year to year rather than as they should, from decade to decade. They were ashamed at the way they betrayed him each spring when they could no longer hold back their flowers and their fragrance. Like me they

could not stand his absence; like me they continually
swooned and faltered. It went on at noon when I visited
the mountain stream—more fortunate than the rest of us
that stream was, for it could move, it could wait for my
father by rushing toward a river which rushed toward the
sea. It continued into the evening when I no longer had
the strength to wait with his dogs and his horses—poor
mortal creatures, incapable by nature of waiting for centuries. I took refuge at that hour among the columns and
statues of his palace. I modeled myself on them. Like them
I stood utterly still in the moonlight, waiting for hours
without thinking, without breathing. I awaited him with
a heart of stone, of marble, of alabaster, of onyx, which
nonetheless beat and shattered my chest—— What would
become of me if there were not times when I still wait,
when I wait for the past, when I still expect him!

Clytemnestra. I wait no longer; I am in love.

Electra. And everything goes well for you now?

Clytemnestra. Very well.

Electra. Do the flowers obey you at last? The birds speak
to you?

Clytemnestra. Yes, the lindens signal to me.

Electra. It's very possible. You've stolen everything from
me in life.

Clytemnestra. Let yourself fall in love. We'll share our
feelings.

Electra. Share love with you? That's as bad as if you
offered to share your lover with me. Who is he?

Clytemnestra. Oh, Electra, have pity! I shall tell you his
name, however much it will make you blush. Just wait a
few days. What will a scandal prove? Think of your
brother. The people of Argos will never let Orestes succeed an unworthy mother.

Electra. An unworthy mother? What are you hoping to
accomplish with such a confession? Are you trying to gain
time? What sort of a trap are you setting for me? What
sort of a covey are you trying to protect by limping, like a
partridge, in the direction of love and unworthiness?

Clytemnestra. Don't force me to face public shame.
Why make me admit that I love beneath myself?

Electra. Some little lieutenant with neither rank nor
family?

Clytemnestra. Yes.

Electra. You are lying. If your lover was some little officer of no particular distinction, if he was the bath attendant or a page, you would love him. But you don't love him; you have never loved. Who is he? Why are you refusing to tell me his name as if it were a key you refused to hand me? What piece of furniture do you fear I will open with it?

Clytemnestra. One that belongs to me: my love.

Electra. Tell me the name of your lover, Mother, and I shall tell you whether you love him. And his name will be a secret between us forever.

Clytemnestra. Never.

Electra. You see! It's not your lover but your secret which you are hiding from me. You are afraid that his name would give me the only evidence which still escapes me in my investigation.

Clytemnestra. Evidence? You're mad!

Electra. Evidence of the crime. Everything tells me that you committed it, Mother. But what I don't yet see, what I must learn from you, is why you committed it. I have tried all the keys, as you call them. Not one works so far. Not love. There's nothing that you love. Not ambition. You couldn't care less about being queen. Not anger. You are cool, calculating. But your lover's name will make everything clear, will tell us everything, won't it? Whom do you love? Who is he?

Enter AGATHA, *pursued by the* JUDGE.

Judge. Who is he? Whom do you love?

Agatha. I hate you.

Judge. Who is he?

Agatha. I tell you it's all over. No more lying. Electra is right! I am in her camp now. Thank you, Electra! You've brought me to life!

Judge. What are you singing about?

Agatha. I am singing the song of a wife. This time you're going to hear the whole of it.

Judge. As if we hadn't had enough already!

Agatha. Yes, here we all are, widowed, or married to uninspiring husbands. And we're wearing ourselves out, every one of us, so that they can live and die more agreeably. Cook them braised lettuce and then they ask you to pass the salt and a smile along with it. And if they smoke, you have to light their horrid old cigar with the flame of your heart!

Judge. Whom do you mean? Have you ever seen me eat braised lettuce?

Agatha. Your puréed spinach, then.

Judge. Your lover doesn't eat spinach or smoke a cigar, I take it?

Agatha. The spinach my lover eats becomes ambrosia. I relish every morsel he leaves on his plate. Everything that is tainted when my husband handles it is purified by the touch of his hands or his mouth—even me—and that's saying something!

Electra. I have it, Mother, I have it!

Judge. Come to your senses, Agatha!

Agatha. But I have come to my senses! At last! There we are, twenty-four hours a day, killing ourselves, committing suicide just to please a husband whose displeasure is our only joy, pretending to enjoy his company when his absence is the only delight we know, fostering the vanity of the man who humiliates us every day with the sight of his big toenails. And then he dares reproach us for depriving him of ourselves for an hour each week! But then, after all, he's right! When this marvelous hour comes, we don't just lie there stiff and cold!

Judge. See what you've done, Electra. As recently as this very morning she was in my arms!

Agatha. I am pretty and he is ugly. I am young and he is old. I am witty and he's a dunce. I have a soul and he doesn't. And he's the one who has everything. Or rather he has me. And I'm the one who has nothing. Or rather, I have him. And until this morning, I who gave everything had to appear overwhelmed with benefits and favors. Why? I polish his shoes. Why? I buff his nails. Why? I make him his coffee. Why? When, if I were to act according to the truth, I would poison him, rub the collar of his tunic with pitch and ashes. Now his shoes, they were one thing I didn't mind—I spat on them when I polished them. I was spitting on you. But that's all over now, all over——Hail to the Truth! Electra has given me some of her courage. It's done, it's done. I would rather die!

Beggar. So that's the song of a wife? Not bad!

Judge. Who is he?

Electra. Listen, Mother! Listen! That's you speaking!

Agatha. Who is he? That's a husband for you! They all believe there can be only one person!

Judge. Lovers! You have more than one lover?

Agatha. And they all think that we deceive them only with lovers. Of course, sometimes we do—— But we deceive you with everything. When I awaken and my hand glides sleepily over the wood of the bed, I commit my first adultery. For once let's use your word adultery. I've turned my back to you when I couldn't sleep and caressed that wood! It's olive wood. How softly grained! And what a pretty word! When I hear the word *olive* spoken in the street, my heart leaps within me. It's my lover's name I hear! I commit adultery for the second time when I open my eyes and see the light of day through the blinds. And for a third time when my foot touches the water of my bath and then when I immerse myself in it. I deceive you with my finger, with my eyes, with the soles of my feet. When I am looking at you, I am deceiving you. When I am listening to you, when I pretend to admire you in court, I am deceiving you. Kill the olive trees, kill the pigeons, kill every five-year-old, boy or girl, kill fire, earth, water! Kill this beggar. You are deceived by them.

Beggar. Thank you.

Judge. And to think that yesterday evening this woman was pouring me my herb tea! She even thought it wasn't hot enough. She even boiled some more water! I suppose all you people are pleased! A little scandal inside a big one is just to your taste!

Beggar. No. It's like a squirrel in a cage. It's what turns the cage.

Judge. And what do you think you are doing, carrying on so in the presence of the queen! You'll forgive us, I hope!

Electra. The queen envies Agatha. The queen would have given her life to be able to treat herself to what Agatha is enjoying today. Who is he, Mother?

Beggar. Do you hear what she's saying, your Honor? Don't allow yourself to be diverted. Almost a minute has gone by since you asked her who he is.

Judge. Who is he?

Agatha. I have already told you. Everyone. Everything.

Judge. It's enough to kill a man! It's like hitting your head against a stone wall!

Agatha. Don't stop because of me. The walls in these old cities were very solidly built.

Judge. Is he young? Is he old?

Agatha. A lover's age—from sixteen to eighty.

Judge. She thinks she can demean me by insults! Your insults strike you alone, O fallen woman!

Agatha. I know. I know. Outrage makes a man majestic. In the street those who look most dignified have just slipped on some dung.

Judge. You'll see what I'm like at last! Whatever they're like, these lovers of yours, I shall kill the first one to pass by!

Agatha. The first to pass by here? You've chosen a very poor spot. You won't even be able to look him in the eyes.

Judge. I will make him kneel, I will make him bow down and kiss the marble.

Agatha. You will soon see how he bows down and kisses the marble when he comes into this courtyard and takes his place on the throne!

Judge. What are you saying, wretch!

Agatha. I am saying that I have two lovers at present and one of them is Aegisthus.

Clytemnestra. Liar!

Agatha. What! She, too!

Electra. You too, Mother?

Beggar. That's strange. I would have said that if Aegisthus had a weakness for anyone, it was for Electra.

Enter a PAGE.

Page [*announcing*]. Aegisthus!
Electra. At last!

Enter the EUMENIDES.

Eumenides. Aegisthus!

Enter AEGISTHUS *with a* CAPTAIN *and soldiers. He is infinitely more majestic and serene than in the first act. High above him hovers a bird.*

Aegisthus. Electra is here—— Thank you, Electra! I will sit here, Captain. We will make this headquarters.

Clytemnestra. I, too, am here.

Aegisthus. I am delighted that you are. Hail, Queen.

Judge. And I, too, Aegisthus!

Aegisthus. Fine, your Honor. You are just the man I need.

Judge. Now he is adding insult to injury!

Aegisthus. What's wrong? Why are you all looking at me that way?

Beggar. What's wrong? The queen is waiting for a man who has perjured himself, Electra is waiting for a man who has been impious, Agatha for a man who has been unfaithful. He doesn't set his sights so high—he is waiting for the man who makes love to his wife—— Don't you see, it's you they are waiting for! And now it's not you who has come!

Aegisthus. Really they don't have much luck, do they, beggar?

Beggar. No, they are unlucky. Imagine waiting for a lot of good-for-nothings, and then in comes a king! I don't mind for the others, but it's going to be hard on that poor little Electra.

Aegisthus. You think so? I think not.

Beggar. I knew it would happen! I told you so yesterday! I knew you were on the verge of becoming what you truly are—a king! Everything conspired—your power, your age, the situation, the presence of Electra. It could have been worse—blood could have flowed. But it's happened this way, and now you have become what you truly are! All the better for Greece. But it's a bit hard on the family.

Clytemnestra. You're speaking in riddles. What are you talking about?

Beggar. All the better for us, too! Since there has to be a scuffle, it's better for Electra to come to grips with nobility rather than turpitude! Tell us how it happened, Aegisthus.

Aegisthus [*studying* ELECTRA]. Electra is here! I knew I would find her standing like this, with her head as still as a statue's. Her eyes seem to see nothing unless the lids are closed! Her ears seem deaf to any human tongue!

Clytemnestra. Listen to me, Aegisthus!

Judge. You chose your lovers well, Agatha! What gall!

Captain. Aegisthus, time is growing short!

Aegisthus. Your ears are purely ornamental, are they not, Electra? The gods said to themselves: since we gave her hands that she may not touch, eyes that she may not see, we cannot give Electra a head without ears! It would be too obvious that she hears no one but us! But if I put my ear up to yours, what would I hear? A roaring, like the roaring of the sea in a shell? Coming from where?

Clytemnestra. Are you mad? Take care! Electra's ears hear you.

Judge. And they blush at what they hear!

Aegisthus. They hear me. I am perfectly convinced of that. A little while ago I was standing on the edge of the woods, at the spot from which one has a view of Argos, when all at once something happened—— Since then my words come from beyond me—— And I know she sees me; she alone sees me. She alone has guessed what it was that happened to me.

Clytemnestra. You are speaking to your worst enemy, Aegisthus!

Aegisthus. She knows why all of a sudden there on the mountain I spurred my horse to a gallop and rode back to the city! The horse seemed to understand, Electra. A light chestnut galloping toward Electra makes a fine sight with the whole squadron thundering after him, all drawn to her as if to a magnet, from the trumpeters' white stallions to the piebald mares of the rear guard. Don't be surprised if my horse pokes his head around one of those columns any moment now and whinnies at you! He knew your name was in his mouth, gagging him like a stopper of gold. I wanted to call out to you and to you alone. Shall I cry your name now, Electra?

Clytemnestra. Stop this scandalous behavior!

Captain. Aegisthus, the city is in danger!

Aegisthus. True. Forgive me!—— Where are they now, Captain?

Captain. Their lances can be seen over the hill tops. No stand of grain ever grew so quickly. Or so thick. There are thousands of them.

Aegisthus. The cavalry couldn't hold them off?

Captain. They retreated with some prisoners.

Clytemnestra. What is happening, Aegisthus?

Captain. The Corinthians have invaded, without any cause and without declaring war. Bands of them slipped into our territory during the night. The outlying districts are already burning.

Aegisthus. What do the prisoners say?

Captain. That they have been ordered to raze Argos.

Clytemnestra. Show yourself, Aegisthus, and they will flee!

Aegisthus. I fear that will no longer be enough, Queen.

Captain. They have agents in the city. They have stolen barrels of pitch which we had in reserve in order to set fire to the houses of our citizens. The mob is gathered around the markets, ready to loot and pillage.

Clytemnestra. If the palace guard is faithful, what is there to fear?

Captain. The guard is ready to fight. But they are grumbling. You know how it is: they are never eager to obey a woman. The same goes for the city. After all, you say "she," don't you, when you talk about an army or a city, and for one reason: they're both women. They both need a man, a king.

Aegisthus. They are right. They will have one.

Judge. He who would be king of Argos must first kill Clytemnestra, Aegisthus.

Beggar. Or simply marry her.

Judge. Never!

Aegisthus. Why never? The queen won't deny that this is the only way to save Argos. I have no doubt that she will assent. Captain, tell the guard the marriage is being celebrated at this very instant. Keep me informed of every development. I shall wait here for your reports. [*Exit* CAPTAIN.] As for you, your Honor, go tell the mob the news in your most enthusiastic manner.

Judge. Never! First I have something to say to you as one man to another, leaving aside what's going on.

Aegisthus. Leaving aside Argos? Leaving aside the war? You're a bit presumptuous!

Judge. My honor is at stake and the honor of the Greek judiciary.

Beggar. If the Greek judiciary based its honor on Agatha's thighs, it has no better than it deserves. Don't bother us at such a moment! Look at Agatha there with her nose in the air! Do you think she's worrying about the honor of the Greek judiciary?

Judge. Her nose in the air? You have your nose in the air at a moment like this, Agatha?

Agatha. My nose is in the air because I am watching the bird which is hovering above Aegisthus.

Judge. Lower it.

Aegisthus. I am waiting for your reply, Queen.

Clytemnestra. A bird? What kind of a bird? Get out from under that bird, Aegisthus!

Aegisthus. Why? It hasn't left me since sunrise. There must be some reason for it. My horse was the first to sense that it was there. He began to kick without any cause. I looked everywhere and finally up there. He was kicking that thousand-legged bird. It's right above me, isn't it, beggar?

Beggar. Right above you. If you yourself had a thousand legs, that's where your head would be.

Aegisthus. It's just like an accent mark, isn't it, on top of a letter?

Beggar. Yes, at present you're the most heavily accented man in all Greece! The problem is that we don't yet know whether the accent is on the word *human* or the word *mortal*.

Clytemnestra. I don't like these hovering birds. What is it? A kite? An eagle?

Beggar. It's too high. I could tell if I could see its shadow. But the bird is too high for its shadow to reach us.

Enter CAPTAIN.

Captain. The palace guard rejoices at your marriage, Aegisthus! They are enthusiastically preparing for combat. They are waiting for you to appear on the balcony with the queen so that they can acclaim you.

Aegisthus. I shall make my vows, and I shall be with you.

Judge. Help me, Electra! What right has this debauched man to give us a lesson in courage?

Beggar. What right? Listen!

Aegisthus. O powers of the earth and air, it is you I

must invoke on the morning of this marriage and this battle! Thank you for the gift I received a while ago at the moment the mist lifted on the hill which overlooks Argos. I had dismounted from my horse, worn out after accompanying the night patrol. I lay down, leaning against the bank; all of a sudden you showed me Argos as I had never seen it. You created it anew for me. You gave it to me. You gave me the whole city, its towers, its bridges, its first breath—the steam rising from the farmers' silos; its first gesture—the pigeons wheeling upward; its first words —the grating clatter of its sluice gates. And every part of this gift is of equal value: Electra, the sun rising over Argos, the last lantern to go out in the city at night, the temple and the hovels, the lake and the tanneries. And your gift was for always!—— This morning I received my city as a mother receives her child. And I wondered anxiously if the gift wasn't greater still, if I hadn't been given far more than Argos. In the morning God does not measure out his gifts: he could have given me the whole world. That would have been horrible. I would have despaired like a man who, expecting a diamond for his birthday, received the sun. You can understand how worried I was, Electra. I imagined anxiously what it would be like to step beyond the confines of Argos. What a joy not to have been given the Orient! I can hear of the plagues, the earthquakes, the famines of the Orient with a smile. My thirst was not of a kind which is quenched by immense tepid rivers flowing between the green lips of a desert; mine is satisfied—I tested it there on the mountainside—by a single drop from an icy spring. Nor does Africa, any part of it, belong to me. The black women can pound their millet on the doorway of their huts, the jaguar can sink his claws into the flank of the crocodile, and not a grain of their cereals, not a drop of their blood is mine. I am as happy with the gifts which were not given to me as I am with the gift of Argos. In a burst of generosity God did not give me Athens or Olympia or Mycenae. What joy! He gave me the cattle market of Argos and not the treasures of Corinth, the short nose of the girls of Argos and not the long nose of the daughters of Pallas, the wrinkled plum of Argos and not the golden fig of Thebes! Here is what has been given to me this morning, to me, the pleasure-loving

parasite, the trickster: a country in which I feel myself
to be pure, strong, perfect—a homeland; and all of a sudden I am king of this homeland in which I was ready to
become a slave! And I swear—hear me, Judge, I am swear-
ing—not only to live and die here in my homeland but to
save it!

Judge. You are my last hope, Electra!

Electra. You can count on me. One has the right to save
one's country only if one's hands are clean.

Beggar. Once a king is anointed he is cleansed of every
misdeed.

Electra. Who has anointed you? How can we tell that
you are to be anointed?

Beggar. Can't you guess? He's to be anointed because
he comes to ask you to anoint him. For the first time he
sees the full force and truth of your being. He came galloping down to the city because he suddenly realized that
Electra was included in the gift of Argos!

Aegisthus. As I came, everything took part in my coronation, Electra! Over the hoofbeats of my horse I heard
trees, children, streams hail me as king. But the holy oil
was missing. Each coronation gift was offered to me by
the most unlikely creature. Until today I was a coward.
But on my way here I received courage from a hare, from
the tips of his ears trembling over the top of a furrow.
I used to be a hypocrite. A fox crossed my path, he gave
me a sly glance and I became truthful. A pair of magpies,
inseparable as ever, gave me independence; an ant hill
gave me generosity. I have hastened to you, Electra, because you are the only being who can impart to another
something of your own essence.

Electra. And what is that?

Aegisthus. I have the impression it is something like
duty.

Electra. My duty is surely the mortal enemy of yours.
You shall not marry Clytemnestra.

Judge. You shall not marry her!

Clytemnestra. Why shouldn't we marry? Why should
we sacrifice our lives to a couple of ungrateful children?
Yes, I love Aegisthus. For ten years I have loved Aegisthus.
For ten years I have put off this marriage for your sake,
Electra, and in memory of your father. Now you are forc-

ing us to it. Thank you—— But not under that bird. That bird bothers me. As soon as it is gone, we shall be married.

Aegisthus. Don't be so upset, Queen. I am not marrying you to bury us still deeper in falsehood. I do not know if I still love you, and the entire city doubts whether you ever loved me. For ten years we alternately forgot or were indifferent to one another. But by marrying we shall inject a little truth into past lies at the same time that we safeguard Argos. We shall marry within the hour.

Electra. I believe that your marriage will not take place.

Judge. Bravo!

Aegisthus. Can't you be quiet! Who do you think you are? A cuckolded husband or a chief justice?

Judge. Both—there's no argument about that.

Aegisthus. Then choose. I have no choice. Choose between doing your duty and going to prison. There's not much time.

Judge. You stole Agatha from me!

Aegisthus. I am no longer the same man who took Agatha from you.

Judge. I suppose the cuckolds of Argos were not one of the gifts you received this morning.

Beggar. Oh, yes. But he's no longer the man who deceived them.

Judge. I understand. The new king forgets the outrages he committed as regent.

Beggar. Agatha is blushing. At least it was an outrage which makes a girl blush.

Aegisthus. A king asks your forgiveness for the insult you received from a debauched man. You should ask for nothing more than that. Listen to what I command: hasten to your tribunal and pass a harsh sentence on the rioters.

Agatha. Yes, be harsh. There's a young lover of mine among them.

Judge. Stop looking at that bird, Agatha. You're getting on my nerves!

Agatha. I'm sorry. It's the only thing in the world that interests me.

Judge. What will you do, you idiot, when it's gone?

Agatha. That's just what I am wondering.

Aegisthus. Didn't you hear me, your Honor? Don't you hear the tumult and shouting?

Judge. I shall not leave! I am going to stay and help Electra prevent your marriage!

Electra. I need your help no longer, your Honor. Your job is done since Agatha gave me the key to the whole problem. Thank you, Agatha.

Clytemnestra. What key?

Aegisthus. Come, Queen.

Clytemnestra. What key did she give you? What new quarrel are you going to pick?

Electra. You hated my father! Ah! How clear everything becomes in the light Agatha casts on it!

Clytemnestra. She's beginning again, Aegisthus! Protect me.

Electra. How you envied Agatha a few moments ago! What exquisite pleasure to scream one's hatred at a hated husband! A pleasure that has been denied you, Mother. Never in your life will you know it. Until the day he died he believed that you admired him, that you adored him! Often at banquets or ceremonies, your face froze and your lips moved although they uttered no sound. At such moments you wanted to cry out that you hated him to every passer-by, to the guests, to the servant pouring your wine, to the guard watching to see that none of the dinner dishes were stolen. Poor mother, you could never go out alone into the countryside and cry out your hatred to the reeds and the rushes. The reeds and rushes all whisper that you adore him!

Clytemnestra. Hear me a moment, Electra!

Electra. That's right, Mother, scream your hatred at me! Since he's no longer here, I am his replacement. Scream at me! It will give you as much pleasure as if you were screaming it at him. Surely you can't die without crying out that you hated him!

Clytemnestra. Come, Aegisthus—— Never mind about the bird——

Electra. If you move a single step, Mother, I shall call for help.

Aegisthus. Whom can you call, Electra? Is there a single person in the world who could take from us the right to save our city?

Electra. Our city of hypocrisy and corruption! There are thousands who could take from you that right. But the purest, the most beautiful, the youngest is here in this courtyard. If Clytemnestra moves as much as a step, I shall call him.

Clytemnestra. Come, Aegisthus!

Electra. Orestes! Orestes!

The EUMENIDES *rise up and block* ELECTRA's *way.*

First of the Eumenides. Poor girl! You really are innocent and simple! You thought we would let Orestes wander about with a sword in his hand. Accidents happen too easily in this palace. We bound and gagged him.

Electra. That's not true! Orestes! Orestes!

Second of the Eumenides. You, too, are about to be seized.

Aegisthus. Electra, dear Electra, listen to me! I want to convince you.

Clytemnestra. You are losing precious time, Aegisthus.

Aegisthus. I am coming! Electra, I know that you alone understand who I am today. Help me! Let me tell you why you must help me!

Clytemnestra. Must we go on forever with these interminable explanations and quarrels? We're not human beings but fighting cocks, crowing and proving ourselves to each other. Must these explanations go on until we've drawn blood, until we've gouged each other's eyes out? Will it take force to separate us?

Judge. I think that will be the only way, Queen!

Captain. Make haste, Aegisthus, I beg you!

Beggar. Haven't you heard what's going on? Don't you understand that Aegisthus will come right along as soon as he has settled this Agamemnon-Electra-Clytemnestra business for all time?

Captain. In five minutes it will be too late.

Beggar. We will all lend a hand and it will be settled in five minutes.

Aegisthus. Take this man away.

Exit the soldiers with the JUDGE. *The rest of the company, with the exception of* ELECTRA, CLYTEMNESTRA, AEGISTHUS, *and the* BEGGAR, *leave the stage. There is a silence.*

Aegisthus. Well, Electra, what do you want?

Electra. You think it's late, Aegisthus. The truth is that it is not coming.

Aegisthus. What are you talking about?

Electra. What you are waiting for in spite of yourself —the messenger of the gods. If heaven wishes Aegisthus to be absolved by his love for the city, to disdain false-hood, to save Argos—in a word to marry Clytemnestra, then this is the moment for a heavenly messenger to alight between the two of you and crown you with laurel. No such messenger is coming.

Aegisthus. You know it has already come. The first ray of the morning sun was the gods' messenger.

Electra. That was a ray of the morning sun and nothing more. The most miserable urchin believes himself to be king if the morning sun touches him.

Aegisthus. You don't think I'm telling the truth!

Electra. Alas, I believe you are. But behind your truth-fulness I detect the hypocrisy and malice of the gods. They have made a just man of the parasite, a husband of the adulterer, a king of the usurper. They thought my job wasn't hard enough as it was. I despised you and now they've made you the soul of honor. But there's one trans-formation they can't manage so easily—they can't make an innocent man out of a criminal. They concede me this much.

Aegisthus. I do not know what you mean.

Electra. Yes, although you have become a king, a part of you still does. Just listen and you will understand.

Aegisthus. Can any of you tell me what she's talking about?

Clytemnestra. Whom has she ever talked about? What has she spent her whole life talking about! About some-body and something she has no idea of. About a father she never even knew.

Electra. Me, not know my father?

Clytemnestra. About a father whom she never saw or touched after the age of five!

Electra. Me, not touch my father?

Clytemnestra. You touched a corpse, an icy image of what your father had been, but not your father himself!

Aegisthus. I beg you, Clytemnestra. This is no time for another argument.

Clytemnestra. We each have a turn to argue. Now it is mine.

Electra. For once you are right. What you've brought up this time is the real argument. From whom would I derive my strength, how would I know the truth was on my side, if I had not touched my father while he was still alive?

Clytemnestra. Precisely. That's why you are so far from the truth. I wonder whether you ever even kissed him. I was careful to see that he didn't slobber all over my children.

Electra. Me, not kiss my father?

Clytemnestra. His corpse when it was already cold, if you insist, but your father himself, no!

Aegisthus. I implore you!

Electra. Ah! Now I see why you confronted me with such self-assurance. You believed that I was unarmed, you believed that I had never touched my father. How wrong you were!

Clytemnestra. You lie.

Electra. The day he returned you both waited for him a minute too long on the staircase of the palace, did you not?

Clytemnestra. How did you know? You weren't there.

Electra. It was I who kept him back. I was in his arms.

Aegisthus. Hear me, Electra.

Electra. I had been waiting for him among the crowd, Mother. I threw myself on him. His escort panicked, thinking someone was attempting to kill him. But he guessed who it was. He smiled at me. He understood that it was Electra's attempt on his life. Courageous father that he was, he gave himself up to me entirely! And I touched him.

Clytemnestra. You touched his leather greaves; you touched his horse. Nothing more!

Electra. He dismounted, Mother. I touched his hands with these fingers; I touched his lips with this mouth. I touched skin you had not touched yourself, cleansed of you by ten years' absence!

Aegisthus. Enough! She believes you!

Electra. With my cheek against his cheek I absorbed my father's warmth. Sometimes in the summer the earth becomes as hot—just barely—as my father was. I grow faint just thinking of how he felt. I embraced him with these arms. I thought I was taking the measure of my love, but I was measuring my vengeance as well. Then he pulled himself free and remounted his horse, more dazzling and graceful than ever. Electra's attempt on her father was finished! He was all the more golden, the more alive as a result of it! I ran toward the palace to see him once more, but even then I was no longer running toward him, I was running toward you, his assassins.

Aegisthus. Come to your senses, Electra.

Electra. I'm all right—just a little out of breath. I have only just caught up with you.

Clytemnestra. Let us rid ourselves of this girl, Aegisthus. Let's give her back to the gardener! Let's lock her up with her brother!

Aegisthus. Stop, Electra! Why must you persist in joining battle at this very moment. I see and love you for the first time. Now that I am no longer ambitious for myself, now that I have become courageous and virtuous, we could get on with one another.

Electra. I have only this moment.

Aegisthus. Do you realize that Argos is in danger?

Electra. We don't agree on what constitutes danger.

Aegisthus. You realize that if I marry Clytemnestra, discontent will die down in the city and the Atrides will be saved? If not, there will be an uprising; the mob will set fire to the city.

Electra. That's entirely possible.

Aegisthus. Do you realize that I alone can defend Argos against the Corinthians? They have already reached the gates of the city. Without me the city will be pillaged and our people massacred.

Electra. Yes, there is no doubt you would win.

Aegisthus. And yet you persist! You prevent me from carrying out my task! You bring ruin down upon me! You sacrifice your country and your family to a dream!

Electra. Do you take me for a fool, Aegisthus? You who claim to know me, do you take me for the kind of person to whom you can say: if you lie and let other people lie, your country will prosper; if you conceal every crime, your country will be victorious? What is this poor ghost of a country that all of a sudden you are slipping between the truth and us?

Aegisthus. Your country—Argos.

Electra. You are unlucky, Aegisthus. I, too, received a gift this morning at the same time that Argos was given to you. I expected it, it had been promised to me, but I did not yet understand what it would be. I had already received a thousand gifts but they seemed ill-assorted, unrelated to one another until during this past night, with Orestes asleep in my arms, I saw that they were all part of one gift. I was given a man on a towpath hauling his barge along with bended back. I was given the smile of a washerwoman suddenly stopping for a moment in the midst of her work and looking at the stream. I was given a fat little child running across the road stark naked while his mother and the neighbors shouted after him to come back. I was given the cry a captured bird makes when it is released and the cry of a mason whom I saw fall one day from his scaffold with his legs akimbo. I was given a water plant which fights the current, alternately struggling and yielding. I was given a consumptive young man who coughs and then smiles and then coughs again. I was given the cheeks of my maid flushed and puffed as she blows on the coals of my fire on a winter morning. I too believed that I was being given Argos, everything in Argos which is modest, tender, beautiful, or wretched. But then, a little while ago, I knew that wasn't true. I knew that I had received far more—I had been given all the cheeks of all the serving girls in the world, whether they are blowing on wood or coal, all the eyes of all the washerwomen, whether round or almond-shaped, all the birds that fly, all the masons that fall, and all the reeds that struggle and then yield in the streams and seas of the world. Argos is no more than a speck in the universe, my country no more than a hamlet in the country of the world. The rays of joy that gleam in a melancholy face, the wrinkles that fret a joyous face with a melancholy shadow, the hope and despair on an indifferent face—of these is my new country made. And it was this morning at dawn when you were being given little Argos that I saw how immense my country was. At the same time I learned its name, although it is a name that is never spoken—my country is called Tenderness and Justice.

Clytemnestra. That's the limit! Electra taking tenderness as her motto! Let us go!

Aegisthus. And you dare claim that this justice which allows your city to be burned to the ground, which lets you condemn your own people to ruin, is the justice of the gods?

Electra. Far from it. In my country the gods are not trusted to dispense justice. Gods are nothing more than artists. To them the beautiful glow cast by a raging fire is justice, the fine green grass on a battlefield is justice. After deliberating on your crime they have decreed that you have made a splendid repentance. I do not accept their verdict.

Aegisthus. Then Electra's justice consists of never passing over even the most minute error, of making every deed irreparable?

Electra. Oh, no! There are years in which trees suffer no injustice from frost and other years when they do. There are convicts one loves, murderers one embraces. But when a crime strikes a blow at human dignity, when it infests an entire nation, when it corrupts their loyalty, it cannot be forgiven.

Aegisthus. Have you any idea what a nation is, Electra?

Electra. A nation is an intrepid pure spirit which looks you straight in the eye.

Aegisthus. Those are the words of a young girl, not a king. A nation is an immense organism which must be governed and nourished.

Electra. I speak as a woman. The spirit of a nation is what counts—the look in its eyes. One would like to capture and hold that dazzling look, but it is evanescent, as the truth always is, no more than fox fire playing on the surface of the world. But it's beautiful, that look of truth gleaming in the eyes of the real nations of the world.

Aegisthus. There are truths which can kill a nation, Electra.

Electra. Sometimes there is a light which never goes out, even in the eyes of a dead nation. Would that this could be the fate of Argos! But ever since my father's death we have been blind; ever since the happiness of our city has been based on crime and injustice, ever since, out of cowardice, we have become accomplices to murder, the light has gone out in our eyes. However prosperous and victorious we may seem, however much we may sing and dance, nevertheless we live in darkness; children at the breast are already blind.

Aegisthus. A scandal will only plunge us deeper into darkness.

Electra. That may be. But I can no longer bear to see that dulled, weak look in the eyes of my people.

Aegisthus. It may cost you thousands of eyes from which all light and life has gone out.

Electra. That is what it always costs. It is not too dear.

Aegisthus. I need this one day. Grant me it. The truth as you see it, if truth it be, will have no trouble coming out at a time better suited to it.

Electra. The day of an uprising is the day for it to come out.

Aegisthus. I beg you. Wait until tomorrow.

Electra. Today is its day. I have seen the truth wither too many times because it waited a second too long. I know what happens to a young girl who puts off saying "No" to what is ugly and vile: within a second she must say "Yes" to anything and everything. It is precisely this which makes the truth so fine and yet so difficult—it is eternal and yet it lasts only as long as a flash of lightning.

Aegisthus. It is my job to save the city, to save Greece.

Electra. That is a minor task. I am saving the look in the eyes of our nation—— You did murder him, didn't you?

Clytemnestra. How dare you say that, girl! Everyone knows that your father slipped on the marble floor!

Electra. Everyone knows because that's the way you told it.

Clytemnestra. He must have slipped, you madwoman, because he fell.

Electra. He didn't slip. For one overwhelming, crystal clear reason: because never once in his life did my father slip!

Clytemnestra. How do you know?

Electra. For eight years I have been questioning the entire household. I have questioned every serving girl, every page. I have questioned everyone who ever escorted him when it rained or hailed. He never once slipped.

Clytemnestra. He was not so nimble after ten years of war.

Electra. I questioned his companions-in-arms. He crossed the Scamander without slipping. He took ramparts by storm without slipping. He slipped neither in water nor in blood.

Clytemnestra. He was in a hurry that day. You had made him late.

Electra. So I am the guilty one? There's the truth according to Clytemnestra. Is that what you think, too, Aegisthus? Agamemnon's murderer is Electra!

Clytemnestra. I admit the servants had put too much soap on the floor. I almost slipped myself.

Electra. So you were in the bath, Mother? What kept you there?

Clytemnestra. Why wouldn't I have been there?

Electra. With Aegisthus, no doubt?

Clytemnestra. With Aegisthus. And we were not alone. Leon, my adviser, was there. Is that not so, Aegisthus?

Electra. The Leon who died the next day?

Clytemnestra. Did he die the next day?

Electra. Yes. Leon also slipped. He was lying in his bed and in the morning he was found dead. He slipped into death; he found a way to slip without slipping, without moving a hair while he was fast asleep. You had him killed, didn't you?

Clytemnestra. Why don't you defend me, Aegisthus! I need your help!

Electra. He can do nothing to help you. You have come to the point where you must defend yourself.

Clytemnestra. O God, to think that I, a queen, a mother, should come to this!

Electra. Come to what? Perhaps you had better tell us!

Clytemnestra. And all because of this daughter who knows neither joy nor love! At least I have my little Chrysothemis. She loves flowers.

Electra. I suppose I don't like flowers?

Clytemnestra. To have come to this! To have taken the whole meaningless journey of life just to reach this point! I, who as a young girl loved nothing better than a quiet life, to take care of my pets, to sew, to enjoy the company of a friend while I dined—I was so gentle, Aegisthus! I swear to you that I was the most gentle of girls. In my native city there are still old people alive for whom Clytemnestra is synonymous with gentleness!

Electra. If they die today, if they die this morning, they can keep the same symbol for gentleness.

Clytemnestra. To have come to this! What injustice! I used to spend my days in the meadow behind the palace, Aegisthus. It was so thick with flowers that I did not need to bend in order to pick them; I sat down and they were all about me. My dog lay at my feet; he used to bark when Agamemnon came to fetch me. I used to tease him with flowers. He ate them to please me. If I had even him today! If I lived anywhere else in the world, if my husband had been Persian or Egyptian, I would be carefree, gay—good! I had a nice voice when I was young and I used to raise birds. I could have been a carefree Egyptian queen who sang; I could have had an Egyptian aviary. And this is what we have come to! What is this family of ours! What have these walls made of us!

Electra. Murderers! They are evil, these walls!

Enter a MESSENGER.

Messenger. My lord, they have forced their way in! The postern is yielding.

Electra. Take heart. Those walls are tumbling down.

Aegisthus. Electra, listen to me one last time. I am willing to forgive all your illusions and all your insults. But can't you see that your country is in its death throes?

Electra. Me not love flowers? Do you think I sat down to pick the flowers for my father's tomb?

Clytemnestra. Then let this father of yours come back, if come back he must! Let him stop playing dead! He is blackmailing us with his silence and his absence! Let him come back with all his pomp and vanity—with his beard! His beard must have grown in the grave—— Still it would be preferable to this!

Electra. What are you saying?

Aegisthus. Electra, I give you my oath that tomorrow, once Argos is saved, the guilty, if any exist, will disappear forever. But for the moment do not persist. You are gentle,

ELECTRA   239

Electra. Your inmost heart is gentle. Listen to what it is telling you. The city is about to perish.

Electra. Let it perish. I can already see my love for Argos vanquished and going up in flames! No! My mother has begun to insult my father—let her finish!

Clytemnestra. What is this about someone being guilty? What are you saying, Aegisthus?

Electra. In one word he has just said everything you deny!

Clytemnestra. What do I deny?

Electra. He has just said that you let Orestes fall, that I am fond of flowers, that my father did not slip!

Clytemnestra. He did slip! I swear that he slipped. Let the truth be written on the face of the heavens! Let a bolt of lightning show that he lost his balance and slipped, armor and all!

Aegisthus. Electra, you are in my power. You, and your brother as well. I can kill you. Yesterday I would have killed you. But I give you my oath that I shall do just the opposite as soon as the enemy is repulsed. I shall leave the throne and return to Orestes what is rightfully his!

Electra. What you are saying is no longer important, Aegisthus. If for once the gods have changed their ways, if they have made you wise and just only to bring about your ruin, that is their concern. What matters to us is to know whether she will dare tell us why she hated my father!

Clytemnestra. Ah! You want to know why I hated him?

Electra. But you won't dare tell me!

Aegisthus. Electra, tomorrow the guilty man—for there is only one guilty person—will be at the foot of the altar where we will be giving thanks for our victory. He will be clothed as a parricide; he will make a public confession of his shame. He will set his own punishment. But first let me save the city.

Electra. Today you have saved yourself in your own eyes and in mine, Aegisthus. I ask no more of you. No! It is she who must go on and finish what she was saying!

Clytemnestra. Ah! You want me to finish what I have begun!

Electra. I defy you to!

Enter a MESSENGER.

Messenger. They have broken into the courtyard of the palace, Aegisthus!

Aegisthus. Let us go, Queen!

Clytemnestra. Yes, I hated him. Yes, now you will know at last what he was like, that admirable father of yours! Yes, after twenty years of silence I shall permit myself the same treat as Agatha! A woman belongs to the entire world. But there is one man in the world to whom she cannot give herself. The only man to whom I could not give myself was he, the king of kings, the father of fathers! From the very day he came, with his curly beard, to tear me from my home, I hated him. He tore me away, but the little finger of the hand which seized me was raised. As usual. He raised it to drink; he raised it to ride, even if the horse bolted; he raised it when he held his scepter— and even when he held me in his arms, I felt on my back the pressure of only four fingers. I thought I would go mad when I saw two little fingers silhouetted against the rising sun as he sacrificed your sister Iphigenia! King of kings, how ludicrous! He was pompous, indecisive, gulli- ble. He was the fool of fools, the simpleton of simpletons! The king of kings was never anything more than that little finger and that beard which nothing could make straight. Nothing did any good—the water of his bath into which I plunged his head, our nights of pretended love when I pulled on it and tangled it, that thunderstorm at Delphi which turned the dancers' hair into horses' manes. With all its ringlets his beard survived bath, bed, downpour—even the passage of time. He used to signal to me with the little finger raised on his hand, and I came smiling. Why?—— And he told me to kiss his mouth in the midst of that fleece of a beard and I ran to kiss it. Why?—— And when as I awakened I deceived him, like Agatha, with the wood of the bed—a more elegant, luxuri- ous bed than Agatha's, of course, a royal bed—he would tell me to talk to him. Since I knew him to be vain, empty, and ordinary, I told him he was modest, magnifi- cent, and distinguished. Why?—— And if he stammered like a fool for me to tell him more, I swore to him that he was a god. King of kings—the only excuse for such a title is that it justifies a hatred to outdo all hatreds. Do you know what I did, Electra, the day he departed for the war while his ship was still in sight? I sacrificed the most tightly curled, the most kinky ram of the flock, and then at midnight I slipped into the throne room all alone and seized the scepter with both hands! Now you know everything. You wanted a hymn to the truth: you have heard the finest!

Electra. Forgive me, Father!

Aegisthus. Come, Queen.

Clytemnestra. Put that girl in prison first. See that she is put in chains.

Electra. Will you ever forgive me for having listened to her, Father! She must die, Aegisthus, must she not?

Aegisthus. Farewell, Electra.

Electra. Kill her, Aegisthus, and I shall forgive you.

Clytemnestra. Do not let her go free, Aegisthus. They will stab you in the back.

Aegisthus. We shall see about that—— Let Electra go. Free Orestes.

Exit AEGISTHUS *and* CLYTEMNESTRA.

Electra. The bird is swooping down, beggar, the bird is swooping down.

Beggar. Look, it is a vulture.

Enter NARSES' WIFE, *followed by a crowd of beggars, cripples, and blind men.*

Beggar. Is that you, Narses' wife? What are you doing here?

Narses' wife. We beggars have come to save Electra and her brother. Lame, halt, and blind, we have come.

Beggar. Justice, in other words.

Narses' wife. Some of our mob have gone to free Orestes.

Beggar. Let me tell you how they killed him, Narses' wife. This is how it happened, and you know I stick to the facts. It was the queen who had the idea of soaping the steps leading down into the bath. The two of them soaped the steps together. While all the housewives in the city soaped their front steps in preparation for Agamemnon's return, the queen and her lover soaped steps leading to his death. Just imagine how clean their hands were when they extended them to greet him. And then, as he put out his arms to her, he slipped; your father slipped, Electra. You are right except on this point. He slipped and slid as far as the middle of the pavement, and you could say it was a royal clatter he made when he fell in his cuirass and helmet of solid gold. And it was she who rushed toward him, to help him up, he thought. Instead she held him pinned to the floor. He did not understand. He did not understand why his beloved wife kept him pinned to the ground unless she was moved by a burst of love; but if that was so, why did Aegisthus remain? That Aegisthus was an indiscreet, blundering young man. He would have to keep his bad manners in mind when the young fellow came asking for a promotion. It's a bit irritating for the master of the world, the conqueror of Troy who has just finished reviewing his navy, his cavalry, and his infantry, to slip the minute he sets foot in his palace, to fall with a clatter as if he were a pile of dishes, and lie there flat on his back with his legs outstretched in front of his loving wife and a young standard-bearer. It is irritating even if not a hair of his curly beard is out of place. Besides, it might be a bad omen. His fall might mean that he was going to die in a year, in five years. But the odd thing was that his beloved wife had seized him by the wrists and was bearing down on him with her full weight as a fisherwoman holds down a tortoise which she has caught in the shallows. She was ill-advised to do so. It didn't add to her beauty to bend over that way so that the blood rushed to her head. He noticed, too, that her neck had become wrinkled since he had been away. Aegisthus, on the other hand, became more handsome each second. The young man obviously wanted to make it easier for him to get up—he was drawing his sword from its scabbard. But both of them were completely silent—that was what was so extraordinary. He talked to them. "Dear wife," he said. "How strong you are!" "Young man," he said, "take the sword by the hilt!" But they were both mute; no one had written him during the ten years he had been away that the queen and the pages had become mute. They were both mute, like people packing a trunk in a great hurry as the moment for departure draws near.

There was something they had to do, fast, before anyone could come in. What sort of baggage was it that had to be packed so quickly? Then all at once he realized everything. Aegisthus kicked his helmet; it was the kind of kick a dying man sees people begin to give his favorite dog. "Let me go, wife!" he cried. "What are you doing to me, wife!" She was careful not to say what she was doing. She couldn't say, "I am killing you, I am assassinating you." But she said it to herself: "I am killing him because there isn't a single gray hair in his beard; I am assassinating him because it's the only way to assassinate that little finger of his." With her teeth she loosed the thongs of his cuirass; and it opened as if it were a mouth made of gold. Then Aegisthus—— So that was why Aegisthus looked so handsome! Agamemnon had seen Achilles suddenly flushed with the same beauty when he was killing Hector and Ulysses, when he was killing Dolon. Then Aegisthus approached with Agamemnon's sword raised over his head. Then the king of kings kicked Clytemnestra in the back. Each time he kicked her she started, her head jerked, and she winced at the pain. But she remained mute. He shouted, but to cover his shouting Aegisthus laughed as loudly as he could, although his face remained rigid and set. Then he plunged the sword deep into the king of kings. The king of kings was not a block of brass and iron as he had imagined, but a mass of soft flesh, as easily pierced as a lamb. He struck too strong a blow; the sword nicked the marble. A murderer makes a mistake if he wounds marble; it harbors a grudge. It was the nick in the marble which gave me a clue to the crime. Then he ceased struggling; he abandoned himself to the two of them, the one becoming more and more ugly and the other becoming more and more handsome. There's this to be said for death: it's a friend as well as an enemy waiting in ambush—a friend to whom you can trust yourself completely, your only friend in fact. And for him there was something familiar about death; it resembled the members of his family. He called his children, the boy Orestes first, to thank him for avenging him one day; then the girl, Electra, to thank her for lending her face and hands to death for a moment. Clytemnestra did not loosen her grip on him. There was a slight froth of foam on her lips; Agamemnon was willing to die, but he was not willing to have this woman spit in his face or on his beard. But she did not spit on him; she was too busy moving around the body, trying to avoid the blood which flowed on the marble. She did not want to step in it with her sandals. She kept moving around him in her red dress, and in his agony he thought he saw the sun wheeling above him. Then darkness followed—they had seized him by the arms and turned him over so that his face was against the floor. He could no longer move four fingers on his right hand. Then, since Aegisthus, not thinking what he was doing, had removed the sword, they turned him over on his back once more and very gently, very carefully replaced the sword in the wound. Young Aegisthus was grateful that the dead man allowed himself to be killed so gently, so very gently this second time. If this were all murder amounted to, one would kill kings by the dozen. But Clytemnestra's hatred grew and increased for this man who had struggled so foolishly, so fiercely, for she knew that she would be tormented by the murder every night in her dreams. And that is exactly what happened. That is what her crime has cost her. She killed him seven years ago; since then she has killed him three thousand times.

ORESTES *has entered during the* BEGGAR's *speech.*

Narses' wife. Here is the young man! How handsome he is!

Beggar. He has the same sort of beauty that young Aegisthus did.

Orestes. Where are they, Electra?

Electra. Orestes, my darling!

Narses' wife. They are in the south courtyard.

Orestes. Electra, in a little while I shall be with you forever.

Electra. Hurry, my love.

Orestes. Don't let me interrupt you, beggar. Go on. Tell them about the death of Clytemnestra and Aegisthus.

Exit ORESTES *with his sword in hand.*

Narses' wife. Tell us about their death, beggar.

Beggar. In a minute. Let them die first.

Electra. He had his sword?

Narses' wife. Yes, daughter.

Beggar. Are you mad, calling the princess your daughter?

Narses' wife. I am calling her my daughter. I am not saying that she is my daughter. But I saw her father many times. There was a fine-looking man for you!

Electra. He had a beard, didn't he?

Narses' wife. Not a beard. A sun. A sun of waves and ringlets. He used to run his hand through it. The most beautiful hand I have ever seen——

Electra. Call me your daughter, Narses' wife, for I am your daughter—— Listen! Someone cried out!

Narses' wife. No, daughter!

Electra. Are you sure he had his sword with him? Are you sure he didn't have to face them without his sword?

Narses' wife. You saw him yourself! He had a thousand swords! Calm yourself. Calm yourself.

Electra. Now I know, Mother, how long that moment was when you waited in the entrance to the bath!

Narses' wife. You don't know what you're talking about! It will be over so fast we won't know it's happened!

Beggar. One minute. He is looking for them. There! He has found them!

Narses' wife. For my part I don't mind waiting. How sweet it is to caress this little Electra. I have only boys, a band of ruffians. It's a lucky woman who has a daughter!

Electra. Yes—lucky—— This time someone did cry out.

Narses' wife. Yes, daughter.

Beggar. Now I can finish my story. Narses' wife and the mob of beggars freed Orestes. He rushed across the courtyard. He did not stop to kiss Electra; he didn't even touch her. He was mistaken not to. He was never to touch her again. He overtook the murderers while they were parleying with the leaders of the uprising. They were standing in a marble niche above the crowd, and Aegisthus was leaning over telling the leaders that everything was fine, that everything would be fine from now on. Suddenly he heard from behind him the cry of a stricken beast. But it was no beast, it was Clytemnestra. But she had been stricken. By her own son. He had closed his eyes and dealt the couple a blow at random. Even an unworthy mother is sensitive and mortal. She called on neither Electra nor Orestes but her youngest daughter, Chrysothemis, so that Orestes had an impression that he was killing not his own mother, but another innocent one. She clutched Aegisthus' right arm—quite right she was, too, to do so, for it was the only way she could hope to keep herself on her feet a moment longer. But in doing so she prevented Aegisthus from unsheathing his sword. He tried to shake himself free, but to no avail; she still kept clutching his arm. And she was too heavy to use as a shield. And that bird was still there, hovering just above him now, slapping him with its wings and pecking at him with its beak. He began to fight. With a dead queen and all her necklaces and other paraphernalia weighing down his right arm, he fought with his left. He had no weapon, but he was desperate. He didn't want to die as a criminal, just when everything in the world had become pure and holy. He did not want to fight because of a crime which was no longer his; he did not want to appear infamous in the eyes of this parricide. Then suddenly a thong of his cuirass caught on the clasp of Clytemnestra's dress and his cuirass opened. He ceased struggling then; he was still, except that he kept shaking his right arm. It seemed that he wanted to be free of the queen, not to fight alone, but to die alone, to sleep in death far from Clytemnestra. He did not succeed. The couple Clytemnestra-Aegisthus exists for eternity. But as he died, he cried a name I shall not repeat.

Aegisthus [*his voice coming from offstage*]. Electra——

Beggar. I went too fast. He's just catching up with me.

Enter the EUMENIDES, *now just the age and height of* ELECTRA. *Also a* SERVANT.

Servant. Flee, all of you. The palace is in flames!

First of the Eumenides. As if Electra didn't have enough light already with the light of the day and the light of the truth! The glow of a fire was all she needed.

Second of the Eumenides. Satisfied, Electra? The city is perishing.

Electra. I am satisfied. For the last minute or so I have known it would be reborn.

Third of the Eumenides. All those people slitting each other's throats in the street, I suppose they will be reborn, too? And what about the people being massacred by the Corinthians? They are attacking us, you know.

Electra. If they are innocent, they will be reborn.

First of the Eumenides. Look where pride has led you, Electra! You no longer amount to anything! Nothing remains to you!

Electra. I have a clear conscience, I have Orestes, I have justice, I have everything.

Second of the Eumenides. A clear conscience! You'll be hearing from your conscience in the wee hours of the mornings that lie ahead. For seven years you couldn't sleep because of a crime others had committed. Henceforth you are the guilty one.

Electra. I have Orestes. I have justice. I have everything.

Third of the Eumenides. Orestes! Never again will you see Orestes. We are about to leave you and start to hound him. We have assumed your age and appearance in order to pursue him. Farewell. We shall never leave him until he begins to rave and then kills himself, cursing his sister.

Electra. I have justice. I have everything.

Narses' wife. What are they saying? What naughty girls they are! What's happening, poor little Electra, what's happening?

Electra. What is happening?

Narses' wife. Yes, explain! I don't catch on very quickly. I can tell that something is happening, of course, but I can't tell what it is. What do you call it when the city is in ruins, sacked and pillaged, and yet morning comes, and there is a freshness in the air? When the city is in flames, when all is lost, when the innocent are killing each other, and yet over in a corner in the morning light the guilty are dying?

Electra. Ask the beggar. He knows.

Beggar. It has a very beautiful name, Narses' wife. It is called dawn.

Curtain.